Popular Victorian women writers

Published in our
centenary year
~ 2004 ~
MANCHESTER
UNIVERSITY
PRESS

For our mothers and our grandmothers –
Joan, Marjorie, Kathleen, Lily, Esther and Winifred

Popular Victorian women writers

edited by Kay Boardman and Shirley Jones

Manchester University Press

Manchester and New York

distributed exclusively in the USA by Palgrave

Published by Manchester University Press
Oxford Road, Manchester M13 9NR, UK
and Room 400, 175 Fifth Avenue, New York, NY 10010, USA
www.manchesteruniversitypress.co.uk

Distributed exclusively in the USA by
Palgrave, 175 Fifth Avenue, New York,
NY 10010, USA

Distributed exclusively in Canada by
UBC Press, University of British Columbia, 2029 West Mall,
Vancouver, BC, Canada V6T 1Z2

British Library Cataloguing-in-Publication Data
A catalogue record for this book is available from the British Library

Library of Congress Cataloging-in-Publication Data applied for

ISBN   0 7190 6450 3 *hardback*

First published 2004

13 12 11 10 09 08 07 06 05 04   10 9 8 7 6 5 4 3 2 1

Typeset by Freelance Publishing Services, Brinscall, Lancs
www.freelancepublishingservices.co.uk
Printed in Great Britain
by CPI, Bath

Contents

List of contributors

Kay Boardman is a Senior Lecturer in English at the University of Central Lancashire

Jane Darcy is a Senior Lecturer in English at the University of Central Lancashire

Helen Debenham teaches English at the University of Canterbury, New Zealand

Shirley Jones teaches in higher education in north-west England

Jennifer H. Litster teaches American History at the University of Edinburgh

Brian E. Maidment is Professor of English at the University of Salford

Valerie Pedlar is a Senior Counsellor at the Open University

Marie Riley is a trainer and freelance writer in north-west England

Valerie Sanders is Professor of English at the University of Hull

Acknowledgements

We wish to thank our fellow contributors for sharing their expertise and enthusiasm for their subjects with us. Thanks also go to colleagues at the University of Central Lancashire and to Paul and Ade, our children, families and friends who have been supportive in all kinds of ways.

Introduction

Kay Boardman and Shirley Jones

In 1893 Helen C. Black published *Notable Women Authors of the Day*, a collection of articles previously published in *The Lady's Pictorial*.[1] Apparently bland biographical pieces, these essays nevertheless provide a useful reference in trying to establish an overview of the woman writer in the late Victorian period. Black writes to a fairly standard formula describing an interview with each of the chosen authors. After detailing her journey to the meeting, Black sets a scene portraying the location, architecture and decor of each author's home (in the style of a modern day celebrity magazine), she then describes the appearance and clothing of each author. Interviewer and interviewee then talk about the writer's career and her writing practice, as well as past and present lifestyle, family, friendships and (usually) pets. With the exception of poet Jean Ingelow, the twenty-six authors included in the collection are writers of fiction in a wide range of genres. Most of the writers also work in other genres, writing articles, travel books, poetry or children's fiction. Black assumes familiarity with the writers' work. Given the source of these articles, it is clear that the original readership of these essays is assumed to be middle-class women, but the wide variety of social positioning within that group is reflected in the diverse depictions of the author's subjects.

Thus the woman writer may live in the midst of London intellectual and artistic society (May Crommelin) or she may live in 'absolute seclusion' (Charlotte Riddell). Her home may reveal a writing 'den' (Mrs Hungerford) or a 'room of a student who prefers books to society' (Edna Lyall), conversely 'no writing-room and no particular table' (Helen Mathers); Mrs Alexander Fraser writes 'in the evening after dinner, with my people chattering all the time'. Black represents many of her writers as paragons of conventional femininity, so Mrs Arthur Stannard ('John Strange Winter') is 'a thoroughly domestic woman', and the children of Mrs L. B.

Walford 'have never been put aside for her work' and 'are constantly with their mother'. Black catalogues the significance of sewing in most of her writers' lives: 'Mrs. Lynn Linton is a great adept with her needle', Miss Iza Duffus Hardy 'is at much at home with the needle as the pen'; Mrs Henry Chetwynd defines herself as a 'great needlewoman' and states 'when I am ruffled by anything I take refuge in sewing a plain seam'; Mrs Lovett Cameron 'hated needlework' in her youth; Adeline Sergeant confesses to having 'done some elaborate embroidery in my time' but now she never uses her 'needle for amusement; only for necessity'.

Many of the writers start writing in childhood and youth and some are determined to be published from an early age (Florence Marryat). Some, like Mrs L. B. Walford and Lady Duffus Hardy do not take 'seriously to novel writing' until after marriage, others stop writing on marriage and return to writing on widowhood (Mrs Alexander). Of the twenty-six authors featured in Black's collection, eleven are unmarried but few live alone, most live with female relatives or companions. Black is intrigued by women who pioneer new ways of living, she is obviously fascinated by the Ladies' Residential Chambers inhabited by Adeline Sergeant. This 'unique' establishment 'was founded for gentlewomen only, of different occupations' and 'conducted entirely upon the principles of a gentleman's club'. Eliza Lynn Linton claims to have supported herself by her pen from the age of twenty-three but she is the only writer who publicly asserts such financial independence. Given that Sergeant's home is part of an institution built to be occupied by women who earn their own living then we might assume a similar self-reliance. The description of home environment therefore becomes the evidence for the reader's suppositions of wealth and income. Many of the homes described are luxurious and artistically ornamented, others are more frugally furnished. Jessie Fothergill's house is described as 'small and ordinary'. She says it is 'all extremely simple and rather shabby' but 'it suits me'. This home is a temporary one as she is interviewed 'on the eve of departure for sunnier climes'. Fothergill claims nevertheless that 'for luxury I do not care. Sumptuous rooms, gorgeous furniture, and an accumulation of "the pride of life" and "the lust of the eye" would simply oppress me, and make me feel very uncomfortable'. Black allows her subjects to represent themselves as they see fit so that although she asks no probing questions, distinctive voices do stand out. Being a woman writer in 1893 is clearly not unusual but each writer has to negotiate her position and define her space in her own way.

Though Black's writers were 'notable' in her day, they are now unknown to the general reader. The Victorian women writers who have become canonical – Charlotte Brontë, George Eliot and Elizabeth Gaskell – were long dead. Although the poets Elizabeth Barrett Browning and Christina Rossetti (who was alive in 1893) were considered of lasting value in their own time, their relationship with both the twentieth-century academy and general reader has been more problematic. Feminist criticism has demanded their inclusion in any study of Victorian poetry but novel reading and adaptations of novels are a part of popular culture in a way that poetry reading patently is not. It is hard to imagine Brontë and Rossetti especially being interviewed in Black's 'celebrity' style – perhaps the inclusion of an author in Black's collection is by definition, a mark of ephemerability? The immortality of those women whose names most contemporary general readers know is already clearly established by the 1890s, although others who were judged to be assured of future fame have not been so valued. Thus Charlotte Brontë and George Eliot appear in *The Queens of Literature of the Victorian Era* (1886) but so do Elizabeth Barrett Browning, Mary Sommerville, Harriet Martineau and Felicia Hemans.[2] In *Women Novelists of Queen Victoria's Reign* (1897), a collection of individually authored essays which takes as its subject matter 'Women novelists deceased', a clear hierarchy of authors is established in the criteria for inclusion:

> the eminence and permanence of the Brontës, George Eliot, and Mrs. Gaskell are universally recognised; the popularity of Mrs. Craik and Mrs. Henry Wood is still admittedly great; the personality of Mrs. Norton will always send students to her works; Mrs. Crowe and Mrs. Clive were pioneers in domestic and 'sensational' fiction; Lady Georgiana Fullerton produced a typical religious novel; Miss Manning made pleasing and acceptable the autobiographico-historical narrative; the authors of 'The Valley of a Hundred Fires', of 'Barbara's History', and of 'Adèle,' have even now their readers and admirers; while 'A.L.O.E.' and Mrs. Ewing were among the most successful caterers for the young.[3]

The 'immortals' seem to transcend genre, after the 'popularity' and 'personality' of Craik and Wood, and Norton (respectively) has been noted, other authors are listed according to their achievements in seemingly specific literary forms. These introductory remarks are not attributed to a specific author. Interestingly, some of the writers who feature as subjects in Black's collection also feature in this 'book of appreciations' as subjects and essayists. (So, for example, Eliza Lynn Linton writes on George Eliot; Edna Lyall writes about Mrs Gaskell; Adeline Sergeant considers Mrs Crowe, Mrs Archer Clive and Mrs Henry Wood.) It is significant that the canonical Victorian woman writer belongs to the early and mid-Victorian

period, but this is not true of male writers. W. L. Courtney's *The Feminine
Note in Fiction* (1904) which takes as its subject women novelists of 'the
modern age and modern novelists', and damns its subjects with faint praise,
includes a whole catalogue of women writers known only to the academic.[4]
At the same time, Courtney's notion of a feminine tradition maintains
the status of the famous four: 'Modern novels, written by women, trace
their descent from two authors, or, rather, two schools of writing. From
George Eliot and Charlotte Brontë comes a line of novels which is
altogether different in character from the school, as we may phrase it, of
Jane Austen and Mrs. Gaskell' (p. xxvii).

By the turn of the century the canon of Victorian women's writing had
largely been set and it was to take another sixty years for a substantive
body of critical work to appear which sought to review and redefine the
tradition of writing by women in the nineteenth century. However before
feminist criticism made its impact on the academy, other scholars sought
to enlarge the understanding of the interested reader in a wider exploration
of the Victorian literary world where the marketplace rather than aesthetics
defined a writer's significance. This relationship to the market is perhaps
one of the reasons why so many writers were written out of the canon;
generally to be popular, best-selling, marketable, a writer had to produce
work suiting the palette of a public eager for reading material in an
increasingly literate and urban culture.

Amy Cruse's pioneering survey of Victorian reading and readership,
The Victorians and Their Books identifies its focus as 'ordinary' readers.[5]
The Victorian reader, states Cruse did not confine himself to 'great' books:

> It is the great books, we know, that make up the literature of a country, but
> there is a sense in which the lesser books are equally important. For a book
> does not become effective, does not really come to life, except in its contacts
> with the reader, and it happens sometimes in the case of even very great
> books that these contacts are comparatively few and slight. The books that
> figure largely in histories of literature are, in many households, those which
> are placed respectfully behind the glass doors of the best bookcase, to protect
> their beautiful and expensive bindings, and are looked at with satisfaction
> as repositories of the higher culture, available when required, though
> required but seldom; while the family reads and re-reads old favourites in
> tattered covers, and devours by dozens new volumes from the circulating
> library. Many of these, too, are probably great books, but certainly not all.
> There are some that have no tincture of the quality that confers immortality
> or even that which promises long life. Yet their contacts are many and close.
> Their lives, though short, are active and potent. From the point of view of
> their readers they are as important as those which take the higher rank. (p. 14)

Here Cruse begins to construct the picture of a representative Victorian family which she will develop further as an upper middle-class micro-community of readers: Papa, Mamma, Caroline, the eldest daughter, her lover Edward, and the imaginary large family which will 'inevitably grow up around them' (p. 20). Although Mamma's moral sense leads to Caroline reading Mrs Gore in secret (p. 18), the reading of the family is expansive, varied in genre, subject matter and religious nuance. Cruse's vision is domestic and thus in opposition to conventional notions of the academy where it is precisely the 'great' books of 'the best bookcase' that are studied. Nevertheless this extract is quoted at length because it opens up so many of the questions of value and significance that twentieth-century critics have debated and that twenty-first-century critics are still grappling with. Contemporary literary history now has to address both the 'repositories of the higher culture', and debate what 'higher culture' might mean and who says so. It also takes stock of 'old favourites in tattered covers', the books that were once 'new volumes from the circulating library' and attempts to quantify their importance to individual readers and the wider society.

The Victorians and Their Books actually considers a wider readership than that outlined and presented in its introduction; Cruse writes about a variety of working-class readers who seek knowledge, advancement, political philosophy, pleasure and escape in their reading. Although readers are frequently categorised according to social status and interests (for example, Cruse refers to 'working men of the higher type', to 'chapel folks', to aesthetes, Philistines, early Victorian ladies, New Women); they also resist labelling and read diversely; and the work of many authors appeals across social boundaries. Cruse examines Victorian reading comprehensively in terms of genre including history, science, journalism, children's fictional and educational works. She assigns significance and worth to texts as they are part of the fabric of people's lives. She is happy to define the canon of the 'great' novelists as without doubt, there are first 'the splendid four – Dickens, Thackeray, Charlotte Brontë, and George Eliot; and in a lower class, not of the greatest, but certainly of the great, Anthony Trollope, Charles Kingsley, and Elizabeth Gaskell. Other names might be added, but these are beyond question' (p. 260). But then she also writes about authors who have never achieved canonical status. Charlotte Yonge is given a whole chapter which places her within the High Church movement; frequent reference is made to other popular novelists such as Mary Braddon, Rhoda Broughton, Marie Corelli, Dinah Mulock, Margaret Oliphant, Ouida, Mrs Humphry Ward and Ellen Wood; lesser reference is made to writers such as Eliza Cook, Catherine Gore, Mrs Gatty, Helen Mathers; Jessie Fothergill, Hesba Stretton, Mary Taylor and Margaret Todd are mentioned. Mathilda Betham-Edwards is named as one of the 'lesser lights' of Victorian fiction and then she features frequently in Cruse's works for her comments as a reader. Cruse's text is inclusive and expansive and in this respect looks forward to a burgeoning critical tradition devoted to the study of popular writing.

Margaret Dalziel's *Popular Fiction 100 Years Ago* also seeks to consider those texts that were immensely popular at the time, texts that addressed contemporary issues in a way that attracted a considerable readership at the time but that did not necessarily display longevity, nor necessarily elicit critical opprobrium.[6] Dalziel's work was also ground-breaking in its own right and provides a detailed survey into a textual landscape that had barely been recreated since its demise. Taking the 'common reader' she looks at what the great majority of people were reading in the mid-nineteenth century; not afraid to disparage many of her findings she does however raise many interesting questions about how we value particular works of 'literature'. Nigel Cross's work on the 'common writer' some thirty or so years later also aims to complete a fuller literary landscape and makes the crucially important point that those books that have survived and thus constitute the canon, belie the reality of the social and economic conditions of authorship and publishing.[7] Writers of distinction, while undoubtedly valuable and interesting, are not necessarily representative, and not necessarily in tune with public taste. Thus scholarship in the area of popular writing has yielded much of interest and in tandem with the burgeoning feminist school of criticism in the 1970s and 1980s has made a significant contribution to the re-discovery of many lost authors and their works and to the stimulation of debates about literary and cultural value and the relationship between social, literary and economic conditions.

If critics from the late nineteenth and early twentieth century had set in motion the establishment of a canon of Victorian women's writing, then the feminist critiques of the last three decades of the twentieth century began to consolidate it. The canon of women's writing, like any other canon, is in a constant process of formation and current scholarship on the subject is moving towards a deeper and more sophisticated understanding out of the work of the first wave of feminist critics writing in the 1970s and beyond. These critics, notably Elaine Showalter in *A Literature of Their Own* and Sandra Gilbert and Susan Gubar in *The Madwoman in the Attic*, have performed a great service in their attempt to reclaim and re-appraise

Victorian women writers.[8] Showalter's survey is the broadest in that she argues for attention to the diversity of nineteenth and twentieth-century women's writing in the knowledge that attention to an elite few had constituted the prime critical focus. In an impressive historical and textual sweep she suggests that the development of the English novel and women's part of that landscape is a desert bounded by four mountains: the four mountains representing the work and reputations of Jane Austen, the Brontës, George Eliot and Virginia Woolf. This metaphor of terrain and of mapping and re-mapping has since become the dominant motif in the reclamation of neglected writers.

For Showalter, to lose sight of the minor novelist is to lose the links in the chain binding generation to generation and this goes on to become an important part of the late twentieth-century feminist project: 'in the past, investigations have been distorted by the emphasis on an elite group, not only because it has excluded from our attention great stretches of literary activity between, for example, George Eliot and Virginia Woolf, but also because it has rendered invisible the daily lives, the physical experiences, the personal strategies and conflicts of ordinary women' (pp. 8–9). Similarly, the identification of recurrent themes, motifs and problems in women's writing forms an important part of her thesis as well as ensuing work on the topic. Central to Showalter's thesis is the identification of three stages of writing by women in the nineteenth and twentieth centuries, which she identifies as feminine, feminist and female. In the feminine phase between 1840 and 1880, women's novels imitate the prevailing modes of the dominant tradition and internalise its standards of art and its view of social roles; in the feminist phase between 1880 and 1920, they protest against those earlier standards and values; in the female phase between 1920 and 1960, women's novels are concerned with journeys to self-discovery and a search for identity.

In spite of the occlusion of writers who do not fall into the set categories, Showalter does have a more inclusive view of the range of women's writing as she considers both radical and conservative writers. However, this is something that does not interest Gilbert and Gubar in their equally ambitious project: focusing on canonical writers such as Austen, the Brontës and Eliot, and also Christina Rossetti and Emily Dickinson, they argue that women's writing of the period is characterised by images of enclosure and escape and that representations of femininity in patriarchal culture oscillate between the angelic and the demonic. Modifying Harold Bloom's work on the anxiety of influence and its effect on major male writers, Gilbert and Gubar suggest women's writing suffers from the 'anxiety of authorship' and this is illustrated by the recurrent figure of the madwoman who serves as the author's double. Gilbert and Gubar take their inspiration from writers who they can read as radical, hence many writers are necessarily excluded. Political judgement as much as any other criteria denies a wider vision of the nineteenth century which would include women such as Charlotte Yonge, Eliza Lynn Linton and Margaret Oliphant who wrote from essentially conservative positions.

However, significant as these feminist classics are, some of their precursors are interesting and ground-breaking in their own right, yet have themselves, like so many of the writers they uncover, been somewhat neglected in surveys of the development of a feminist critical tradition. Patricia Meyer Spacks's *The Female Imagination* and Vineta Colby's *The Singular Anomaly* both pre-date the work of Showalter and Gilbert and Gubar and along with Ellen Moers's *Literary Women* published in the same year as *A Literature of Their Own*, begin to address female experience and its relationship to women's writing.[9] Spacks and Moers provide broad surveys of women's writing: Spacks looks at a similar chronological sweep to Showalter, from the eighteenth to the twentieth century, and Moers looks at writers from the English, French and American traditions; Colby's sweep is less broad, focusing on the work of specific Victorian writers. The embryonic Anglo-American feminist tradition can be seen very clearly in both *The Female Imagination* and *Literary Women* in the focus on innate female experience and its manifestations such as the 'female Gothic' and Colby's work with its more specific focus looks forward to a whole series of detailed studies of selections of women writers. Other early, key texts including the work of Francoise Basch and Patricia Stubbs, do not exclusively focus on women writers, but do subscribe to a broadly feminist methodology in their consideration of the history and development of the novel and its relationship to women's experience.[10]

But what was, perhaps the most ground-breaking aspect of Showalter's contribution to the re-excavation of neglected women writers, was her willingness to consider non-canonical writers as worthy of more attention. Colby's *The Singular Anomaly* had already set this agenda with its attention to Eliza Lynn Linton, Olive Schreiner, Mrs Humphry Ward, John Oliver Hobbes and Vernon Lee, but a central part of her thesis was to suggest that these writers were 'women of intellect, taste, and talent, but they were not artists'.[11] For Colby, Jane Austen, the Brontës and George Eliot set the standard for nineteenth-century women's writing and the authors she considers, while interesting in terms of their purpose and popularity, fall some way below the mark of the aesthetic and intellectual genius of this pioneering group. Dorothy Mermin's study of women's writing from 1830 to 1880 continues in this vein in that she argues that Eliot's *Daniel Deronda*, with the exception of Oliphant's *Autobiography*, is the last major work by a Victorian woman writer.[12]

This rather bleak assessment of women's output in the *fin de siècle* years also concurs with Gaye Tuchman's thesis in *Edging Women Out*, which suggests that women were edged out from their position of prominence as writers of the high-culture novel by men and their manipulation of major literary institutions.[13] Yet as Valerie Sanders points out, Tuchman bases her argument on the Macmillan archive; but a wider consideration of the publishing industry suggests that at the end of the nineteenth century women writers still enjoyed success and adapted well to the changes in publishing patterns and indeed many of the recent collections of essays on *fin de siècle* writing corroborate this.[14] But Colby was willing to evaluate as well as to interpret the work of her chosen authors and this is worthy of note; there has been a strong and healthy tradition in modern feminist criticism of looking at major and minor writers together, of being inclusive;[15] but some critics have been more open to evaluation as well as interpretation than others and some have been more critical in their appraisal of certain writers and output at certain times such as Dorothy Mermin in *Godiva's Ride* for instance.

The areas that have been covered by feminist critics since the 1970s are very comprehensive and the most prevalent are: thematic concerns, studies of specific genres and studies of single authors. Most dedicated to themes look at a range of issues and either focus at the level of representation such as sexuality, marriage, maternity and domesticity,[16] or they focus on issues of textual production and consumption such as publishing, reading, reviewing, reception.[17] A number of recently edited collections covering both of these areas give an indication of current scholarly and critical areas of interest and provide a focus on questions of current concern. Nicola Thompson's *Victorian Women Writers and the Woman Question* addresses the rich ramifications of the woman question as seen through the work of a number of non-canonical writers.[18] Joanne Shattock's *Women and Literature in Britain 1800–1900* pulls together international scholarship and surveys and evaluates women's literary and cultural output throughout the whole century.[19] While Leah Harman and Susan Meyer's *The New Nineteenth Century* and Emma Liggins and Daniel Duffy's *Feminist Readings of Victorian Popular Texts* do not focus exclusively on writing by women they do reflect current interest in both feminist critique and the notion of the popular, both areas of seminal concern in this collection.[20]

Studies of single authors also reflect the commitment to extend the canon of women's writing and many recent studies have focused on writers who have come back into the frame and who deserve more attention such as Margaret Oliphant, Eliza Lynn Linton, Harriet Martineau, Rosa Nouchette Carey, Mrs Humphry Ward, Mary Elizabeth Braddon and Rhoda Broughton.[21] Those dedicated to specific genres are also plentiful and reflect areas of specific critical concern and interest such as sensation writing, new woman writing and writing for adolescents and children.[22] It is worth noting that consideration of women writing for specific audiences has been largely pushed to the margins, as has been the case with writing for the working class, or has appeared in different critical contexts, such as writing for children which has so far been best served by attention from critics working in the tradition of children's literature. It is surprising that these and other areas have been largely neglected by feminist critics, but it is perhaps symptomatic of the depth, richness and complexity of the field that so much interesting work has yet to be explored.

Thus the amount of critical material produced on Victorian women writers since the 1970s is impressive both in terms of volume and quality; yet if we are to move towards a more sophisticated understanding of Victorian women's writing more work remains to be done. But this takes us back to the rather knotty question of interpretation and evaluation, as critics as diverse as Dalziel and Thompson remind us.[23] This may not be something the critic aiming at inclusivity wants to confront yet it cannot be avoided; if a tradition of writing is to be fully explored then all avenues must be journeyed and all the material assessed. The canon of Victorian women's writing as it has emerged in the late twentieth century is filled with writers who fit into the Anglo-American frame of reference, concerning themselves with women's experience in one way or another and as the boundaries have been stretched to include conservative writers, it has been less amenable to writers writing in different modes or with different agendas. The process of discovering, re-discovering and analysing texts is the task of the critic and in this process the critical landscape is re-drawn. This re-mapping takes into account new findings such as 'lost' authors and new perspectives on themes, genre, production and consumption.

This collection presents three strands or themes: radical writing through the work of Mary Howitt, Eliza Metyard and Jessie Fothergill; writing for and about children through the work of Charlotte Yonge, Louisa Molesworth and Juliana Ewing; and sensation and romance writing through the work of Ellen Wood, Mary Braddon and Rhoda Broughton.

We give particular emphasis to these three areas because they are significant in the development of a tradition of popular women's writing. There is a healthy tradition of radical writing by women but the work of the three chosen authors has been neglected; they all write with very clear ideals and principles and use their writing as a tool or spur to social change. The reasons for their neglect are complex and differ in relation to each individual writer as the essays themselves seek to explain. However, it is fair to say that questions of genre and audience are particularly pertinent in relation to Howitt and Meteyard who largely addressed audiences marginalised or at least distanced from the metropolitan literary and cultural centre by either their class, their gender or their provinciality. A significant proportion of their work was journalistic, usually in the form of essays, articles, and short fiction and the periodicals to which they contributed were not prestigious, but this in itself should not debar them from serious consideration. It is also worthy of note and perhaps even faintly ironic that the work of these writers is not radical in the sense that Gilbert and Gubar envisage in their re-reading of nineteenth-century women's writing through its interest in the palimpsestic impulse and metaphors of enclosure and escape; rather, much of Howitt and Meteyard's work is domestic, didactic and sentimental, all arenas not traditionally lauded or laden with aesthetic or intellectual 'value' and certainly still posing some consternation for contemporary critics. In the case of Jessie Fothergill the radicalism lies in the agnosticism expressed in her writing and this contributed to many of the critical and technical difficulties she faced in the fluctuating late nineteenth-century market. The status of all three as minor writers both then and now tells us much about the politics of literary form, mode and genre.

Although many of the most famous nineteenth-century writers for children are men (for example Carroll and Kingsley) writing for children was a significant career option for women, and many of those who were well respected by their contemporaries are unknown to a modern audience. As discussed earlier, writing for specific audiences, in this instance for children and young adults, has been pushed to the margins in the developing tradition of feminist critique and once again questions of value begin to emerge. The essays on all three writers in this group raise a number of interesting questions about readership and genre. In the case of Yonge we see a shifting sense of projected readership and for all three the question of their writing in a recognisably female tradition which locates home, children, parenting, story-telling and instruction at the centre of the fictional worlds becomes something of a double-edged sword in terms of their ensuing critical reputations. It is most definitely the case that writing for children lacks the status of writing for adults, something which the relatively new critical tradition of children's writing has sought to redress; yet it remains to be seen whether women's writing for children will be considered as interesting and insightful as writing for adult women and those arenas already considered part of a tradition of women's writing.

Although the collective works of Wood, Braddon and Broughton constitute a large number of volumes, the reputations of these authors were made and continue to rest on a very limited number of novels produced during one decade, the 'sensational' 1860s. The phenomenon of sensation fiction with its mix of realism and melodrama, domesticity and criminality, and its fascination with constructs of femininity has become part of the curriculum of Victorian literary studies. Wood's *East Lynne* (1861) and Braddon's *Lady Audley's Secret* (1862) in particular are now intrinsic to the study of popular Victorian writing, but as the chapters on Ellen Wood and Mary Braddon assert there are other angles and other aspects of their work which merit further attention and reconsideration. Wood's corpus of work, as well as providing one of the most famous examples of sensation fiction in *East Lynne*, offers insight into a writer very much in tune with her public and her celebration of bourgeois values has much to tell us about the textual construction of class and gendered cultural identity. Braddon too, demonstrates versatility in theme and genre in her work and the focus on the intensity of visual experience derived from her theatrical experience contributes to the mass appeal of much of her fiction. Broughton's work is less studied, probably because it fits definitions of sensation less well. Categorising Broughton's work as romantic is more apt but hardly conveys the wit, subtlety and diversity of her work. Categorisation is a practical descriptive necessity but obviously it is limited by its generalisations. At the same time, the politics of generic description has been important to women's creative work in many forms. Romantic fiction is of course the archetype of the gendered genre. Despite the fact that romance would seem to be an almost essential element of fiction (especially that produced in the nineteenth century), fiction defined specifically as 'romantic' has been designated as for women and placed on the lowest rung of the literary hierarchy. Contemporary feminist critics have found this both instructive and enlightening.[24] The connection between the status of readers and their reading is relevant also to the production of works for and about children. Current discussion of the boundaries of child/adult reading is helping to bring consideration of Victorian 'children's' writing to the fore and we hope that continued work in the field of radical writing will also stimulate more debate on questions of audience and address. Insight into the ideological assumptions that shape generic definition features in many of the essays in this book as does a notion of the hybridity of each individual author's work. All of the contributors to this collection argue for a more extensive and developed understanding of their subject.

These areas are also worthy of attention because of their relation to the market and their role in both stimulating and meeting its needs; the growth of niche markets such as those for juvenile literature and the increasingly literate working class and the response to the public's need for sensation and romantic fiction. The method is broadly empirical with a particular emphasis on the material conditions of production. All of the writers fall under the aegis of the popular writer in one way or another and we seek to demonstrate the richness and complexity of this term. Some of our writers were popular in the sense that their works sold well and others struggled to make a living in a competitive and saturated market. Some enjoyed more critical success than others, both at the time and subsequently and others were very aware of the minor status of their work, even during their career. Those that edited periodicals were both influential and resourceful, often using the periodical as a site for marketing their work and career. Some wrote primarily to entertain, some to educate and some for particular audiences. Many of the writers produced their work within the context of a highly developed sense of their readership. All made use of professional, intellectual and social networks so important at a time when women were largely excluded from formal education and the usual trappings of professional life. The entirety of the texts discussed in this collection represents a wide range of women's perspectives of their world. As the discussion of Helen C. Black's work at the beginning of this introduction outlines and as feminist critics have repeatedly emphasised, a woman writer's reputation is formed in relation to ideologies of femininity as much as in relation to notions of aesthetics. Thus, when a woman writer markets her work she also markets 'herself'. Within and across this collection writers address notions of life as a daughter, spinster, lover, wife and as the earlier reference to Showalter indicates, we ignore these links in the chain at our peril.

Presented in three groups, each in loosely chronological order, the essays will present their own reading of the author's works or particular topic of interest but will also demonstrate the way each writer negotiated her place in the market, her place in the contemporary critical and commercial context and the late twentieth-century critical canon. We aim to bring attention to writers who have been barely or only recently begun to be considered such as Howitt, Meteyard and Fothergill; to bring interesting and new perspectives on those who have come to the fore since the advent of modern feminist criticism such as Wood, Braddon, Broughton and Yonge; and to consider writers who have most often elicited interest from other critical communities such as Molesworth and Ewing and have been somewhat neglected by feminist critics.

In the first essay of the collection Brian Maidment looks at the way in which Mary Howitt recognised both the ideological functions of mass circulation literature and the importance of literature as a means of social progress. Looking at a range of her writing both in its own right and in relation to the work she did with her husband William, he situates Howitt as a writer at the centre of progressive politics and as playing a key role in writing women into this discourse. In the essay on Eliza Meteyard, Kay Boardman considers the struggles of the minor writer and the way in which Meteyard negotiated her place in a fiercely competitive market and how often she felt she had to compromise her artistic integrity in order to make a living. Focusing also on her contribution to social critique and progressive politics, this chapter seeks to demonstrate how Meteyard dedicated her writing to the pursuit of a principle. Helen Debenham's chapter considers Jessie Fothergill, a determinedly regional writer, who was successful in her lifetime, and who grappled with the moral dilemmas of the 1870s and 1880s. Her work also highlights the effects of the increasing divergence between serious and popular fiction. Debenham's discussion of Fothergill's novels reveals an original and challenging author who merits further scholarly interest.

Valerie Sanders focuses on the work of Charlotte Yonge and her exploration of the vicissitudes of family life through the family chronicle. The detailed recreation of the psychological and physical pleasures and hardships of large families is Yonge's achievement here. Her emphasis is on the child's experience of the family and their moral development within this validates both the child as character and the child or adolescent reader. In Chapter 5 Jane Darcy considers the work and career of Louisa Molesworth, who although very popular in her day has not attained the status of a classic 'golden age' children's writer. Molesworth's work moves away from the didactic domestic fiction of the previous generation towards a more balanced attention to both domestic realism and fantasy. Looking at a whole range of writing produced throughout Molesworth's long career, Darcy argues that she was a writer who trod successfully the thin and difficult line between satisfying the expectations of the market and expressing something more individual and personal. Jennifer Litster's chapter on Juliana Ewing traces the career of a writer born into a very particular eccentric and educational milieu where a distinctive creative identity had to be developed. Within a relatively short chronological period Ewing produced a wide variety of children's fiction and approached her writing with a seriousness of intent that demands contemporary review. Litster argues that Ewing's best work was innovative and child-centred and that she was always willing to experiment creatively.

In Marie Riley's essay on Ellen Wood she pays particular attention to Wood's relationship to the marketplace. Wood knew and understood her audience and offered them products which defined and affirmed them. Further, Wood's knowledge of the market allowed her to re-package and re-cycle her work extensively. Mary Elizabeth Braddon is the subject of Chapter 8 and Valerie Pedlar provides a detailed discussion of her use of the theatre and theatrical imagery. Sketching in Braddon's personal experience of theatrical life as a young actress, Pedlar then goes on to explore ideas of staging, scene-setting, role-playing and performance across a range of Braddon's novels. The final chapter in the collection considers Rhoda Broughton's writing of romance. For over fifty years Broughton produced novels on the same subject, love, and Shirley Jones argues that these works are diverse and experimental rather than limited and formulaic. Whether or not Broughton was initially inspired to write by personal experience, her novels deal with romantic love imaginatively and expansively.

If part of the task of extending the canon is to offer up neglected writers for attention and to encourage new perspectives on those who have received attention then surely part of that task is to engage with questions of literary value, of interpretation and evaluation as Vineta Colby suggested at the beginning of late twentieth-century feminist critique. No matter how much the canon is still largely self-perpetuating, no matter what the aesthetic agenda is on literary merit and how it might be redrawn, we believe that all the authors covered are eminently engaging and worthy of our attention. Many of the works of the authors covered here are no longer in print rendering them largely inaccessible to a wide range of potential readers, but it is hoped that these essays will bring the work of largely unknown authors and the neglected works of known authors, to critical and public attention.

Notes

1 Helen C. Black, *Notable Women Authors of the Day, Biographical Sketches* (Glasgow: David Bryce and Son, 1893).

2 Eva Hope, *The Queens of Literature of the Victorian Era* (London: Walter Scott, 1886).

3 Mrs Oliphant et al., *Women Novelists of Queen Victoria' s Reign: A Book of Appreciations* (London: Hurst and Blackett, 1897), p. viii–ix.

4 W. L. Courtney, *The Feminine Note in Fiction* (London: Chapman and Hall, 1904), p. viii.

5 Amy Cruse, *The Victorians and Their Books* (London: George Allen and Unwin, 1935). Subsequent page references are given in the text.

6 Margaret Dalziel, *Popular Fiction 100 Years Ago* (London: Cohen and West, 1957).

7 Nigel Cross, *The Common Writer. Life in Nineteenth-Century Grub Street* (Cambridge: Cambridge University Press, 1985). See also Guinevere L. Griest, *Mudie's Circulating Library and the Victorian Novel* (Newton Abbot: David and Charles, 1970) and R. C. Terry, *Victorian Popular Fiction, 1860–1880* (London: Macmillan, 1983).

8 Sandra M. Gilbert and Susan Gubar, *The Madwoman in the Attic. The Woman Writer and the Nineteenth-Century Literary Imagination* (New Haven, CT: Yale University Press, 1979); Elaine Showalter, *A Literature of Their Own: British Women Novelists from Brontë to Lessing* [1977] (London: Virago Press, 1978). Subsequent page references are given in the text.

9 Vineta Colby, *The Singular Anomaly. Women Novelists of the Nineteenth Century* (New York: Garland Press, 1970); Ellen Moers, *Literary Women* (London: W. H. Allen, 1977); Patricia Meyer Spacks, *The Female Imagination. A Literary and Psychological Investigation of Women's Writing* (London: George Allen and Unwin, 1972).

10 Françoise Basch, *Relative Creatures. Victorian Women in Society and the Novel, 1837–1867,* trans. Anthony Rudolf (New York: Schocken Books, 1974); Patricia Stubbs, *Women and Fiction. Feminism and the Novel, 1880–1920* (Brighton: Harvester Press, 1979); see also Jenni Calder, *Women and Marriage in Victorian Fiction* (London: Thames and Hudson, 1976).

11 Colby, *The Singular Anomaly,* pp. 10–11.

12 Dorothy Mermin, *Godiva's Ride. Women of Letters in England, 1830–1880* (Indianapolis, IN: Indiana University Press, 1993).

13 Gaye Tuchman with Nina Fortin, *Edging Women Out. Victorian Novelists, Publishers, and Social Change* (London: Routledge, 1989).

14 Valerie Sanders, 'Women, Fiction and the Marketplace', in Joanne Shattock (ed.), *Women and Literature in Britain 1800–1900* (Cambridge: Cambridge University Press, 2001), pp. 142–61.

15 See, for example, Shirley Foster's *Victorian Women's Fiction: Marriage, Freedom and the Individual* (London: Croom Helm, 1985) which looks at

the work of Dinah Mulock Craik and Elizabeth Sewell alongside that of Charlotte Brontë, Elizabeth Gaskell and George Eliot.

16 See, for example: Nina Auerbach, *Communities of Women, an Idea in Fiction* (Cambridge, MA: Harvard University Press, 1978); Jill L. Matus, *Unstable Bodies: Victorian Representations of Sexuality and Maternity* (Manchester: Manchester University Press, 1995); Kimberley Reynolds and Nicola Humble, *Victorian Heroines. Representations of Femininity in Nineteenth-Century Literature and Art* (Hemel Hempstead: Harvester Wheatsheaf, 1993); Patricia Thomson, *The Victorian Heroine. A Changing Ideal, 1837–1873* (London: Oxford University Press, 1956).

17 See, for example: Sally Mitchell, *The Fallen Angel: Chastity, Class and Women's Reading, 1835–1880* (Bowling Green, OH: Bowling Green University Press, 1981); Kate Flint, *The Woman Reader, 1837–1914* (Oxford: Clarendon Press, 1993); Barbara Onslow, *Women of the Press in Nineteenth-Century Britain* (Basingstoke: Macmillan, 2000).

18 Nicola Diane Thompson (ed.), *Victorian Women Writers and the Woman Question* (Cambridge: Cambridge University Press, 1999).

19 Shattock (ed.), *Women and Literature.*

20 Barbara Leah Harman and Susan Meyer (eds), *The New Nineteenth Century. Feminist Readings of Underread Victorian Fiction* (London: Garland Publishing, 1996; Emma Liggins and Daniel Duffy (eds), *Feminist Readings of Victorian Popular Texts: Divergent Femininities* (Aldershot: Ashgate, 2001).

21 See Nancy Fix Anderson, *Woman Against Women in Victorian England. A Life of Eliza Lynn Linton* (Indianapolis, IN: Indiana University Press, 1987); Jennifer Carnell, *The Literary Lives of Mary Elizabeth Braddon: A Study of her Life and Work* (Hastings: The Sensation Press, 2000); Elaine Hartnell, *Gender, Religion and Domesticity in the Novels of Rosa Nouchette Carey* (Aldershot: Ashgate, 2000); Elisabeth Jay, *Mrs. Oliphant: A Fiction to Herself. A Literary Life* (Oxford: Clarendon Press, 1995); Jane Moore, *Mrs. Molesworth* (Sussex: Pratts Folly Press, 2002); Margarete Rubik, *The Novels of Mrs. Oliphant: A Subversive View of Traditional Themes* (New York: Peter Lang, 1994); Valerie Sanders, *Reason over Passion: Harriet Martineau and the Victorian Novel* (Sussex: Harvester, 1986); John Sutherland, *Mrs. Humphrey Ward* (Oxford: Clarendon Press, 1990); D. J. Trela, *Margaret Oliphant: Critical Essays on a Gentle Subversive* (Selinsgrove, PA: Susquehanna University Press, 1995); Robert Lee Wolff, *Sensational Victorian* (New York: Garland Press, 1979); Marilyn Wood, *Rhoda Broughton (1840–1920), Profile of a Novelist* (Stamford: Paul Watkins, 1993).

22 On New Woman writing see, for example: Ann Ardis, *New Women, New Novels: Feminism and Early Modernism* (New Brunswick, NJ: Rutgers University Press, 1990); Gail Cunningham, *The New Woman and the Victorian Novel* (London: Macmillan, 1978); Ann Heilmann, *New Woman Fiction: Women Writing First-Wave Feminism* (London: Macmillan, 2000); Sally Ledger, *The New Woman: Fiction and Feminism at the Fin de Siècle*

(Manchester: Manchester University Press, 1997). On sensation writing see, for example: Ann Cvetkovich, *Mixed Feelings: Feminism, Mass Culture, and Victorian Sensationalism* (New Brunswick, NJ: Rutgers, 1993); Pamela K. Gilbert, *Disease, Desire, and the Body in Victorian Women's Popular Novels* (Cambridge: Cambridge University Press, 1997); Winifred Hughes, *The Maniac in the Cellar: Sensation Novels of the 1860s* (Princeton, NJ: Princeton University Press, 1980); Lyn Pykett, *The 'Improper' Feminine: The Women's Sensation Novel and the New Woman Writing* (London: Routledge, 1992). On writing for children and adolescents see, for example: Mary Cadogan and Patricia Craig, *You're a Brick Angela! The Girls' Story, 1839–1985* (London: Victor Gollancz, 1976); Shirley Foster and Judy Simons, *What Katy Read: Feminist Rereadings of 'Classic' Stories for Girls, 1850–1920* (London: Macmillan, 1995); Kimberley Reynolds, *Girls Only? Gender and Popular Children's Fiction in Britain, 1880–1910* (Hemel Hempstead: Harvester, 1990); Judith Rowbotham, *Good Girls Make Good Wives: Guidance for Girls in Victorian Fiction* (Oxford: Basil Blackwell, 1989).

23 Thompson, *Victorian Women Writers*; Dalziel, *Popular Fiction.*
24 See Tania Modleski, *Loving with a Vengeance* (New York: Methuen, 1984) and Janice A. Radway, *Reading the Romance: Women, Patriarchy, and Popular Literature* [1984] (London: Verso, 1987).

Bibliography

Anderson, Nancy Fix, *Woman Against Women in Victorian England. A Life of Eliza Lynn Linton,* Indianapolis, IN: Indiana University Press, 1987.

Ardis, Ann, *New Women, New Novels: Feminism and Early Modernism,* New Brunswick, NJ: Rutgers University Press, 1990.

Auerbach, Nina, *Communities of Women, an Idea in Fiction,* Cambridge, MA: Harvard University Press, 1978.

Basch, Françoise, *Relative Creatures. Victorian Women in Society and the Novel, 1837–1867,* trans. Anthony Rudolf, New York: Schocken Books, 1974.

Black, Helen C., *Notable Women Authors of the Day, Biographical Sketches,* Glasgow: David Bryce and Son, 1893.

Cadogen, Mary and Patricia Craig, *You're a Brick Angela! The Girls' Story, 1839–1985,* London: Victor Gollancz, 1976.

Calder, Jenni, *Women and Marriage in Victorian Fiction,* London: Thames and Hudson, 1976.

Carnell, Jennifer, *The Literary Lives of Mary Elizabeth Braddon: A Study of her Life and Work,* Hastings: The Sensation Press, 2000.

Colby, Vineta, *The Singular Anomaly. Women Novelists of the Nineteenth Century,* New York: New York University Press, 1970.

Courtney, W. L., *The Feminine Note in Fiction,* London: Chapman and Hall, 1904.

Cross, Nigel, *The Common Writer. Life in Nineteenth-Century Grub Street,*

Cambridge: Cambridge University Press, 1985.

Cruse, Amy, *The Victorians and Their Books,* London: George Allen and Unwin, 1935.

Cunningham, Gail, *The New Woman and the Victorian Novel,* London: Macmillan, 1978.

Cvetkovich, Ann, *Mixed Feelings: Feminism, Mass Culture, and Victorian Sensationalism,* New Brunswick, NJ: Rutgers, 1993.

Dalziel, Margaret, *Popular Fiction 100 Years Ago,* London: Cohen and West, 1957.

Elwin, Malcolm, *Victorian Wallflowers,* London: Jonathan Cape, 1934.

Flint, Kate, *The Woman Reader, 1837–1914,* Oxford: Clarendon Press, 1993.

Foster, Shirley, *Victorian Women's Fiction: Marriage, Freedom and the Individual,* London: Croom Helm, 1985.

Foster, Shirley and Judy Simons, *What Katy Read: Feminist Rereadings of 'Classic' Stories for Girls, 1850–1920,* London: Macmillan, 1995.

Gilbert, Pamela K., *Disease, Desire, and the Body in Victorian Women's Popular Novels,* Cambridge: Cambridge University Press, 1997.

Gilbert, Sandra M. and Susan Gubar, *The Madwoman in the Attic. The Woman Writer and the Nineteenth-Century Literary Imagination,* New Haven, CT: Yale University Press, 1979.

Griest, Guinivere, *Mudie's Circulating Library and the Victorian Novel,* Newton Abbot: David and Charles, 1970.

Harman, Barbara Leah and Susan Meyer (eds), *The New Nineteenth Century Feminist Readings of Underread Victorian Fiction,* London: Garland Publishing, 1996.

Hartnell, Elaine, *Gender, Religion and Domesticity in the Novels of Rosa Nouchette Carey,* Aldershot: Ashgate, 2000.

Heilman, Ann, *New Woman Fiction: Women Writing First-Wave Feminism,* London: Macmillan, 2000.

Hope, Eva, *The Queens of Literature of the Victorian Era,* London: Walter Scott, 1886.

Hughes, Winifred, *The Maniac in the Cellar: Sensation Novels of the 1860s,* Princeton, NJ: Princeton University Press, 1980.

Jay, Elisabeth, *Mrs. Oliphant: A Fiction to Herself. A Literary Life,* Oxford: Clarendon Press, 1995.

Ledger, Sally, *The New Woman: Fiction and Feminism at the Fin de Siècle,* Manchester: Manchester University Press, 1997.

Liggins, Emma and Daniel Duffy (eds), *Feminist Readings of Victorian Popular Texts: Divergent Femininities,* Aldershot: Ashgate, 2001.

Matus, Jill L., *Unstable Bodies: Victorian Representations of Sexuality and Maternity,* Manchester: Manchester University Press, 1995.

Mermin, Dorothy, *Godiva's Ride. Women of Letters in England, 1830–1880,* Indianapolis, IN: Indiana University Press, 1993.

Mitchell, Sally, *The Fallen Angel: Chastity, Class and Women's Reading, 1835–1880,* Bowling Green, OH: Bowling Green University Press, 1981.

Modleski, Tania, *Loving with a Vengeance,* New York: Methuen, 1984.

Moers, Ellen, *Literary Women,* London: W.H. Allen, 1977.

Moore, Jane, *Mrs. Molesworth,* Sussex: Pratts Folly Press, 2002.

Oliphant, Mrs, et al., *Women Novelists of Queen Victoria's Reign: A Book of Appreciations,* London: Hurst and Blackett, 1897.

Onslow, Barbara, *Women of the Press in Nineteenth-Century Britain,* Macmillan: Basingstoke, 2000.

Pearce, Lynne and Jackie Stacey (eds), *Romance Revisited,* New York and London: New York University Press, 1995.

Pykett, Lyn, *The 'Improper' Feminine: The Women's Sensation Novel and the New Woman Writing,* London: Routledge, 1992.

Radford, Jean (ed.), *The Progress of Romance: the Politics of Popular Fiction,* London: Routledge and Kegan Paul, 1986.

Radway, Janice A., *Reading the Romance: Women, Patriarchy, and Popular Literature* [1984] London: Verso, 1987.

Reynolds, Kimberley, *Girls Only? Gender and Popular Children's Fiction in Britain, 1880–1910,* Hemel Hempstead, Harvester, 1990.

Reynolds, Kimberley and Nicola Humble, *Victorian Heroines. Representations of Femininity in Nineteenth-Century Literature and Art,* Hemel Hempstead: Harvester Wheatsheaf, 1993.

Rowbotham, Judith, *Good Girls Make Good Wives: Guidance for Girls in Victorian Fiction,* Oxford: Basil Blackwell, 1989.

Rubik, Margarete, *The Novels of Mrs. Oliphant: A Subversive View of Traditional Themes,* New York: Peter Lang, 1994.

Sanders, Valerie, *Eve's Renegades. Anti-Feminist Victorian Women Novelists,* Basingstoke: Macmillan, 1996.

——'Women, Fiction and the Marketplace', in Joanne Shattock (ed.), *Women and Literature in Britain 1800–1900,* Cambridge: Cambridge University Press, 2001, pp. 142–61.

——*Reason over Passion: Harriet Martineau and the Victorian Novel,* Sussex: Harvester, 1986.

Shattock, Joanne (ed.), *Women and Literature in Britain 1800–1900,* Cambridge: Cambridge University Press, 2001.

——(ed.), *The Oxford Guide to British Women Writers,* Oxford: Oxford University Press, 1993.

Showalter, Elaine, *A Literature of Their Own: British Women Novelists from Brontë to Lessing,* London: Virago Press, 1977.

Spacks, Patricia Meyer, *The Female Imagination. A Literary and Psychological Investigation of Women's Writing,* London: George Allen and Unwin, 1972.

Stubbs, Patricia, *Women and Fiction. Feminism and the Novel, 1880–1920,* Brighton: Harvester Press, 1979.

Sutherland, John, *Mrs. Humphrey Ward,* Oxford: Clarendon Press, 1990.

Rubik, Margarete, *The Novels of Mrs. Oliphant: A Subversive View of Traditional Themes,* New York: Peter Lang, 1994.

Terry, R. C., *Victorian Popular Fiction, 1860–1880*, London: Macmillan, 1983.

Thompson, Nicola Diane (ed.), *Victorian Women Writers and the Woman Question*, Cambridge: Cambridge University Press, 1999.

Thomson, Patricia, *The Victorian Heroine. A Changing Ideal, 1837–1873*, London: Oxford University Press, 1956.

Trela, D. J., *Margaret Oliphant: Critical Essays on a Gentle Subversive*, Selinsgrove: Susquehanna University Press, 1995.

Tuchman, Gaye with Nina Fortin, *Edging Women Out. Victorian Novelists, Publishers, and Social Change*, London: Routledge, 1989.

Walbank, Felix Alan (ed.), *Queens of the Circulating Library*, London: Evans Brothers, 1950.

Wolff, Robert Lee, *Sensational Victorian*, New York: Garland, 1979.

Wood, Marilyn, *Rhoda Broughton (1840–1920), Profile of a Novelist*, Stamford: Paul Watkins, 1993.

1

'Works in unbroken succession': the literary career of Mary Howitt

Brian E. Maidment

Famously, Mary Botham was born a Quaker in 1799 but died a Catholic, as Mary Howitt, in 1888. Her posthumously published *An Autobiography* (1889) describes this spiritual journey as well as the way in which Mary Botham became half of a highly respected professional writing team called the Howitts. Brought up a Quaker, the daughter of an entrepreneurial though not always successful surveyor, Mary Botham in 1821 married a restless and ambitious young Quaker, William Howitt, whose nascent career as an apprentice carpenter soon gave way under the weight of his literary aspirations. The Howitts moved to central Nottingham in 1822 where William ran a druggist's shop. Despite the demands of a growing family and a strong engagement in local political and religious life, the young couple launched themselves into literary careers, working both collaboratively and individually on poems, topographical, historical and polemical subjects. Their generosity of mind, unwavering belief in the importance of literature as a means of social progress and their gift for friendship drew them into a wide network of literary and political acquaintance, and made them a rallying point for literary activities. Despite being responsible for their growing family, and living through a variety of local disturbances centred on the Reform Bill, they began to undertake journeys and travels which, as well as providing them with much of their literary material, fed their intellectual curiosity and furthered their awareness of social differences. They were several times visitors to the literary salons of London, so that it was hardly surprising that they moved to Esher in Surrey in 1836, a move that publicised their commitment to careers as freelance writers. William Howitt had already published controversial articles on religious history in *Tait's Edinburgh Magazine* as well as successful travel-cum-cultural history books, and was beginning to establish himself in the marketplace. Mary, like William, was moving on from poetry, but was looking more towards didactic and improving literature, especially 'tales' for children. An adventurous three year stay in Germany (1840–43) was prompted by both a sense of literary opportunity (the Howitts had taught themselves German over several years and wanted to exploit, through translations, British curiosity about German Romanticism) and by their never failing interest in the social and intellectual life of others. Their interest in translation also derived from a commitment to introducing 'progressive' literature to Britain regardless of its source, and Mary became well known as a translator of Scandinavian literature.

The next, extended, phase of their lives was spent in semi-rural London suburbs, turning their deeply felt and modestly moralised concern for the education and moral well-being of artisans into series of publications aimed at furthering 'popular progress', publications which often shifted the boundaries between established literary genres and which re-worked the British literary tradition for new propagandist purposes. The most complete representation of this project was a co-edited weekly periodical *Howitt's Journal* which ran from 1847 to 1849. This periodical, wrought out of evident support for the intellectual and cultural development of the working classes, combined William's polemical enthusiasm with Mary's concern for the social inclusion of women and children. During these years around London, William and Mary drew their large and often talented family members into a range of co-authored projects and offered generous continuing support to a broad range of struggling writers, thus becoming widely and affectionately recognised in the changing contexts of mid-Victorian professional literary life.

In 1870, as well established writers, the Howitts left their Esher home for Switzerland, travelling on to Rome later in the year. Over the next few years, Mary Howitt used travels in Switzerland, Italy and Austria as the basis for articles in periodicals like *The Leisure Hour* and *The Argosy*. In 1879, William died at their home in the Austrian Tyrol at the age of 86. In the wake of his death, Mary was accorded a small civil list pension. Much to the astonishment of friends and even her family, Mary Howitt converted to Catholicism before her death in 1888.

To those Victorians whose opinions we have, Mary Howitt was primarily a poet, widely anthologised and hence widely visible across the century. Her vast output of over one hundred volumes nonetheless comprised fiction, children's books, verse, topographical and travel writing and some journalism. Yet, for reasons to be explored later in this essay, her work could easily be dismissed for its lack of ambition, its privileging of the social above the 'literary', for its address to social groups without cultural privileges – children, artisans, working women, for example – and for its cheerful re-working of established literary ideas and forms. The two book length biographical studies of the Howitts, both of which date from the 1950s, stress their decency, their intellectual curiosity and their family life at the expense of their literary achievement – indeed Amice Lee summarises Mary's literary output as 'tales and ballads' and notes that while she 'had truly dreamed of fame' she had won only 'homely laurels' and 'plenty and many friends'.[1] A few scattered attempts have since been made to redeem Mary Howitt from 'homeliness' and decency into someone whose generic experimentation, sense of audience, and social mission informed and energised rather than compromised her writing. The most important of these is Linda Peterson's recognition that Mary Howitt's autobiography represents the outcome of a highly wrought professional career, but some other slight attempts have been made to explore further the significance of the Howitts as entrepreneurs of artisan literature and to recognise their contribution to the development of working-class culture.[2] But there is still some fundamental work to be done in acknowledging Mary Howitt's considerable literary achievements. Such work needs to begin by looking at the ways in which her contemporaries constructed her as an essentially minor writer because these reveal a considerable amount about the politics of literary form, mode and genre in the early Victorian period.

In the massive ten-volume survey of a century of nineteenth-century poetic production, A. H. Miles's *The Poets and Poetry of the Century*, A. H. Japp describes Mary Howitt as 'one of the most graceful, versatile and voluminous writers of the earlier half of the century'.[3] As *A New Spirit of the Age* noted in 1844 'our authoress sends forth her delightful works in unbroken succession, to the four quarters of the globe.'[4] It is hard to disagree with Japp's summary. *The Cambridge Bibliography of English Literature* entry for Howitt, notes after a substantial listing of poetry and fiction (much of it published under an American imprint), that 'Mrs. Howitt wrote, edited and translated some 110 works. Among her more notable [translations] are various tales from the Danish of Hans Andersen, and the novels of Fredrika Bremer from the Swedish in 18 vols.'[5] So 'voluminous' and 'versatile' are not difficult to establish, though these are not entirely terms of praise. 'Graceful', which might allude specifically to Howitt's literary style or more broadly to a spiritual project which informs all her work, is more difficult to interpret, even though the word seems entirely apposite.

Inevitably, by implication, 'voluminous' and 'versatile' also mean 'minor'. Mary Howitt's 'minorness' was, for the late Victorians, compounded out of a number of factors. First of all she was a woman writer, and late Victorian recognition of her significance was inevitably filtered through the lens of gender politics. She appears in the volume Miles devotes to women poets, who 'form a characteristic feature of [nineteenth century] literature ... As such it has been thought well to separate it [poetry by women] from the general body of poetry of the period and present it in a form calculated to show its progress and development. It is hoped that the result will be found of sufficient interest to justify this special treatment.'[6] The special pleading with which late Victorian commentators sought to make writing by women poets of 'sufficient interest' of course manifested itself in several other anthologies of writing by women poets. Mary Howitt is invariably accorded a modest presence in such volumes. The most challenging of these, Mrs William Sharp's wide-ranging *Women's Voices*, sought to represent 'each of our women-poets by one or more essentially characteristic poem' rather than offer 'their most indifferent productions' after the fashion of previous thematic or chronological anthologies.[7] But Sharp's project is driven by a polemical teleological vision:

> Women have had many serious hindrances to contend against – defective education, lack of broad experience of life, absence of freedom in which to make full use of natural abilities, and the force of public and private opinion, both of which have always been prone to prejudge her work unfavourably, or at best apologetically. These deterrant influences are gradually passing away, with the result that an ever-widening field for the exercise of their powers is thus afforded to women.[8]

Thus Mary Howitt, represented in Sharp's anthology by 'The Fairies of The Caldon-Low', a jolly pastiche of a traditional ballad, complete with riddling structure, in which a child sees a nocturnal vision of fairies fulfilling human need, was regarded to some extent as a product of her age, an essentially early Victorian figure whose popularity, despite Sharp's claims for the formation of a tradition of women's writing, was circumscribed by the opportunities available to her. Another later Victorian survey, Eric S. Robertson's *English Poetesses*, offers a much more precisely dismissive sense of Mary Howitt as both a minor writer and as an anachronism: 'Four names popularly honoured – though chiefly in a bygone age – must here be mentioned. Of these the first three belong to women who have best distinguished themselves by efforts other than the poetical.'[9] Robertson goes on to cite Howitt along with Mary Cowden Clarke and Frances Anne Kemble [Mrs Butler] in this category. This concentration on Howitt's *poetry* as presenting to her contemporaries her best case for literary survival is an interesting one given her wide range of publications. While of course it is much easier to anthologise poems than prose or 'tales', nonetheless the relegation of her fiction and journalism to the realm of the 'non-literary' seems to me to derive largely from a recognition of the overt social purposiveness of her work in these genres. Howitt's determination to bring together education, social reform and literature was something that made her more genteel readers uncomfortable, a discomfort which has distorted awareness of her work for succeeding generations.

So, for the late Victorians, four immediate factors militated in favour of relegating Mary Howitt's literary output to a 'minor' status. Firstly, she wrote too much. Secondly, she belonged unequivocally to a tradition of 'women's writing' which, if it could be identified and rehabilitated at all, still remained marginalised within literary history. As we shall see, her self-imposed affiliation with a view of writing as a necessarily gendered activity forms one of the most interesting aspects of Howitt's career. Thirdly, Mary Howitt was an anachronism, important for a society when literature served a particular ideological purpose, but essentially someone belonging to a bygone age. Fourthly, there remained an unresolved tension between Howitt's role as a educationalist concerned with the moral welfare of the nation and any artistic ambitions she might have had as a writer. As Japp puts it – 'It would be wholly unjust to try many of her pieces, written with an eye to certain evils special to the time – by the highest standard of what we are nowadays taught to consider "high-art."'[10]

These late Victorian filters are not, however, the only difficulties in getting Mary Howitt's writing into clear focus. Her most famous book for late Victorians was in many respects her most controversial – the two volume *Mary Howitt: An Autobiography* edited by Howitt's daughter Margaret and published in 1889 after Mary's death.[11] The book had a complicated publishing history: begun as a memoir for her children, and increasingly incorporating family letters and papers, it was partially serialised in *Good Words*, revised for book issue by Mary Howitt just before her death and finally published under the editorship of her daughter. *An Autobiography*, which draws extensively on Howitt's family letters and journals, as well as providing an important glimpse of the literary and social world that the Howitts occupied, more unusually provides a female equivalent to the celebrated line of Victorian male spiritual autobiographies that runs from Mill's *Autobiography* and Newman's *Apologia* through Froude to 'Mark Rutherford's' *Autobiography* and *Deliverance*. In *Traditions of Victorian Women's Autobiography*, Linda Peterson has written about how

the formation of a Victorian tradition of distinctively female autobiographies was constructed out of a recognition of the relevance of
seventeenth-century spiritual autobiographies and domestic memoirs
written by women which 'provided Victorian women with a means of
contributing to an increasingly popular genre; while their male
counterparts established the narrative structures and interpretive modes
of the classic *res gestae* and developmental forms, women tried alternative
structures and added a "feminine sensibility to the genre, a deeper
revelation of sentiments, more subjectivity and more subtle self-analyses".'[12]
She notes further that Howitt's book, while it does, in the tradition of
spiritual autobiography, examine a conversion from a pious Quakerism
into a fervent, if characteristically modest and humble, Catholicism,
combine family material and expound the collective Howitt activities, and
conform to the notion of a 'domestic memoir' it also, more radically, offers
an account of 'the family's professional achievement'.[13] Such 'incipient
versions of the professional woman's life written as "domestic memoir"'
formed 'not only a formal model but ... an ideological model for the
woman artist's work'.[14] Yet for all its engagement with Mary Howitt's
professional life, *An Autobiography* does have a genuine spiritual intensity.
Noting in her final illness that 'I assuredly believe that the wonderful power
of Catholic prayer, not for my life, but for the fulfilment of God's will,
whether I were to live or die, prevailed, and that for some purpose or
other I was raised up again', she is quick to add in a letter to Miss Leigh
Smith 'This seems arrogant, does it not? I feel it so.'[15] In many ways *An
Autobiography*, with its earnest good sense and vision of social meliorism
overlaid by spiritual energy was a startling book for Mary Howitt to write.
In using, and feminising, a combination of literary genres and
acknowledging a tradition of women's autobiographies which stretch back
to the seventeenth century, Mary Howitt's *An Autobiography* is a fitting
conclusion to her professional career.

   If the combination of socio-political vision, professional competence
and spiritual intensity expressed by *An Autobiography* to some extent
confounded the late Victorian constructions of her career, Mary Howitt
also contradicted conservative ideas of what women authors should be
through both her internationalism, especially her work as a translator,
and her role as a magazine editor. In neither activity was she unique –
Marian Evans ['George Eliot'] had, of course, begun her literary career as
a translator, and by the 1840s women had become quite widely involved
in the management, financing and editing of periodicals as well as
contributing extensively to periodicals.[16] A number of periodicals, most

notably *Eliza Cook's Journal*, depended for their success on a feminised awareness of the traditional content of popular monthlies. But in drawing attention to, and making available, the existence of valuable and socially progressive literature, especially literature for children, from such diverse sources as Denmark, Sweden and the United States, Mary Howitt was unusual. The alliance of Mary Howitt's European eclecticism and William Howitt's determined efforts to make sure that new ideas about social justice and communitarianism emerging, in particular, in France should be better known in England, give the idea of 'making available' a new intensity and cultural force which culminated in the various magazines co-edited and co-projected by the Howitts, especially *Howitt's Journal* which ran from 1847 to 1849. These magazines will form the focus of much of this chapter.

The mere mention of William Howitt inevitably brings into play the most complex reason why it is hard to focus on the literary and cultural importance of Mary Howitt – her long-lived personal, literary and political partnership with William Howitt. While the *Cambridge Bibliography* entry at least manages to separate out the literary work of the two Howitts, most other commentators have been happy enough to regard their work as somehow the product of an elided 'William and Mary' – an understanding not helped by the historical echoes of their combined name or by the fact that several of their early volumes of poems had been published under their joint names. Both of the modern biographies are joint ones.[17] The essay on the Howitts in R. H. Horne's *A New Spirit of the Age*, written as early as 1844, opened with the comment that 'the numerous literary labours of William and Mary Howitt, are so inextricably and so interestingly mixed up with their biographies, that they can only be appropriately treated under one head'.[18] Another contemporary, Ebenezer Elliott, was recalled by Spencer T. Hall, a personal friend of the Howitts, as being in the habit of remarking 'that their names always reminded him of a "William and Mary" shilling, with the two heads side by side'. Hall adds 'And when one thinks of the arduous career through which they have solaced each other, and how much the literary world owes to their beautifully united labours, certainly the symbol is not an inapt one.'[19] Hall, perhaps unconsciously, here elides the Howitts' literary activities into a single career. When the various literary and artistic contributions and collaborations of William and Mary's children were added in – Peterson notes of *An Autobiography* that 'since William and Mary Howitt were well-published poets and journalists, their daughter Anna Mary was a prominent painter in the 1840s and 1850s, and their daughter Margaret a professional translator, this autobiography represents a family memoir *cum* professional artist's life'[20]

– it is perhaps hardly surprising that the Victorians, and to some extent subsequent criticism has invented a single author called 'The Howitts'.

Notwithstanding the elisions of these various Howitts into a singular 'William and Mary', with all the potential this might have for subordinating Mary to her more controversial and publicly visible husband, there is no doubt that the Howitts themselves not only accepted but actually made capital out of the perception of their separate work as part of a single socio-literary project. Indeed, they seem in many respects to have gone out of their way to reinforce what might seem nowadays a highly conservative and restrictive 'separate spheres' approach to the making of their literary output. William's volume-length writings were largely devoted to history (both religious and secular) and topography, although these categories rather belie the polemical turn of much of what he wrote – in his hands, history became the history of colonialisation, priestcraft and national identity. Indeed, his great topic was the attempt to re-appropriate traditions from the ownership of the powerful in order to reformulate them in modes and forms which made them accessible to the artisan and the cottager. He also published some fiction and a considerable amount of poetry in volume form. His journalism covered a broad range of similar topics. Overall his work raided literary history and scoured British topography in order to maintain, re-invent or secure specifically British traditions of understanding – an important project in developing a shared popular cultural heritage. In particular, he sought to write the artisan experience back into British history and to describe a perceived continuity of rural experience in an increasingly urbanised and industrial culture. His work is very 'male' – that is, his implied readership is serious-minded artisans or the 'labour aristocracy' with whom he conducts a dialogue about public events and debates the constitution of their shared, but occluded, cultural, literary and national inheritance.

Mary's work, on the other hand, derived from both a highly developed sense of women and children as her target audience and from a sense of those literary genres which might be most appropriately written by women. Her work comprised literature aimed at children (long and short fiction, verse, fables); fiction for adults, usually of an exhortatory or didactic nature using the full range of narrative possibilities and genres; translations, often of fairy tales or moral fables; volumes of poems; and, as already described, an extended spiritual and professional autobiography. Collections of her poems, usually grouped with other British women poets, were widely published in the United States. Even her most appreciative critics acknowledged that her work was essentially didactic and purposive:

her special claim to praise is that, whatever the subject, whatever the purpose, she managed in her treatment to infuse into the work so much subdued imaginative colour, that it may well be claimed for her, that however definite her purpose or pronounced her moral aim she very rarely or, indeed, never failed to produce what has the true note of poetry, observation, fancy, and happy, figurative illustration.[21]

If William's main aim was to offer artisans a version of British culture which would give them a sense of their own identity and social significance, Mary's predominant interest was making available a Christianised and often liberal social tolerance (she was, for example, a fervent opponent of capital punishment and vigorously supported the more humane treatment of animals) which stressed kindness, charity, forgiveness and self-scrutiny through literary means less complex and intimidating than those of the dominant literary tradition. While William tried to re-evoke the British literary tradition biographically and topographically in books like *Visits to Remarkable Places* (1840 and 1842) and *Homes and Haunts of the Eminent British Poets* (1847), Mary's re-working of the same tradition was largely in terms of literary acknowledgement. She recognised that there were simple, direct and affecting literary forms and languages available for the newly or barely literate within the literary tradition and saw her role as that of 'translator'. 'Translation' might mean the rendering of profound truths to be found within 'great' literature into accessible language and form in order to support everyday good conduct and moral self-awareness, but it might also mean 'a rare power of raising the conventional or properly prosaic … to a higher level.'[22] Certainly, the 'properly prosaic' is a field in which we might appropriately locate Mary Howitt's work.

Mary Howitt's poetry in particular re-worked or 'translated' the English literary tradition. She contributed, for example, to an interesting anthology called *Childhood* put together by Hannah Mary Rathbone in 1841. The anthology offered a 'selection from the poets' aimed at helping readers to consider 'the expressions of the feelings excited by the contemplation of children'.[23] Mary Howitt, while by no means the most voluminous contributor, nonetheless is given particular prominence. Her poem 'Little Children' forms the volume's epigraph, and is one of the few poems in the British tradition that specifically acknowledges Blake as its source:

Sporting through the forest wide;
Playing by the waterside;
Wandering o'er the heathy fells,
Down within the woodland dells;

Dwelleth many a little child!
In the baron's hall of pride,
By the poor man's dull fireside;
'Mid the mighty, 'mid the mean,
Little children may be seen,
Like the flowers that spring up fair,
Bright and countless, everywhere! [24]

Such a brave re-working of the opening poem of *Songs of Innocence and Experience* in such uninspired verse might seem both pretentious and lacking in self-awareness if it was not for the considered modesty of the poem and the determination to replace Blake's sustained symbolism with something more easily related to contemporary society. Howitt, without in any way thinking herself the equal of Blake, is nonetheless one of few early nineteenth-century authors to acknowledge the subversive 'simplicity' and symbolic energy of his *Songs,* which themselves, of course, derived from a dynamic re-conceptualisation of functional and naive children's verse.

If Blake is the avatar of this poem in the anthology, Wordsworth functions in similar ways for other of Howitt's poems reprinted elsewhere in *Childhood.* Her long narrative poem 'A Forest Scene. In the Days of Wickliffe', which, by means of an extended ballad narrative, celebrates the simplifying of the Bible into English vernacular consciousness through the Wycliffe translation, is more truly a 'lyrical ballad' than anything Wordsworth wrote. One of the central sections in the poem draws together the interrogative structures of 'We Are Seven' and 'Expostulation and Reply' (themselves of course derived from the ballad tradition) to form an exposition of simple child-like piety:

The butterfly went flitting by,
 The bees were in the flowers,
But the little child sate stedfastly,
 As she had sate for hours.

'Why sit you here, my little maid?'
 An aged pilgrim spake;
The child looked upward from her book,
 Like one but just awake.

Back fell her locks of golden hair,
 And solemn was her look,
And thus she answered witlessly,
 'Oh, sir, I read this book!'

'And what is there within that book
To win a child like thee?
Up, join thy mates, the merry birds,
And frolic with the bee!'

'Nay, sir, I cannot leave this book,
I love it more than play:
I have read all legends, but this one
Ne'er saw I till this day

'And there is something in this book
That makes all care be gone,
And yet I weep, I know not why,
As I go reading on.'[25]

Of course the line here between feeble imitation and empowering pastiche is a fine one, yet I think there are moments – most notably here the deployment of the allusive and complex adverb 'witlessly' – which re-enact Wordsworthian 'simplicity' to considerable effect. The faux-naivety of the verse seems to me a justified strategy in avoiding the priggishness of overt didacticism. The evocation of Wordsworth serves as a timely reminder of previous theoretical debates over such poetic possibilities as the expression of the profound through the simple and the uses of narrative in dramatising the workings of the human consciousness. Given this careful con-textualising of her verse within the history of British poetry, Howitt has managed to provide here both an acceptable lecture on popular poetry and its uses for adults and a fast moving and memorable moral narrative in ballad form for her child readers.

Yet, while it is possible to approach the work of Mary and William Howitt through ideas of 'difference' constructed by gender, literary intention or style, their own determined elision of their literary output argues against the value of any such enterprise. Indeed they both implicitly argued that for them difference is more an issue about readership and audience than of artistic purpose or individual creativity. In pursuing these aims they are almost post-modern in their recognition of the value of pastiche, hybridity and intertextuality as creative possibilities. On many occasions Mary and William wrote on the same topic or used the same literary genres in ways which suggest collaboration rather than coincidence. In almost all of these instances, they were 'translating' each other's work into forms and modes of address peculiar to either the domestic and feminised discourses Mary had established for herself or to the more public and male-centred modes of publication and address that William had adopted. Three examples from various parts of the vast Howitt oeuvre should make this point clear.

One of William's best known and successful books was *The Year Book of the Country; or, The Field, The Forest and the Fireside* which was published by Henry Colburn in 1850 with wood engravings after Birket Foster.[26] The book, which drew for its format on a number of Howitt's previous publications like *The Book of the Seasons* (1831) and the two volume *Rural Life in England* (1838), combined the old almanac and year book functions with meditations on the significance of the seasons which sought both to sustain the idea of the agricultural year, with all its festivals, memorialisings, and cyclical hopefulness and to translate it into a new structure which would seek to introduce, or even reconcile, more urban artisans to older pre-urban ideas of ceremony and popular celebration.[27] Yet, however rooted William's book might have been in his earlier expositions of rural life and its traditions, it was Mary who had re-thought the year book idea first in two publications – *The Children's Year* (1847), which Mary herself described as 'an experiment in children's books', and, more radically still, *Our Cousins in Ohio* first published in 1849.[28] Characteristically, *Our Cousins in Ohio* expressed ideas of family in its conception, its production and its subject. The book recounted the fictionalised year of a family living in rural Ohio through a narrative that was implicitly drawn from letters home. These seem to have been letters between children – the 'cousins' of the title – which had been 'translated' by Howitt into a year book narrative. In the Preface Howitt asserted the truthfulness of the narrative, and memorialised the dead sister whose family had provided the basis for the volume. So here again Howitt turned her own domestic experience into fiction. Mary's daughter Anna Mary Howitt drew the designs from which the four soft ground etchings which embellished the book were taken, furthering the idea of a collaborative artistic and didactic project which informed the cultural production of the entire family. The year book format in Mary Howitt's hands combined detailed descriptions of seasonal country tasks, observations of the seasonal changes in flora and fauna, interpolated narratives and anecdotes (many of a gently moralising or admonitory nature) and accounts of travels within the United States. While drawing on an ancient tradition of educational textbooks structured round the calendar year, the generic instability and innovativeness of Howitt's book justified her own term 'experimental' in this instance. There can be little doubt that *The Children's Year* and *Our Cousins in Ohio* formed the blueprints for William's subsequent equivalent volume which was self-consciously addressed to adult artisan readers. It is entirely typical of both Howitts that this trio of successful books should have raided a variety of traditional and popular literary forms in order to produce a hybrid entirely appropriate to its purpose.

A second example shows Mary entering, on her own carefully articulated terms, the traditionally male world of political journalism. One of the central campaigns of *Howitt's Journal* had been against the use of the death penalty as the mainstay of the British justice system. Following on from a series of closely reasoned articles, laid out as a philosophical treatise, that William Howitt had written for the second volume of the *Journal* in 1847 on the Game Laws, the editors commissioned a similar series of essays from Frederic Rowton, the Secretary to the Society for the Abolition of Capital Punishment, which were published at fortnightly intervals in the same volume.[29] Rowton's essays were sober, thoughtful, yet passionate polemics, sometimes illustrated with detailed statistics, and centrally concerned with the moral and ethical aspects of capital punishment.[30] These essays were entirely in William's own chosen manner for his political writings in the *Journal* – carefully structured, pre-empting likely objections one by one, and aimed at a serious-minded, well informed and open-minded readership. Unremittingly progressive but self-consciously logical, deeply felt without ever seeming subjective, outspoken but not confrontational, these essays by Rowton were entirely within the idiom and address which William Howitt had adopted as appropriate for the discussion of contentious topics of the day in his magazine.

Mary's intervention into the same discussion, published in the same journal between Rowton's third and fourth essays, could hardly have been more different in tone, address and purpose.[31] It comprises an open letter 'To the Women of Great Britain and Ireland', which introduces a 'Humble Petition' to the Queen. The petition in turn gives way to a note urging like-minded readers to replicate the petition or else add their names to the original. So Mary's article seeks to establish a discourse within practical politics rather than reproduce the earnest analytical and philosophical arguing characteristic of the *Journal*'s political coverage. Both the open letter and the petition foreground the feminine as the source of their arguing – the arguments are 'maternal' and 'womanly' in their interests and mode. What this means in practice is that Mary Howitt argues against capital punishment by seeking out an individualised moment where the barbarity of execution is conceived as abhorrent in particularly feminised ways. A young pregnant woman, doubtless guilty of the murder charge brought against her, has been given a stay of execution not in the hope of reform or mitigation but rather to allow her to give birth to her child. Thus her ordeal is to be inhumanely dragged out so that her child can be immediately rendered motherless. Howitt seizes on the manifest ethical contradictions of this situation, which, she argues, can only be fully appreciated by women. The Queen, herself 'as a woman and a mother, as the chief woman of the nation and the mother of her people … cannot be behind the greater portion of your female subjects in desiring to set aside the barbarism now impending over one of your own sex' (p. 291). The carefully constructed evocation of a concept of national womanhood established by Howitt here is remarkably powerful. While using exactly Rowton's arguments for the abolition of capital punishment, Mary Howitt individuates (and thus feminises) her polemic and shapes it into a series of interconnecting and purposive statements that work out from a sense of individual empathy and outrage to a public declaration of mission. The tone, address and chosen literary forms here all insist on the particular value of the female point of view – Christian, compassionate, empathetic and driven by moral certainty, the women of England are asked to influence legislation on behalf of their 'common nature'.

While *Howitt's Journal* offers many such examples of clearly diff-erentiated but ultimately complementary 'masculinised' and 'feminised' discourses, perhaps the most telling example of this process is to be found in the poem each wrote on the death of their son – William's poem is called 'A Father's Lament' and Mary's 'The Lost One'.[32] While both poems traverse a therapeutic path from bewildered grief to a reconciliation with loss and a recognition of the possibility of heavenly bliss, William's poem is essentially concerned with his own inner anguish and an analysis of the 'dark dream' and 'agony of pain' which cause him 'pangs and suspense that inly make me quake' –

> I turn and turn, and ponder o'er and o'er
> Insatiate, all that sad and dreamy time
> Thy words thrill through me – in my fond heart's core
> I heard thy sighs, and tears shed for no crime,
> And thy most patient love sent from a happier clime.

Mary's poem has its origins not within the grieving and self-recriminating mind of the poet but rather in the empty space within the household –

> We meet around the hearth – thou art not there,
> Over our household joys hath passed a gloom;
> Beside the fire we see thy empty chair,
> And miss thy sweet voice in the silent room. –

So even at moments when their writing is framed in terms of the most intensely personal and individual feelings William and Mary formulate their response in terms of clearly demarcated gender identities, with William offering an inner monologue on loss, responsibility, and introverted male anguish while Mary begins her poem by surveying the family space, here conventionally rendered as the emblematic hearth.

These three examples of the ways in which the Howitts offered separate but complementary gendered versions of the same texts for differing audiences are meant to represent their willing construction of differentiated male and female voices in all their work, a construction which was, in my view, both self-conscious and voluntary. While apparently conservative in their acceptance of the male voice as belonging to the sphere of public utterance and the female as representing domesticity, the family and womanly empathy, it is nonetheless possible to read the Howitts, both individually and collaboratively, as positing in their work a progressive, even subversive, vision of *inclusivity*. 'Inclusivity' here might be understood primarily in terms of the pragmatics of readership, niche marketing, and literary address, an aspect of the professionalism of the Howitts as freelance authors in the emerging Victorian literary marketplace. But of course 'inclusivity' was also a form of social vision, less radical than the largely politicised energy of Chartism, but nonetheless progressive, if not radical, in its recognition of the political and ideological significance of literary culture. 'Male' and 'female', 'child' and 'artisan', the Howitts argued, might need to be constructed and addressed differently, and might occupy differing spheres of interest and action, but such diversity ought properly to be understood as part of a single *project*. The most evident record of the nature and significance of that project is the relatively short lived *Howitt's Journal*, which the Howitts co-edited between 1847 and 1849.[33]

Before turning directly to *Howitt's Journal*, however, it is important to situate the Howitts' project alongside the other sustained attempts to provide the emerging class of literate and socially aware artisans of the 1830s and 1840s with a range of reading materials. The most famous of these, of course, were the institutionalised and politicised interventions of organisations like the Society for the Diffusion of Useful Knowledge and the Society for the Propagation of Christian Knowledge, best exemplified in their 'useful knowledge' publications, especially *The Penny Magazine* and *The Saturday Magazine*.[34] These two organisations had in their publishers Charles Knight and John Parker two of the most astute apologists for the 'march of intellect', men who understood the politics and the practicalities of the development of a new mass readership. But alongside these self-consciously ideological ventures were the less overtly political and more entrepreneurial commercial publishers like the Chambers Brothers and John Cassell who were developing 'programmes' of niche-marketed reading.[35] Often based on precedents drawn from mass circulation vernacular or sectarian literature, such texts aimed to foster the development of artisan culture as a desirable form of social progress. But of course they also aimed to establish reading, especially the reading of periodical literature, as a commercial activity with new opportunities and a continually widening market. Other publishers in this period, like William Tweedie, developed specialist lists of publications aimed at artisan readers and thus became important elements in defining what 'the people' might purchase and read as both to fill their available leisure and to establish their cultural capital. Publishers who had previously specialised in children's literature, most notably Harvey and Darton, extended their lists to include the just and newly literate among their target readership. On at least one occasion, an individual author, Edwin Paxton Hood, took it upon himself to try to write and publish a complete library for artisans that would combine history, biography and exemplary literature with poetry.[36] It is helpful to consider all these various developments as in some ways 'projects' comparable to the Howitts' literary endeavour. All have aspects in common – a considered mode of address which took into account the presumed interests of artisans, an awareness of niche marketing as an important aspect of mass circulation publishing, a recognition and consequent exploitation of traditionally popular genres, a willingness to translate genteel cultural traditions into something more accessible and 'popular', and a rapid adoption of the new cheap mechanisms for the reproduction of graphic images, especially wood engraving.

Howitt's Journal then, is only one of a number of periodicals aimed at establishing a range of common interests through which a reading community of both thoughtful artisans and liberal intellectuals from within the professions, trades and new urban managerial classes might be constructed.[37] There is not room here to discuss the magazine in detail, and it is only possible to sketch some of its key elements. In doing this it may be useful to use the concepts of 'translation' and 'inclusivity' established above as characteristic of the Howitts' work more generally. Furthermore, in discussing *Howitt's Journal* it is impossible to establish precisely the division of labour between the two editors, and thus I shall continue to use the model of 'the Howitts' as a single figure which divides itself into individual gendered voices as the occasion requires.

Despite an initial declaration by the editors that 'we are bound to no class', *Howitt's Journal* defines both its readership and its primary interest as 'the million' and its progress. These aims are to be manifested in the journal by attention to the 'onward and sound movements of the time', which include peace, temperance, sanitary reform, universal education, free trade, 'free opinion', and human rights alongside the 'pleasures of an enlightened intellect'.[38] As we have already seen, the later numbers of the magazine ran several series of articles on progressive 'issues' like the abolition of capital punishment and the injustices of the game laws as well as long discussions on the colonies and their management. But if the main declared focus of *Howitt's Journal* was on the progress of the labouring and artisan classes:

> not the less do we regard the rights and enjoyments of every other class ... Between the employer and the employed, between the more and less wealthy classes, there lies one common ground of truth and sacred right, which the efforts of the wise will only make more clearly seen, more solidly and securely felt. All that separates and embitters are the briers and brushwood of old error, which advancing knowledge will show in their true deformity, and which the axe of education, and the fire of wise discussion, will consume out of the way.[39]

On the whole this remains a useful summary of the editorial policy of the *Journal*, which did seek out 'one common ground of truth and sacred right' and attack 'all that separates'.

Inclusiveness was a key strategy in pursuing these aims, and is manifested in the magazine in a variety of ways. The contents were nothing if not varied. The genres and kinds of journalism which made up each issue of *Howitt's Journal* included politicised polemic, detailed and informative accounts of topical public issues, travel writing and topographical description, biography and reminiscences, articles containing 'useful knowledge' or information, short fiction, poetry, and articles on the calendar in the William Howitt's new almanac and year book style.[40] Each weekly issue included a two-page supplemental 'Weekly Record' listing news of events related to popular progress. Here, as elsewhere in the magazine, the Howitts solicited their readers to engage in the writing of the *Journal* – 'In this department of our Journal we mean not only to state candidly our own earnest opinion on any matter of importance ... with equal sincerity we solicit the opinion of all classes –be they rich or poor, be they masters or men, be they men or women. We work FOR all, and we desire to work WITH all.'[41] Artisans were frequently invited to contribute unsolicited material to the magazine, and occasionally did so, though sometimes to the discomfiture of the editors.[42] The *Journal* made extensive use of women journalists like Mary Gillies and Eliza Meteyard, and was an important element in establishing women in the writing professions – a theme explored elsewhere in this volume.[43] There was a strong focus on international issues which included a running debate about the purposes of the colonies and the moral issues raised by colonialism. There was a determined effort to seek out progressive movements and events abroad which were comparable to social change in Britain – Mary Howitt's series of *Memoirs of Remarkable Americans*, for example, which was partially serialised in the *Journal*, included the struggles of the little known Elihu Burritt and Frederick Douglass. India, Italy, Germany, Hungary and Ireland as well as the United States all feature in the first two volumes. Translations from several European languages – one of Mary's specialist areas of expertise – were frequently printed. 'The Child's Corner', suggesting an orderly notion of everything being in its rightful place rather than jostling for attention, was an occasional feature.

And, crucially, *Howitt's Journal* was illustrated, at first with full-page wood engraved portraits, but increasingly with reproductions of paintings. Quite aside from the importance of their early recognition that the rapidly developing technology for the reproduction of images by wood engraving was transforming mass circulation literature, the Howitts also immediately understood that it was a key mechanism for translating art images into popular consciousness. I do not believe they have been given sufficient credit for their part in democratising high art images. The dominant scholarly accounts of the history of wood engraving have emphasised its aspirations to counterfeit or replicate the condition of 'art' in a tradition that runs from Bewick into *The Illuminated Magazine* in the 1840s and on to the art edited journals of the 1860s like *Good Words, The Cornhill Magazine* and *Once a Week*, where full-page wood engravings hovered somewhat uncomfortably between illustrations and art images.[44] Alternatively, wood engraving has been seen as an important medium for the dissemination of the information which drove many of social transformations embodied in those areas of mass circulation literature associated with the 'march of intellect'.[45] But *Howitt's Journal*, well before the usually cited examples to be found in John Cassell's publications in the 1850s, used wood engraving extensively to translate the images of high art into accessible forms for consumption by 'the million'.

Howitt's Journal, then, epitomises the literary endeavour that the Howitts sustained over several decades, but which belongs particularly to the 1840s. To this extent, I think the later Victorians were probably right to regard Mary Howitt's work as anachronistic. The *Journal* seeks to translate diversity, manifested in social class, age and gender, into a single social project. In pursuit of this aim, its editors accept the need to construct differing modes of address, differing literary forms and differing literary persona to speak separately, but with a common purpose, to diverse readers.

At the centre of this project, then, is a potentially disabling belief that women should be addressed through a range of specifically feminine, and feminised, discourses. Yet it is hard to think of Mary Howitt, for all her literary conventionality and willing acceptance of her role as a woman writer, as a reactionary or conventional figure. Nor is the volume and occasional nature of her work sufficient in itself to condemn her to 'minorness'. What the Howitts offered in their vast and sustained literary endeavour (as well as in their personal generosity to individuals), was a vision of artisan reading and cultural advance driven less by a vision of social control than the SDUK (Society for the Diffusion of Useful Knowledge) or the SPCK (Society for the Propagation of Christian Knowledge) and less by a sense of commercial opportunity than the Chambers Brothers or John Cassell. Nor did they have Edwin Paxton Hood's fervent sense of religious mission, although they were driven by a profoundly moral sense of purpose. In pursuit of this social project they accepted every element of the British cultural tradition as being available to their purposes. In raiding tradition they sought to translate, which very often meant subvert, the genteel into the popular and the progressive, defamiliarising and re-directing well known texts in the process. Mary's central contribution to this immensely ambitious project, however compromised she may have been by circumstance and belief, and however much she may have surrendered her individual identity to a broader vision, was to write women firmly into this discourse both as contributors and as audience. Despite all the evident shortcomings of her work as literature, her recognition of the ideological functions of mass circulation literature and of the role women needed to play in its production remains a significant and unique achievement.

Notes

1 Amice Lee, *Laurels and Rosemary: The Life of William and Mary Howitt* (Oxford: Oxford University Press, 1955), p. 289.
2 Linda H. Peterson, *Traditions of Victorian Women's Autobiography – The Poetics and Politics of Life Writing* (Charlottesville, VA: University of Virginia Press, 1999). For the Howitts' role as entrepreneurs of artisan literature see Brian E. Maidment, 'Magazines of Popular Progress and the Artisans', *Victorian Periodicals Review*, 17:3 (Fall 1984), 82–94.
3 A. H. Miles (ed.), *The Poets and Poetry of the Century*, 10 vols (London: Hutchinson n.d.), vol. 10, p. 81. This volume of Miles's massive anthology, *From Joanna Baillie to Mathilde Blind*, forms the final volume in the series.
4 R. H. Horne (ed.), *The New Spirit of the Age*, 2 vols (London: Smith, Elder &

Co., 1844), vol. 1, p. 198.

5 Joanne Shattock (ed.), *The Cambridge Bibliography of English Literature*, vol. 4 (third edn, Cambridge: Cambridge University Press, 1999), p. 2157.

6 Miles (ed.), *Poets and Poetry*, vol. 10, p. v.

7 Elizabeth A. Sharp (ed.), *Women's Voices – An Anthology of the most Characteristic Poems by English, Scotch, and Irish Women* (London: Walter Scott, n.d.), p. vii.

8 Sharp (ed.), *Women's Voices*, p. ix.

9 Eric S. Robertson, *A Series of Critical English Poetesses' Biographies with Illustrative Extracts* (London: Cassell and Co., 1883), p. 381.

10 Miles (ed.), *Poets and Poetry*, vol. 10, p. 86.

11 Margaret Howitt (ed.), *Mary Howitt – An Autobiography*, 2 vols (London: William Isbister Ltd., 1889).

12 Peterson, *Traditions*, p. 21. There is obviously not the space here to deal properly with *An Autobiography*. Peterson's book, as well as providing a full context for the autobiography, also engages with the considerable body of critical work which seeks to construct traditions of women's autobiographical writing.

13 Peterson, *Traditions*, p. 153.

14 Peterson, *Traditions*, p. 153.

15 Howitt, *Mary Howitt*, vol. 2, p. 327.

16 See Margaret Beetham, *A Magazine of Her Own? Domesticity and Desire in the Woman's Magazine, 1800–1914* (London: Routledge, 1996) and Barbara Onslow, *Women of the Press in Nineteenth-Century Britain*, (Basingstoke: Macmillan, 2000) for information on women's roles in the development of periodical literature during the nineteenth century.

17 Carl R. Woodring, *Victorian Samplers: William and Mary Howitt* (Lawrence, KS: University of Kansas Press, 1952); Lee, *Laurels and Rosemary*.

18 Horne, *A New Spirit of the Age*, vol. 1, p. 180.

19 Spencer T. Hall, *Biographical Sketches of Remarkable People Chiefly From Personal Recollection* (London: Simpkin, Marshall, 1873), p. 312.

20 Peterson, *Traditions*, p. 153.

21 Japp, *Poets and Poetry*, vol. 10, p. 86.

22 Japp, *Poets and Poetry*, vol. 10, p. 86.

23 H. M. R. [Hannah Mary Rathbone] (ed.), *Childhood, Illustrated in a Selection from the Poets* (London: Harvey and Darton, 1841), p. v.

24 The most precise allusion is to 'The Introduction' to *Songs of Innocence* (1789) which begins: 'Piping down the valleys wild/Piping songs of pleasant glee/ On a cloud I saw a child/And he laughing said to me.' The English poetic tradition is famously lacking in imitators of Blake, with only the late nineteenth-century artisan poet Joseph Skipsey, who had become aware of Blake through his acquaintance with the Rossettis, as a professed disciple.

25 H. M. R, *Childhood*, pp. 249–50.

26 For a brief overview of the year book and almanac form see Brian E.

Maidment, 'Re-arranging the Year: the Almanac, the Day Book and the Year Book as Popular Literary Forms, 1789–1860', in Juliet John and Alice Jenkins (eds), *Re-Reading Victorian Culture* (London: Macmillan, 2000), pp. 64–80.

27 For an account of the writing and publication of *The Book of the Seasons* see Lee, *Laurels and Rosemary*, pp. 80–1. As Mary's letters make clear, it is actually extremely hard to separate out the roles Mary and William had in the compiling of the book, which was in effect joint authored.

28 Preface to *Our Cousins in Ohio* (second edn, London: Darton & Co., n.d.). In the same Preface Howitt makes it clear that *Our Cousins in Ohio* is a companion volume to *The Children's Year*.

29 *Howitt's Journal*, 1 (1847), 218, 244, 265, 299, 348, 386.

30 Rowton states his arguments in the first essay: 'the infliction of death by the law, is a barbarous, useless, and injurious practice, answering no good purpose, but demoralizing the whole community; Secondly, that it is, in the highest sense of the term, immoral man, having no right nor commission to enforce it; and, Thirdly, that it is an impious assumption of the divine prerogative, a punishment totally opposed to the spirit and precepts of Christianity.' *Howitt's Journal*, 2 (1847), 219.

31 'To the Women of Great Britain and Ireland', *Howitt's Journal*, 2 (1847), 291. Subsequent page references are given in the text.

32 While there is some uncertainty over the date of the first publication of these two poems, which were reprinted in several anthologies, I assume the poems refer to Claude Middleton Howitt, who was born in December 1833 and died unexpectedly in 1843, see Lee, *Laurels and Rosemary*, p. 90 and p. 158. As the poems appear, however, in *Childhood*, which was published in 1841, it is possible that Lee has made a mistake about the date of Claude's death or that the poems were written as matching exercises in parental empathy about an imagined death or about an acquaintance.

33 There are considerable difficulties to be overcome in untangling the complex of magazines which form *Howitt's Journal*, *The People's Journal* and *The People's and Howitt's Journal*. These complexities largely derive from a widely publicised dispute between the Howitts and John Saunders, the proprietor of *Howitt's Magazine*. For the purposes of this article I am defining *Howitt's Journal* as the volumes published between 1847 and 1849 variously by Darton and Co., William Lovett and John Saunders under the title of *Howitt's Journal of Literature and Popular Progress*. The magazine was published weekly and cost 1½d unstamped and 2½d stamped. Each weekly issue comprised 14 pages of the magazine proper, extensively illustrated with wood engravings, and a two-page supplement called 'The Weekly Record' which comprised news items relevant to the interests of a broadly defined idea of 'popular progress'.

34 This is not the place for a detailed discussion of these kinds of initiatives. Richard Altick's *The English Common Reader* (Chicago, IL: University of Chicago Press, 1957) still offers the best introduction to such issues.

35 For Chambers see the above and also W. Chambers, *Memoir of Robert Chambers* (Edinburgh: Chambers Bros., 1872). For Cassell's increasingly sophisticated recognition of the artisan market for printed matter and the development of carefully considered niche markets see Brian E. Maidment, 'Entrepreneurship and the Artisans: John Cassell, the Great Exhibition and the Periodical Idea', in Louise Purbrick (ed.), *The Great Exhibition of 1851* (Manchester: Manchester University Press, 2001), pp. 79–113.

36 See Brian E. Maidment 'Popular Exemplary Biography in the Nineteenth Century: Edwin Paxton Hood and his Books', *Prose Studies*, 7:2 (September 1984), 148–67.

37 Maidment, 'Magazines of Popular Progress'.

38 'William and Mary Howitt's Address to their Friends and Readers', *Howitt's Journal*, 1 (2 January 1847), 1.

39 *Howitt's Journal*, 1 (2 January 1847), 2.

40 W. B. Carpenter's long running series on 'Physiology for the People' is a good example of the way in which the Howitts nudged on past traditional definitions of 'useful knowledge' to find information that genuinely helped working people understand and care for themselves.

41 These remarks are taken from the strap title of 'The Weekly Record' section of the *Journal*.

42 The most illuminating example of editorial embarrassment at their own generosity of spirit is to be found in *Howitt's Journal*, 1, 132 where the publication of a poem called 'Just Instinct and Brute Reason' by a Manchester operative is accompanied by the following editorial disclaimer – 'Our operative is severe, but perhaps his sufferings are, and for misery we must make ample allowance. At all events he is a *poet*, and poets "learn in suffering." EDS.'

43 One of the contributors was Elizabeth Gaskell whose first narratives of industrial life were published in *Howitt's Journal* under the pseudonym of 'Cotton Mather Mills'. This clever pseudonym is very much in the allusive Howitt idiom and elides together the piety of Cotton Mather with the industrial realities of the Manchester 'mills'.

44 Both Gleeson White's 1897, *English Illustration – the Sixties* and Forrest Reid's *Illustrators of the Eighteen Sixties*, first published in 1928, were extremely influential in establishing a 'fine art' tradition in Victorian wood engraving which dominated understanding of the history of nineteenth-century wood engraving, as well as collecting, for several generations.

45 Patricia Anderson, *The Printed Image and the Transformation of Popular Culture 1790–1860* (Oxford: Clarendon Press, 1991) is a good example of this approach.

Bibliography

Altick, Richard, *The English Common Reader*, Chicago, IL: University of Chicago Press, 1957.

Anderson, Patricia, *The Printed Image and the Transformation of Popular Culture 1790–1860*, Oxford: Clarendon Press, 1991.

Beetham, Margaret, *A Magazine of her Own? Domesticity and Desire in the Woman's Magazine, 1800–1914*, London: Routledge, 1996.

Chambers, William, *Memoir of Robert Chambers*, Edinburgh: Chambers Bros., 1872.

Hall, Spencer T., *Biographical Sketches of Remarkable People Chiefly from Personal Recollection*, London: Simpkin, Marshall, 1873.

Horne, R. H. (ed.), *The New Spirit of the Age*, 2 vols, London: Smith, Elder & Co., 1844.

Howitt, Margaret (ed.), *Mary Howitt – An Autobiography*, 2 vols, London: William Isbister, 1889.

Howitt, Mary, *The Children's Year*, London: Darton and Co., 1847.

—— *Our Cousins in Ohio*, London: Darton and Co., 1849.

Howitt, Mary and William (eds), *Howitt's Journal of Literature and Popular Progress*, London: Darton and Co, William Lovett and John Saunders, 1847–49.

Howitt, William, *The Year Book of the Country; or, The Field, the Forest and the Fireside*, London: Henry Colburn, 1850.

Lee, Amice, *Laurels and Rosemary: The Life of William and Mary Howitt*, Oxford: Oxford University Press, 1955.

Maidment, Brian E., 'Magazines of Popular Progress and the Artisans', *Victorian Periodicals Review*, 17:3 (Fall 1984), 82–94.

——'Popular Exemplary Biography in the Nineteenth Century: Edwin Paxton Hood and his Books', *Prose Studies*, 7:2 (September 1984), 148–67.

——'Re-arranging the Year: The Almanac, the Day Book and the Year Book as Popular Literary Forms, 1789–1860', in Juliet John and Alice Jenkins (eds), *Re-Reading Victorian Culture*, London: Macmillan, 2000, pp. 64–80.

Miles, A. H. (ed.), *The Poets and Poetry of the Century*, 10 vols, London: Hutchinson, n.d.

Onslow, Barbara, *Women of the Press in Nineteenth-Century Britain*, Basingstoke: Macmillan, 2000.

Peterson, Linda H., *Traditions of Victorian Women's Autobiography – The Poetics and Politics of Life Writing*, Charlottesville, VA: University of Virginia Press, 1999.

H. M. R. [Rathbone, Hannah Mary] (ed.), *Childhood, Illustrated in a Selection from the Poets*, London: Harvey and Darton, 1841.

Robertson, Eric S. (ed.), *A Series of English Poetesses' Biographies with Illustrative Extracts*, London: Cassell and Co., 1883.

Sharp, Elizabeth A. (ed.), *Women's Voices – An Anthology of the most Characteristic Poems by English, Scotch, and Irish Women*, London: Walter Scott, n.d.

Shattock, Joanne (ed.), *The Cambridge Bibliography of English Literature*, vol. 4, third edn, Cambridge: Cambridge University Press, 1999.

Woodring, Carl R., *Victorian Samplers: William and Mary Howitt*, Lawrence, KS: University of Kansas Press, 1952.

2

Struggling for fame: Eliza Meteyard's principled career

Kay Boardman

In the semi-autobiographical *Struggles for Fame,* Eliza Meteyard's first novel, the heroine Barbara struggles to make her way in the world. After enduring a childhood of abuse at a baby farm and then kidnap at the hands of an itinerant dancing troupe, she finally makes it to London to become a writer and although it was difficult 'Yet it was independence'.[1] Armed with her first manuscript she arrives at various publishing houses only to be turned away unceremoniously by all of them; an old bookseller advises her to write for one of the popular magazines and a 'great author' who likes her work also advises her to continue writing. Spurred by these signals of support Barbara decides to battle on and 'to steer onward in the good cause of self-help, and honest independence' (p. 291). Some years later an old friend, Lord Trafford re-appears offering her marriage and a comfortable future, but she declines on the basis that the duties of wife and of literature are not compatible and declares 'the woman who wishes to excel in literature must be alone from the cradle to the grave' (p. 367). In this uncannily prophetic projection of Meteyard's own career, we are offered an insight into the pain and the pleasure of what was to become a fairly typical experience for the common writer, that of struggling for fame and, for the unmarried woman writer in particular, the price and value of independence.[2] Yet Meteyard, an author of some esteem in her lifetime has, like many others before and after, almost slipped out of literary history; but her career has much to tell us about the choices and disappointments facing the committed, yet unexceptional minor writer as well as having something useful to tell us about a career devoted to the pursuit of an ideal. Although known mainly for the biography of Josiah Wedgwood published in 1865, Meteyard was a prolific writer of fiction for adults and for children, in both volume and serial form, and of essays on a wide range of social topics and of antiquarian works; well before the Wedgwood fame she had gained a solid reputation as a writer interested in a whole range of social issues. Like many writers of the time she entered the profession through journalism, but unlike some of her more successful contemporaries like Elizabeth Gaskell and George Eliot, her subsequent novels were not well received and she continued writing for the periodical press in order to make a living.[3]

Meteyard, the daughter of a Shropshire military surgeon, was born in Liverpool in 1816. When she was two years old her father was transferred back to Shropshire and the family settled in Shrewsbury where she lived until she was thirteen. For the next thirteen years of her life she lived with her mother's family in Norfolk and in 1842 she moved to London where she remained until her death in 1879. She began her literary career in 1843 with 'Scenes in the Life of an Authoress', an earlier version of *Struggles for Fame* which appeared in three instalments in *Tait's Edinburgh Magazine* between 1843 and 1844.[4] This was the beginning of a career of writing fiction and articles for the periodical press and of nearly a decade of prolific writing for a particular group of periodicals, identified as magazines of popular progress and committed to the promotion of progressive principles: these include *Howitt's Journal*, *Douglas Jerrold's Shilling Magazine* and *Eliza Cook's Journal*.[5] It was also at this time that she took up the pseudonym Silverpen, a name conferred on her by Douglas Jerrold whilst she was working under his editorship of his eponymous *Shilling Magazine*. In the 1850s she began to contribute to *Sharpe's London Magazine* where she contributed a number of lead pieces and for the women's press, most notably *The Ladies' Cabinet*.[6] In the 1860s she appears to have developed long-standing interests in the antiquarian and the decorative arts in a more specialised way working for journals such as *The Reliquary*, *Good Words* and *The Oddfellow's Magazine*. The interest in the decorative arts in particular culminated in the two-volume *The Life of Josiah Wedgwood* but throughout her career until her death in 1879, Meteyard continued her lifelong commitment to progressive principles.

The first novel, the three-volume *Struggles for Fame* appeared in 1845 and was reviewed by one critic as a work not appropriate for a female author: 'the talent of the fair author has been exercised upon an uncongenial and ungrateful soil'.[7] This uncongenial soil was undoubtedly the Newgate novel, the influence of which can be seen in much of her earlier fiction. The second novel, for children, *The Doctor's Little Daughter*, also semi-autobiographical, appeared in 1850. These were the first of eleven works of fiction, most of them short tales for children, with the exception of the three-volume *Mainstone's Housekeeper* (1860), *The Lady Herbert's*

Gentlewomen (1862) and the antiquarian *Hallowed Spots of London* (1862). None of the books appear to have been very successful, although eight of them did go into a second edition or a reprint. In spite of this unpropitious start to her novelistic career with poor sales and tepid reviews[8] it was to be the biography of Wedgwood that ultimately sealed Meteyard's reputation and led to the award of civil list pensions in 1869 and 1874.[9] Yet this acknowledgment of her significant contribution to literature and publishing generally masks the years of struggle that preceded these awards. Meteyard applied to the Royal Literary Fund for financial support on no less than five occasions and the letters of application demonstrate just how precarious the profession was at the time and detail how as a professional writer, she had to be both versatile and willing, on occasion, to compromise her artistic aims to make a living.[10]

There is plenty of further evidence from accounts of the period to support the idea that this kind of versatility was essential for survival in a precarious profession and a saturated market.[11] It is no coincidence then that it was almost immediately after the demise of the magazines of popular progress and the decline in regular income, that Meteyard succumbed to the fate of many struggling authors of the time and made her first application to the fund for financial support.[12] In one of her letters of application she complains about the 'inferior class of writers', a class she identifies as dilettantes and amateurs who are willing to write cheaply or for no fee at all.[13] In the period between 1850 and 1880 the market for reading material grew immensely and the market for fiction was particularly buoyant, this also meant that it was also extremely competitive.[14] As Valerie Sanders notes the publishing industry was marked by immense productive activity and as such relationships between publishers and novelists became very personal and intense.[15] Women writers in particular tended to stay with the same publishers far longer than did their male counterparts. Meteyard placed her novels with a range of publishers from the prestigious firms such as Chapman and Hall and Routledge, keeping company with Elizabeth Gaskell, Alfred Tennyson and Geraldine Jewsbury, to Hurst and Blackett at the other end of the spectrum. Nigel Cross claims that Hurst and Blackett was the first port of call for second-rate writers,[16] yet *Mainstone's Housekeeper* which was originally published by them in 1860 was reprinted in a yellow back edition by Chapman and Hall in 1865, probably on the back of the success of the Wedgwood biography. *Dr Oliver's Maid* was published in London by Hall and Virtue and was available in a Tauchnitz edition, ensuring that at least one of her works was known in Europe. Yet the placing of work with publishers and the subsequent receipt of payment was not without difficulty for many writers and in this Meteyard was no exception; the letters of application to the Royal Literary Fund detail her earnings and also give accounts of incompetence and negligence at the hands of some of the more unscrupulous editors and publishing houses. By the third application to the fund, Meteyard charts a fast decreasing annual wage from her literary labours from earnings of £82 4s in 1855 to £12 in 1859, the actual year of application. Ill health and adverse circumstances are most often cited as the reasons for application, but she also mentions moments of disappointment such as not getting paid when promised and not getting paid as much as originally agreed, which was the case with one of Hurst and Blackett's reprints of *Mainstone's Housekeeper*. Even the apparent success of the Wedgwood biography shielded disappointment with Meteyard feeling aggrieved that in spite of the large advance, she had to incur the loss of £216 to pay for the engravings which the publisher had originally agreed to pay.[17]

At a time when work options for women were severely limited it was not surprising that writing had become a popular choice for women since it did not require special training, money or materials and it could be performed from home. Meteyard was not able to follow the traditional route to governessing taken up by other single middle-class women because she was very deaf. She fits the typical profile and pattern of the self-supporting woman writer of the time in that she was a spinster, middle-class, took a direct route into authorship and produced a significant amount of journalistic work.[18] In her study of women's journalism in the nineteenth century Barbara Onslow points out that shared knowledge and a commitment to niche markets compensated to some degree for limited access, not only to the legislative process, but to formal education, club-land networks and also to funding.[19] Looking at Meteyard's network of professional colleagues and friends on the literary scene we can see that this network provided her with crucial ideological, intellectual and practical support. Her early friendship with both Mary and William Howitt, Samuel Smiles, Eliza Cook and Douglas Jerrold in particular were instrumental in launching her career.[20] Not only did she produce a significant amount of work for *Douglas Jerrold's Weekly Newspaper*, *Douglas Jerrold's Shilling Magazine*, *Howitt's Journal* and *Eliza Cook's Journal* but the Howitts helped secure the large advance on the Wedgwood biography and it was through Mary Howitt that she met prominent women from the literary scene, including Elizabeth Gaskell, Bessie Parkes and Harriet Martineau.[21] The comparison with Martineau is quite coincidental as

Meteyard also began her career writing about political economy and she too was deaf and carried an ear trumpet. Anna Mary Howitt, the artist and daughter of Mary and William also illustrated one of her children's books. Contacts in the antiquarian world also proved useful and she maintained strong friendships with leading figures such as Samuel Carter Hall and Charles Roach Smith, to whom *The Hallowed Spots of London* was dedicated.[22]

On numerous occasions Meteyard gives accounts of her experience of being a professional writer and details both her successes and tribulations. In the preface to *The Nine Hours Movement*, a repackaging of three stories which were serialised many years earlier, she looks back on her career and writes that she is proud of her literary endeavours, claiming that crowds gathered outside the bookseller's shop eagerly awaiting the next instalment of her serialised fiction.[23] This confident self-mythologising emerges in a number of ways in her writing: there are a number of cameos of the single woman writer in her fiction, in *Lilian's Golden Hours* the figure in question even has an ear trumpet, both *Struggles for Fame* and *The Doctor's Little Daughter* are semi-autobiographical and in *The Lady Herbert's Gentlewomen* the characters sit down to read a serialised story from a magazine 'loving the hand that wrote it, listen with interest and an attentive ear' and it is in fact one of her own, 'A Winter and its Spring' which had appeared in *The Ladies' Cabinet* eight years earlier.[24] What also emerges from Meteyard's accounts of her career in prefaces to various editions of her volume works and in the letters lodged in the files of the Royal Literary Fund is the very clear sense that for her, the writing for the periodicals constituted her main form of income but that it all too often affected her status and reputation and this need to derive an income, whatever the cost, precluded her from producing the kind of work of which she really felt herself capable. In the preface to *The Doctor's Little Daughter* she talks of this more creative writing, 'the fruit of the mind's holiday' as a release from the drudgery of writing for the periodical press and in a letter to the Royal Literary Fund she talks of her hope for some new work which will be 'more consonant to my tastes, and more worthy of my own intellectual sense'.[25]

Making five applications to the Royal Literary Fund for financial support demonstrates the precarious nature of making a living by writing and the difficulty of maintaining a consistently successful career; but there is also a degree of irony in the fact that applicants had to have a good reputation as writers in order to gain the award. In spite of her obvious disappointment at not being free to pursue the kind of writing that she would have wished, Meteyard did manage to balance the need to make a living with the ideological and creative needs she had and her reputation during her lifetime was good. She enjoyed time as a lead writer for *Douglas Jerrold's Weekly Newspaper, Eliza Cook's Journal* and *Sharpe's London Magazine* and was listed as one of the eminent authors that *Howitt's Journal* had managed to procure. A cover page devoted to her career in *The Lady's Own Paper* suggests her contemporary profile and assumes that, at the very least, a female, middle-class audience would be familiar with her work; although the Wedgwood biography undoubtedly brought her name to a much wider audience.[26] After her death she did not attract much critical attention until her mention in criticism nearly a century later.[27] The few critics that have looked at her works have focused on the representation of independent women and the figure of the seamstress in 'Lucy Dean; The Noble Needlewoman', one of her most celebrated stories that appeared in *Eliza Cook's Journal*.[28] More recently she has been the subject of interest to historians interested in the significance of women's contribution to radical writing of the 1840s, but as yet no full-length critical study of her work exists.[29]

Throughout her career Meteyard wrote in a range of modes and genres on a wide variety of topics. Although the need to earn a living was always a consideration she managed, in the main, to write about topics that interested her and these include: sanitary reform, political and domestic economy, educational reform, working conditions, temperance, antiquarianism, the role of women in public life and the role of art. Half of her fiction published in volume form was for children, yet she appears not to have been known at the time or more recently for this. Most are short *Bildungsromans* centring on a young heroine and are written in a sentimental mode and reflect many of Meteyard's wider concerns such as animal welfare and the importance of harmony and respect between classes. In spite of Meteyard's prefaces stating how much she enjoyed writing these works, it is very likely that they were produced partly as opportunities to make an income from the lucrative and fast growing market for juvenile writing. The three three-decker novels produced for an adult audience were not generally well received by the critics and did not sell well. *Mainstone's Housekeeper* is densely plotted and has a mystery at its heart. *The Lady Herbert's Gentlewomen* is a series of connected narratives about a group of elderly gentlewomen who live in a charitable institution. Similar to Gaskell's *Cranford* it chronicles in meticulous detail the daily lives and tribulations of this group of women. It is strong on description and humour and provides a very sympathetic portrayal of a fallen woman, but as the reviewer for *The Athenaeum* suggested the stories are a little too dis-connected and the plotting a little slipshod.[30] Much of the volume fiction was reviewed and critics were almost unanimous in the assertion that characters were often too perfect and the style too sentimental and this seems to me to be a fair assessment.

Meteyard was much more prolific and successful with the articles and short, serialised fiction she produced for the periodicals. The articles are usually polemical which most often suited the context of publication and her style in this mode of writing is clear and accessible. She produced a lot of domestic fiction for the periodicals and at its best it is well-plotted and descriptive; at its worst it is didactic and sentimental. Meteyard fits the typical profile of the common writer in that she produced a lot of material for a market hungry for units of production, did not write ahead of public taste but for it, addressed the concerns of the time and presented her work to her audience in a lively and accessible way. In the work produced for the magazines of popular progress in the first phase of her career she was consistent in the promotion of the ideological position espoused by the magazines' firm editorial line. This was as much a personal as a professional commitment as demonstrated by her membership of clubs associated with the reform movement such as the Whittington Club, which supported the provision of libraries and recreational facilities to members of the working class.[31] Although the magazines she contributed to in the 1850s and beyond did not have quite the same cohesive ideological impetus; nevertheless Meteyard continued to produce work 'with a thesis' as Gallagher suggests of her early work, and indeed throughout her career a significant amount of her work subscribes to the philosophical and ideological vision of the early years.[32]

In a letter to Meteyard, Eliza Cook, a fellow single, self-supporting poet, writer and editor of *Eliza Cook's Journal* wrote 'Old times come before me when we were both engaged, heart, head and hand in the ardour of literary work, and we may both take some credit in having striven to help our fellow creatures on the road to wisdom and happiness … and have often wished we had more such women to guide and strengthen mankind.'[33] This offers us some insight into the altruistic ideals embedded in the work of both authors and very importantly, the significance of women's contribution to this kind of social and literary endeavour; both Meteyard and Cook were heavily involved in the work and commitments of the magazines of popular progress in the 1840s. According to Brian Maidment they 'were a small group of essentially literary magazines with interests in the intellectual and social progress of "the people" and in humanitarian and progressive causes' and Meteyard along with a small but influential group of other authors and editors, including William and Mary Howitt, Eliza Cook and Douglas Jerrold, sought to promote association and cooperation between the classes, through a process of 'cultural negotiation'.[34] Working broadly in support of progressive social and political reform, those associated with the magazines of popular progress also extended their ideas and philosophy to ventures such as the Whittington Club. Women were fully involved in the activities of the Whittington Club, both social and literary, and a Ladies' Committee was established with Meteyard and Mary Howitt, co-editor of *Howitt's Journal* and a close friend, as members. Kathryn Gleadle states that these magazines also acted as a central forum for the burgeoning feminist movement, arguing that the seeds of Victorian feminism lie, not in the work of the Langham Place Circle of the late 1850s, but in this preceding decade.[35] This relocation of early feminist engagement and critique to an earlier point stresses the instrumental role that those associated with the idea of popular progress played in the promotion of self-advancement, self-help and individualism. It is no surprise that a movement concerned primarily with social amelioration and conciliation should be so significantly associated with women, considering the long tradition of cultural assignment of this role to them. It seems that women's involvement was two-fold in that they were involved because of their traditional role, but also because this cultural milieu provided an opportunity to carve out a space to participate in a legislative process from which they were formally excluded.

Although Meteyard's first published work dealt with a heroine struggling to make her living as an author and this was to become a perennial theme in her work, she soon embarked on the Condition of England debate as it was fast becoming discussed in the magazines of popular progress. As Kestner argues, women entered the tradition of social narrative much earlier than men.[36] This debate was concerned primarily with the social and spiritual well-being of the population and with the disharmony between classes at a time of great social and political unrest. Meteyard soon began to write consistently about single issues symptomatic of the problems precipitated by industrialisation and urbanisation and began to articulate her own answer to the problems experienced by all groups of society. She locates this in the problem of social fragmentation and the difficulties of pursuing social and spiritual well-being in this kind of environment, and uses her writing as did Gaskell and Howitt for instance, to intervene in the debate, intending this intervention to be not merely a stage toward reform, but as a function of reform (p. 14). In the fiction in particular she uses the imaginative possibilities germane to the genre to personalise social problems and render them manageable. This also gives fiction an elevated status, as Kestner argues, and this became of seminal importance in the work of the magazines of popular progress whose very ethos was of contemplation and debate about social cooperation and its concomitant improvement. Indeed as Maidment argues, these magazines engaged in an open form of cultural dialogue, which exploited literature as a common ground for discussion.[37]

This is evident in Meteyard's work where she continues to engage in debates about the amelioration of social life through fiction. Catherine Gallagher argues that in 'Lucy Dean; The Noble Needlewoman', Meteyard identifies family problems as social problems and this is also the case for her work generally.[38] In 'Lucy Dean' she resolves the dilemma of the over-worked and exploited seamstress by taking her off to Australia to make a new life.[39] The plight of the seamstress and the question of female emigration were both topics of debate at the time and this choice of topic is indicative of most of the fiction produced for the journals of popular progress. The early closing movement, temperance concerns, education and domestic economy were all covered and in almost every case involve a woman at the centre of the narrative. Indeed most of her fictional work is littered with single women earning a living and helping their community, usually through personal contact and philanthropy. In 'A Soul Amongst the Vagrants' published in *Eliza Cook's Journal* in 1849 we see the engagement with the question of community and the role and responsibility of members of all classes to ensure social harmony.[40] In this story a reformed vagrant girl assists in running a lodging house set up by liberal philanthropists. This is a typical example of many of her stories written as part of the Condition of England debate and appearing fast on the heels of Gaskell's *Mary Barton,* where Meteyard re-emphasises the importance of collective responsibility and cooperation between classes. Like Gaskell, in this story and numerous others, she also represents members of the working class in a sympathetic light, using dialect with skill and sensitivity and she works particularly hard to show the dignity of labour. There is a plethora of positive working-class role models in her fiction, as there is a plethora of strong, independent female role models.

Female influence in particular is crucial as a humanising antidote to the fierce world of competition and in emphasising the relationship between the individual and the community she returns consistently to the ideas of self-help – presented through individualism; and altruism –

presented through the community. As women's lives were essentially experienced through the domestic, Meteyard writes about middle-class women performing cross-class mediation through traditional feminine channels: thus mistresses advise and support servants, spinsters foster abandoned children and single women live independent lives. Two stories published in the latter part of Meteyard's career demonstrate the continued interest in women's lives, dilemmas and influence, in each we have a single woman and a married woman respectively. 'The Shop at Barrow-in-Furness' is the story of Mary and her three sisters who fall on hard times because of a poor investment.[41] An old aunt presents the sisters with a cheque, the last of the family money and advises them to use it wisely. Mary takes the aunt's advice and wants to invest the money but her sisters disagree so she moves north to Barrow and opens a little shop. The story ends with Mary finding 'peace and independence' and running a successful business, using part of the profits to help her sisters. This success story is forged through Mary's indomitable commitment to hard work and thrift and she is offered as a role model for single middle-class women looking for a place for themselves in the community but outside of marriage. In 'Lis's Culture', Lis the daughter of a cabinetmaker signs up for women's classes at a local people's college and after years of study she finally wins a place at Girton.[42] The narrative ends with Lis married to a prosperous tradesman and we are told that she has no desire to have a place in parliament but that she wants to raise the physical, moral and intellectual condition of all classes of women in her native town. Published just two years before her death, in this story Meteyard continues to engage in the question of women's role in the community and her relationship to public life. As a role model, Lis represents the educated wife and mother who utilises her knowledge and wisdom to affect change from within the home. In this story and its concern with the life of a married and fulfilled woman Meteyard does not seek to de-emphasize the importance of marriage, just to suggest that significant cultural power is still assigned to the feminine. In the parting description of Lis she is described as clothed in 'garments of antique art' (p. 293); presumably a medieval style of dress which very subtly demonstrates Meteyard's interest in the decorative arts and in this instance textile design as one area of this field.

Meteyard had a lifelong commitment to the development of the decorative arts and the humanising effects of art and beauty and wrote many short stories around this theme. The 1840s witnessed the origins of the Arts and Crafts movement with the work of Pugin and Henry Cole;[43] Meteyard was very committed to the idea that art and good craftsmanship in particular could be a redemptive force in society but she also believed, along with Pugin, that machine processes were acceptable as long as they were used properly and ensured the integrity of design. 'Art in Spitalfields' is just one of a number of stories about textile art and its promotion.[44] Between 1842 and 1852 the government created twenty-one new schools of design and the London school was in Spitalfields. *The People's Journal,* the site of publication for this story was a magazine targeted at an artisan readership, so the creation of funded design schools offering training to artisans on designing for manufacture was a topic of importance and interest to readers. In this story, the heroine Sarah Chapman, recovering from the disappointment of learning that her sister has secretly married the man she loves finds solace in textile design. Living in Spitalfields among the weavers Sarah is convinced of the benefits that a knowledge of skilled design and application can bring to this section of the community; 'One steady conviction arose that the fundamental principles of art in their application to design, must become an essential portion of education' (p. 40). In defiance of her domineering father she is helped by an old woman for whom she is supposed to be acting as companion, to go to the British Library to draw the Elgin Marbles as a new textile design. The design is so good it is acclaimed in the House of Commons as an example of fine British textile art. On her death we learn that Sarah has been instrumental in raising the profile of textiles from her humble origins in Spitalfields. Her example illustrates, not just what application and perseverance can yield, but it also serves as a reminder of how much society can learn, in both theory and practice, from the principles of applied art. As Mitchell argues 'environmental determinism is wholly reversible; when conditions are changed people improve'.[45] Beyond the Condition of England writings Meteyard uses her ideas on art and aesthetics to provide a way forward.

In 'The Beauty Brought Home' and 'The Hatton Garden Spoon' published in *The Ladies' Cabinet*, Meteyard suggests the moralising capabilities of art and aesthetic appreciation in a more abstract manner.[46] 'The Beauty Brought Home' is a story of a middle-class family who befriend a rural family with a son, to whom their maid is eventually married. This domestic narrative is essentially interested in the return to homely values found in rustic life and in the good relationships between mistresses and servants, one of Meteyard's perennial concerns; but as part of this literal and figurative marriage of country and city, cultivation and industry it suggests that an appreciation of the natural beauty of simple things, both manufactured and natural, is essential to social and domestic harmony. At the close of the story with the young couple entertaining visitors, the narrator breaks the frame of the narrative to state 'Did I not say, educate; and deformity and waste should be turned to beauty and proportion'(p. 74). The heroine of 'The Hatton Garden Spoon', a young woman who embarks on design work for cutlery, laments the difficulties women have in finding time to pursue art 'if only for the sake of its own moral and refining influence' (p. 58).

In another story focusing specifically on textile design 'My Work as a Decorator' published in *Sharpe's London Magazine,* a rare male narrator tells the story of his career which includes training in France which had the best reputation in Europe for design schools and for producing good designers.[47] He suggests that good design work is for all classes, decorative art in particular is just at home in lowly cottages as it is in the homes of the middle and upper classes. 'But one prerogative of the decorative art eminently pleases me – this is their general alliance with moral principles. They bestow, as it were, upon me a *teaching power*' (p. 307). It is this educational function of art as much as its aesthetic qualities that attracts Meteyard and there are numerous stories and articles that work this through. In 'Blue to Brown' a story published in *Country Words*, a provincial magazine, Meteyard discusses once again the nature of art in the cottage home.[48] Here, the young housewife, Sukey learns to appreciate the beauty of simple pottery. The story ends thus 'For ornamental beauty is amongst the mind's necessities; and beauty of effect, and beauty of decoration, are absolute wants to an advancing and highly civilised people' (p. 25). This story, which appeared later in her career is entirely consistent with the critique on art offered in the 1840s. The cultivation and appreciation of art is synonymous with progress. Indeed the 'deformity and waste' referred to in 'The Beauty Brought Home' suggests the degenerative qualities and price of the ignorance of aesthetic principles. This view of art is essentially in keeping with a career that has been devoted entirely to progressive principles.

But Meteyard began her writing career on the topic of authorship and as artistic endeavour it is inevitably connected to wider ideas about art and its role and potential. As a professional writer, writing was a means of earning money, but as a topic the interest was two-fold. It provided one theme among many others with which she could work and there are many plots with a writer or the act of writing at the heart of the narrative; but it also provided an opportunity to develop and extend ideas on the role that writing could play as a humanising and civilising force. An early letter to *Douglas Jerrold's Weekly Newspaper* on the Whittington Club discusses this vital role and suggests that women in particular utilise it as a means of livelihood and as a means of spreading ideas and influence. [49] In 'The Flint and Hart Matronship' a story about the importance of education for pauper children she writes of 'the iron pen', a pre-eminently industrial image suggesting the power and status of writing. [50] But it is in the later fiction that this topic is most often found and Meteyard takes many opportunities to explore what writing can offer both to the individual and to the community. These opportunities are always accessed via depictions of women writers, which also enables Meteyard to consider the value – the influence and prestige; and the price – the drudgery and exploitation, involved in this 'struggle for fame'.

'A Winter and its Spring' the story read by the characters in *The Lady Herbert's Gentlewomen,* is a sentimental story of a writer, Alice Newport who meets her former lover, William Fitzgerald in a strange twist of fate. [51] He is very ill and reveals the regret that he now has about finishing their relationship rather hastily. On hearing this revelation she says she will now marry him as an act of duty and honour, but the selfless Fitzgerald declines, insisting she build her new relationship with Dr Burnell which she does and they marry. In an equally magnanimous move, Dr Burnell sees Alice is torn and accepts her wish to nurse William on his deathbed; indeed so secure is Burnell in the knowledge that his new wife holds no other feelings than noble ones for Fitzgerald, he suggests he join them in their honeymoon cottage. Fitzgerald does just that and after a short time he dies. What is interesting about this story in relationship to writing is that Alice and William, when young lovers, had grown together through their love of literature and learning. For Alice, William, thirteen years her senior, had not only been a teacher but an intellectual soul-mate 'and for the first time in my life I felt that I had someone for a friend who sympathised with and understood my intellectual yearnings' (p. 190). While Alice was tending him on his sick-bed the narrator reveals 'Alice and William were now no more than friends – but friends whose pure and divine spirit of friendship augmented day by day. They read together, talked together, and to his fine taste – antiquarian, legal, and philosophical – she was again a scholar' (p. 297). What legitimises Alice's rather unconventional nursing of Fitzgerald is the integrity of their past endeavours and the nobility of their desire to fill his last days with literary and philosophical pursuits. Here we see the ennobling quality of literature and knowledge explored through domestic tableaux and once again Meteyard suggests that art, in this case literary endeavour, has tremendous power and principle.

In *The Doctor's Little Daughter,* a semi-autobiographical novel for children, Meteyard once again engages with the energising principles of art.[52] Evoking the Romantic model of the importance of childhood and of memory, Meteyard tells the story of an exemplary childhood. While walking in the hills one day Alice, the heroine, contemplates the landscape and has a moment of epiphany, realising that one day she will become an artist. This tendency to valorise and celebrate the possibilities of art and creativity is a perennial theme in her work. But these positive images work alongside others that acknowledge that not all writing is spontaneous and creative and not all writing is produced in ideal circumstances, as Meteyard reminded the committee of the Royal Literary Fund when she gave an account about the writing of this novel as a release from the tedium of writing for the periodical press. This image of not only the sacrifices, but also the sheer drudgery involved for the professional woman writer is never far away from many of the stories dealing with this topic. For instance, in 'The Thorn and Then the Rose', a story of a man who falls for the wrong woman, we are told about the trials and tribulations facing the female author.[53] Anne, the author in the story tells her friend 'I am a writer, and so get my bread by my pen. It is hard-won bread – scanty bread, but I have peace of mind and independence' (p. 172). Anne criticises unscrupulous publishers who exploit writers and suggests they ride in fancy carriages whilst their authors endure great poverty. This bitterness clearly derives from Meteyard's own experience as the letters to the Royal Literary Fund attest.

But it is on 'A Woman's Pen' published in *The Englishwoman's Journal* that I want to end this piece.[54] Mary Howitt had introduced the editor Bessie Parkes to Meteyard and this is her only contribution to this publication. Aimed at a female, educated, middle-class readership *The Englishwoman's Journal* was the mouthpiece of the Langham Place Circle and as such was deeply committed to the improvement and enhancement of women's role and position in society. This story is about a successful iron master who, while on holiday comes across a writer Mary Cresset, now an old lady. It transpires that Mary's books had had an enormous influence on his life and principles and in a fit of deep gratitude he attempts to award her an annuity to help her in old age. In conversation they discuss her aims and the attributes which women in particular bring to literature and culture. Mary says 'but the time is coming when science and imagination will coalesce and work harmoniously; and woman's peculiar faculty be recognised as one of intrinsic value in furthering the loftiest purposes of human advancement' (p. 253). As the conversation progresses it begins to read as a manifesto for the improvement of the lot of the average woman writer who experiences both success and failure at different

times in her career. In this story Meteyard manages to cover a comprehensive list of the joys and pains of literary labour. Mary is adamant
that her writing, while constituting her livelihood, was not just undertaken
for that aim alone, that it was produced in order to contribute to 'human
advancement'. But these lofty claims for literature are balanced against the
hardships endured by many writers and Mary suggests ways forward for
instances like this, such as the establishment of pensions and funds for
struggling authors. Meteyard, in her own life, had by this time already
been in that predicament and so there is no doubt that personal experience
informs many of the character's comments. Indeed one of Mary's
stipulations for a Benefit Society for female authors is that the applicant
need not explain their private affairs to the committee. This is surely a
reference to Meteyard's own experience with the Royal Literary Fund where
applicants had to prove, not only their literary worth but also their moral
worth and Mary declares 'I only know I would rather end my days in a
garret, than condescend to such humiliation; and the majority of literary
women would, I think, share my opinion' (p. 255). So, Meteyard's career
shows us the choices and disappointments facing the committed writer
who was always, it seems, 'struggling for fame', starting out as a radical
writer Meteyard's career took a number of turns. It may be reasonable to
assume that a writer who relies almost entirely on contributions to
periodicals tailors copy to suit demand and indeed there are instances
when this appears to be the case. However, equally apparent is the
continuing commitment to the positive principles so evident in the writing
of the first decade of her career, albeit in a different form and addressed to
a different audience. Eliza Meteyard, like her first character Barbara, did it
seems, 'steer on in the good cause of self-help and honest independence'.[55]

Notes

1 Eliza Meteyard, *Struggles for Fame*, 3 vols (London: T.C. Newby, 1845), vol.1,
   p. 51. Subsequent page references are given in the text.
2 For a useful discussion of the common writer see Nigel Cross, *The Common
   Writer. Life in Nineteenth-Century Grub Street* (Cambridge: Cambridge
   University Press, 1985).
3 Like Meteyard, Elizabeth Gaskell also published in *Howitt's Journal* in the
   early part of her career.
4 'Scenes in the Life of an Authoress', *Tait's Edinburgh Magazine*, 10 (1843),
   765–75; 11 (1844), 36–42, 245–54.
5 See Brian E. Maidment, 'Magazines of Popular Progress and the Artisans',
   Victorian Periodicals Review, 17:3 (Fall 1984), 82–94. Other magazines of

popular progress include *Chamber's Journal* and *The Working Man's Friend and Family Instructor*, to both of which Meteyard contributed.

6 There is much work still to be done on both magazines and I have discovered that they merged in 1858; however this is not noted in *The Waterloo Directory of Victorian Periodicals, 1824–1900*. Other women's magazines Meteyard contributed to include *The English Woman's Journal*, a radical journal and organ of the Langham Place Circle and *The Ladies' Treasury* a more mainstream domestic magazine.

7 *The Literary Gazette* (25 October 1845), 704.

8 Her work was widely reviewed and in the main they were satisfactory but *The Hallowed Spots of London* received a vitriolic review from W. H. Dixon in *The Athenaeum* (18 January 1862), 77–9.

9 See Mary Howitt's autobiography, Margaret Howitt (ed.), *Mary Howitt, An Autobiography*, 2 vols (London: William Isbister, 1889) for an account of the ground-breaking advance Meteyard received from the publisher for the biography.

10 The Royal Literary Fund was set up in 1790 to help authors in difficult circumstances. Meteyard's letters of application are in the archive and give detailed accounts of her career and earnings. Many of the letters give pre-*New Grub Street* accounts of how she felt she had to compromise her artistic integrity to make a living and at one point she writes about wanting to be 'less a hack of the press', Nigel Cross, *The Royal Literary Fund 1790–1918* (London: World Microfilm Publications, 1984), case file no. 1269, 7 June 1854. For a fascinating study of applications to the RLF at this time see S. D. Mumm, 'Writing for their Lives, Women Applicants to the Royal Literary Fund, 1840–1880', *Publishing History*, 27 (1990), 27–47.

11 Cross, *The Common Writer*, p. 38.

12 Meteyard applied to the RLF on five occasions, in 1851, 1854, 1859, 1862 and in 1868. A year after the final award she received the first of the two civil list pensions but records her dismay at the amount offered, RLF case file no. 1269, 8 April 1869.

13 RLF case file no. 1269, 2 May 1859.

14 See John Sutherland, *Victorian Novelists and their Publishers* (London: Athlone Press, 1976).

15 Valerie Sanders, 'Women, Fiction and the Marketplace', in Joanne Shattock (ed.), *Women and Literature in Britain 1800–1900* (Cambridge: Cambridge University Press, 2001), pp. 142–61.

16 Cross, *The Common Writer*, p. 189.

17 RLF case file no. 1269, 31 March 1868.

18 For profiles see John Sutherland's 'Foreword: The Underread', in Barbara Leah Harman and Susan Meyer (eds), *The New Nineteenth Century. Feminist Readings of Underread Victorian Fiction* (London: Garland Press, 1996), pp. xi–xxv, and also Mumm, 'Writing for their Lives'.

19 See Barbara Onslow, *Women of the Press in Nineteenth-Century Britain*

(Basingstoke: Macmillan, 2000).

20 Samuel Smiles and Mary and William Howitt also wrote letters of support to the RLF on her behalf.

21 Howitt, *Mary Howitt,* p. 155.

22 Meteyard also wrote for *Sharpe's London Magazine* which was edited by Anna Carter Hall, wife of Samuel Carter Hall.

23 Preface to *The Nine Hours Movement: Industrial and Household Tales* (London: Longmans, Green and Co., 1872), p. ix.

24 Eliza Meteyard, *The Lady Herbert's Gentlewomen,* 3 vols (London: Hurst and Blackett, 1862), vol. 3, p. 25.

25 Eliza Meteyard, *The Doctor's Little Daughter* (London: Arthur Hall, Virtue and Co., 1850), p. v (this story was also serialised in *Eliza Cook's Journal* in the same year); and RLF case file no. 1269, 9 June 1851.

26 *The Lady's Own Paper* (20 July 1867), 545.

27 See Margaret Dalziel, *Popular Fiction 100 Years Ago* (London: Cohen and West, 1957).

28 Notably Kay Boardman, '"The Glass of Gin": Renegade Reading Possibilities in the Classic Realist Text', in Sara Mills (ed.), *Gendering the Reader* (Brighton: Harvester Wheatsheaf, 1994), pp. 199–216; Catherine Gallagher, *The Industrial Reformation of English Fiction: Social Discourse and Narrative Form, 1832–1867* (Chicago, IL: University of Chicago Press, 1985); Joseph Kestner, *Protest and Reform. The British Social Narrative by Women 1827–1867* (London: Methuen, 1985); Sally Mitchell, *The Fallen Angel: Chastity, Class and Women's Reading, 1835–1880* (Bowling Green, OH: Bowling Green University Press, 1981).

29 See Kathryn Gleadle, *The Early Feminists. Radical Unitarians and the Emergence of the Women's Rights Movement, 1831–1851* (New York: St Martins Press, 1995) and Helen Rogers, 'From "Monster Meetings" to "Fireside Virtues"? Radical Women and "the People" in the 1840s', *Journal of Victorian Culture,* 4:1 (Spring 1999), 52–75.

30 *The Athenaeum* (8 March 1862), 328.

31 See Christopher Kent, 'The Whittington Club: A Bohemian Experiment in Middle Class Social Reform', *Victorian Studies,* 18:1 (1974), 31–55.

32 Gallagher, *The Industrial Reformation,* p. 136.

33 Manuscript letter dated 13 May 1872 in the private possession of Kevin Desmond.

34 Maidment, 'Magazines of Popular Progress', p. 83.

35 Gleadle, *The Early Feminists,* p. 181; Gleadle also states that Barbara Leigh Smith and Bessie Parkes, leading figures of the Langham Place Circle, both subscribed to *Howitt's Journal* and *Eliza Cook's Journal.*

36 Kestner, *Protest and Reform,* p. 33. Subsequent page references are given in the text.

37 Maidment, 'Magazines of Popular Progress', p. 87.

38 Gallagher, *The Industrial Reformation.*

39 Eliza Meteyard, 'Lucy Dean; The Noble Needlewoman', *Eliza Cook's Journal*, 2 (1850), 312–17, 329–31, 340–4, 360–4, 376–9, 393–5.
40 Eliza Meteyard, 'A Soul Amongst the Vagrants', *Eliza Cook's Journal*, 1 (1849), 164–7, 186–91.
41 Eliza Meteyard, 'The Shop at Barrow-in Furness', *The Odd-Fellows Magazine*, 7 (1870), 353–60.
42 Eliza Meteyard, 'Lis's Culture. A Story in Four Chapters', *The Odd-Fellows Magazine*, 11 (1877), 74–80, 137–44, 215–22, 284–94. Subsequent page references are given in the text.
43 See Gillian Naylor, *The Arts and Crafts Movement* (London: Studio Vista, 1971).
44 Eliza Meteyard, 'Art in Spitalfields', *The People's Journal*, 2 (1846), 40–2, 52–4. Subsequent page references are given in the text.
45 Mitchell, *The Fallen Angel*, p. 31.
46 Eliza Meteyard, 'The Beauty Brought Home', *The Ladies' Cabinet*, 2, new series (1853), 71–4; 'The Hatton Garden Spoon', *The Ladies' Cabinet*, 5, new series (1854), 1–6, 57–61, 113–16, 169–74, 231–6. Subsequent page references are given in the text.
47 Eliza Meteyard, 'My Work as a Decorator', *Sharpe's London Magazine*, 5 (1854), 305–8, 328–35. Subsequent page references are given in the text.
48 Eliza Meteyard, 'From Blue to Brown', *Country Words*, 1 (1866), 22–5. Subsequent page references are given in the text.
49 Eliza Meteyard, 'The Whittington Club and the Ladies', *Douglas Jerrold's Weekly Newspaper*, 1 (1846), 343.
50 Eliza Meteyard, 'The Flint and Hart Matronship,' *Howitt's Journal*, 1 (1847), 18–20, 36–8.
51 Eliza Meteyard, 'A Winter and its Spring', *The Ladies' Cabinet*, 4, new series (1854), 188–92, 230–5, 294–8. Subsequent page references are given in the text.
52 Meteyard, *The Doctor's Little Daughter*.
53 Eliza Meteyard, 'The Thorn and Then the Rose', *The Ladies' Treasury*, 4 (1860), 34–7, 66–70, 98–103, 170–2, 202–5, 234–9. Subsequent page references are given in the text.
54 Eliza Meteyard, 'A Woman's Pen', *The Englishwoman's Journal*, 1 (1858), 246–59. Subsequent page references are given in the text.
55 Meteyard, *Struggles for Fame*, p. 291.

Bibliography

Boardman, Kay, '"The Glass of Gin": Renegade Reading Possibilities in the Classic Realist Text', in Sara Mills (ed.), *Gendering the Reader*, Brighton: Harvester Wheatsheaf, 1994, pp. 199–216.
Cross, Nigel, *The Royal Literary Fund 1790–1918*, London: World Microfilm

Publications, 1984.

—— *The Common Writer. Life in Nineteenth-Century Grub Street*, Cambridge: Cambridge University Press, 1985.

Dalziel, Margaret, *Popular Fiction 100 Years Ago*, London: Cohen and West, 1957.

Gallagher, Catherine, *The Industrial Reformation of English Fiction: Social Discourse and Narrative Form, 1832–1867*, Chicago, IL: University of Chicago Press, 1985.

Gleadle, Kathryn, *The Early Feminists. Radical Unitarians and the Emergence of the Women's Rights Movement, 1831–1851*, New York: St Martin's Press, 1995.

Harman, Barbara Leah and Susan Meyer, *The New Nineteenth Century. Feminist Readings of Underread Victorian Fiction*, London: Garland Press, 1996.

Howitt, Margaret (ed.), *Mary Howitt – An Autobiography*, 2 vols, London: William Isbister Ltd., 1889.

Kent, Christopher, 'The Whittington Club: A Bohemian Experiment in Middle Class Social Reform', *Victorian Studies*, 18:1 (1974), 31–55.

Kestner, Joseph, *Protest and Reform. The British Social Narrative by Women 1827–1867*, London: Methuen, 1985.

Maidment, Brian. E, 'Magazines of Popular Progress and the Artisans', *Victorian Periodicals Review*, 17:3 (Fall 1984), 82–94.

Meteyard, Eliza, 'Scenes in the Life of an Authoress', *Tait's Edinburgh Magazine*, 10 (1843), 765–75; 11 (1844), 36–42, 245–54.

——*Struggles for Fame*, 3 vols, London: T. C. Newby, 1845.

——'Art in Spitalfields', *The People's Journal*, 2 (1846), 40–2, 52–4.

——'The Whittington Club and the Ladies', *Douglas Jerrold's Weekly Newspaper*, 1 (1846), 343.

——'The Flint and Hart Matronship', *Howitt's Journal*, 1 (1847), 18–20, 36–8.

——'A Soul Amongst the Vagrants', *Eliza Cook's Journal*, 1 (1849), 164–7, 186–91.

——*The Doctor's Little Daughter*, London: Arthur Hall, Virtue and Co., 1850.

——'Lucy Dean; The Noble Needlewoman', *Eliza Cook's Journal*, 2 (1850), 312–17, 329–31, 340–4, 360–4, 376–9, 393–5.

——'The Beauty Brought Home', *The Ladies' Cabinet*, 5, new series (1853), 71–4.

——'The Hatton Garden Spoon', *The Ladies' Cabinet*, 5, new series (1854), 1–6, 57–61, 113–16, 169–74, 231–6.

——'My Work as a Decorator', *Sharpe's London Magazine*, 5 (1854), 305–8, 328–35.

——'A Winter and its Spring', *The Ladies' Cabinet*, 4, new series (1854), 188–92, 230–5, 294–8.

——*Dr Oliver's Maid*, London: Arthur Hall, Virtue and Co., 1857.

——*Lilian's Golden Hours*, London: G. Routledge and Co., 1857.

——'A Woman's Pen', *The Englishwoman's Journal*, 1 (1858), 246–59.

——*Dora and her Papa*, London: George Routledge and Sons, 1860.

——*Mainstone's Housekeeper*, London: Hurst and Blackett, 1860.

——'The Thorn and Then the Rose', *The Ladies' Treasury*, 4 (1860), 34–7, 66–70, 98–103, 170–2, 202–5, 234–9.

——*Give Bread, Gain Love*, London: William Tegg, 1861.

——*The Little Museum Keepers*, London: William and Robert Chambers, 1861.

——*The Hallowed Spots of London*, London: E. Marlborough and Co., 1862.

——*The Lady Herbert's Gentlewomen*, 3 vols, London: Hurst and Blackett, 1862.

——*The Life of Josiah Wedgwood*, 2 vols, London: Hurst and Blackett, 1865–66.

——'From Blue to Brown', *Country Words*, 1 (1866), 22–5.

——'The Shop at Barrow-in-Furness', *The Odd-Fellows Magazine*, 7 (1870), 353–60.

——*The Nine Hours Movement: Industrial and Household Tales*, London: Longmans, Green and Co., 1872.

——'Lis's Culture. A Story in Four Chapters', *The Odd-Fellows Magazine*, 11 (1877), 74–80, 137–44, 215–22, 284–94.

——*The Children's Isle*, London: Hodder and Stoughton, 1878.

Mitchell, Sally, *The Fallen Angel: Chastity, Class and Women's Reading, 1835–1880*, Bowling Green, OH: Bowling Green University Press, 1981.

Mumm, S. D, 'Writing for Their Lives, Women Applicants to the Royal Literary Fund, 1840–1880', *Publishing History*, 27 (1990), 27–47.

Naylor, Gillian, *The Arts and Crafts Movement*, London: Studio Vista, 1971.

Onslow, Barbara, *Women of the Press in Nineteenth-Century Britain*, Basingstoke: Macmillan, 2000.

Rogers, Helen, 'From "Monster Meetings" to "Fireside Virtues"? Radical Women and "the People" in the 1840s', *Journal of Victorian Culture*, 4:1 (Spring 1999), 52–75.

Sanders, Valerie, 'Women, Fiction and the Marketplace', in Joanne Shattock (ed.), *Women and Literature in Britain 1800–1900*, Cambridge: Cambridge University Press, 2001, pp. 142–61.

Sutherland, John, *Victorian Novelists and Their Publishers*, London: Athlone Press, 1976.

——'Foreword: The Underread', in Barbara Leah Herman and Susan Meyer (eds), *The New Nineteenth Century. Feminist Readings of Underread Victorian Fiction*, London: Garland Press, 1996, pp. xi–xxv.

3

'Almost always two sides to a question': the novels of Jessie Fothergill

Helen Debenham

'Où allait donc, Mademoiselle de Saint Geneix, en pleine nuit, et en pleine montagne, dans un pays perdu?'[1] Unlike George Sand's heroine, fleeing into the night from a false accusation, the nobly self-sacrificing Aldyth Sweynson, to whom these words are applied in Jessie Fothergill's *Aldyth* (1877), never realises that she has wandered into peril, and certainly not that her steady religious faith itself constitutes the 'pays perdu' – 'a lost land of the vaguest hope and conjecture' (p. 290). Nor would Fothergill have realised that Sand's question could equally apply to her own situation as a novelist. Now largely forgotten, like many other women writers whose careers began as George Eliot's ended, Fothergill was highly successful in her day, best known for an exotic romance but also acclaimed as a regional writer and for her investigation of social, moral and political 'questions of the day'.[2] From the start she had no doubts about her own philosophical and intellectual position: rejecting Christianity, she agreed with the narrator of *Aldyth* that, although 'in certain exalted moments we believe that we believe in what we call God', He is only 'an abstraction quite apart from us, our earth, our lives, our hopes – opposed to them in fact' (p. 68), and she endeavoured to live resolutely and clear-sightedly without Him. What she could not know was the extent to which the agnostic beliefs which underpin every aspect of her fiction would contribute to the critical and technical difficulties she faced in the changing late nineteenth-century literary market.

Her rejection of religious belief was central to Fothergill's literary aspirations. At the end of *Aldyth*, faced with bitter disappointment, the heroine seeks comfort, as Maggie Tulliver does, from the writing of Thomas à Kempis, a consolation which the narrator condones but thinks mistaken. The echo of Eliot is one of the ways in which the young author signals the readers she hopes to attract, ones who are, like herself, liberal-minded, serious and unafraid of 'advanced' views. In her first published novel, *Healey* (1875),[3] the heroine, Katharine, discusses *Romola* with her cousin, who finds it depressing: 'I feel all hope dead when I have finished it. It shuts me in like a high wall, and there is nothing beyond'. This is precisely why Katharine likes it, because '… it is so true'. She herself '… could never have a definite hope. I should be always reminding myself that I had no higher authority for it than my own imagination' (vol. 1, p. 123). Although Katharine learns to be more hopeful, essentially her views, and her refusal of compromises and false consolations, are endorsed by all Fothergill's work. There is no 'beyond'; there is only the here and now, this world, in which every action has its consequences, and no harmful action can be fully redeemed. The outlook can be bleak – 'the sins of the fathers are visited upon the children daily, hourly, inevitably', insists Bernard in *Kith and Kin* (1881) – and there is no reward for good behaviour, 'except the one which Christianity says is not sufficient to keep a man straight – the conviction that you have done right and been honest, cost what it might, and that whatever you have suffered from others, no others shall suffer by you'.[4]

Fothergill thus makes explicit what Eliot presents more circumspectly, the problems of living in a world where religious sanctions no longer apply. At times she also parallels, or foreshadows, Thomas Hardy: 'Oh, I don't believe in God!' cries a character in *Healey*, 'in a voice of extreme anguish', 'I don't believe He is good; if He were good, we should not be so miserable!' '"Hast ne'er found out that afore?" said Sara, with a concentrated scorn' (vol. 2, p. 161). Sara, a betrayed and dying factory girl, 'had begun to feel, to question, to reason, since her great grief had come about. She did not know that, formulated scientifically,' the narrator continues sarcastically, '"Life is the continuous adjustment of internal conditions to external conditions" but she did know that if "things had been different," she might have lived, and might have been happy instead of miserable'(vol. 3, pp. 69–70).[5] Fothergill's characters live in a self-consciously modern world: the literate among them read, as she did, George Sand, and Eliot and the Brontës; they admire Dickens and Scott and Thackeray. They also read Darwin, Ruskin, Mill, Morris and Spencer at a time when to profess scepticism or indeed anything 'distinctly opposite to the opinions of the *Record*, the *Church Times*, and other religious papers' was still to incur profound suspicion: 'vague, disjointed sounds, such as "Colenso," "German Rationalism," "Materialists," "Communism," seemed to float in the air in connection with it. People said one or two of these words (in a whisper), nodded their heads, and *looked*. "*Westminster Review*, my dear; John Stuart

Mill, and all those *dreadful* people!"' [6] Whether they live in busy industrial cities or remote country villages, the characters face the clash of old and new value systems. Religious and moral beliefs, social institutions, class structures, work possibilities, gender roles and sexual relations, all are in a process of rapid change, which Fothergill valiantly attempts to depict and to understand.

Whatever the appeal of such topics for scholarly readers today, there was little profit in them for a young writer beginning to publish in the mid-1870s. *Healey* and *Aldyth*, in Fothergill's own words, 'fell flat and dead to the ground'.[7] The novel which brought her first and greatest popular success, *The First Violin* (1877), is in some respects the least characteristic of her works. Exuberantly romantic in every sense, it features, alongside a vivid depiction of the contemporary world of professional musicians in Germany, a heroine outstanding in looks, talents and virtues, a disguised hero nobly bearing another's guilt, a fairy godmother and wicked baronet in minor roles, and a plot which relies on outrageous coincidences. It also sympathetically presents a married woman's affair with another man. It throbs with the discovery of a new life, new music, new possibilities of all kinds, and it is very readable. Rejected by Fothergill's first publisher, as likely to damage her (and presumably his) reputation, and by another firm, it reputedly caused a sensation when finally brought out by Richard Bentley and Son in *Temple Bar* and then as a three-decker.[8] It remains the best known of her novels and was particularly popular in the United States, running to many separate editions before the end of the century and helping to ensure a ready market for her later works.[9] It is probably also a major reason why her novels were deemed 'sensational and immoral' by the American Library Association in 1881[10] and later consigned to critical oblivion as yet another of the minor sensationalists who filled the fiction pages of weekly journals and the shelves of lending libraries. In 1878, Fothergill entered the *Bolton Weekly Journal*'s first fiction contest with *The Lasses of Leverhouse*, a relatively gentle domestic story written a few years earlier and unlikely to shock too many of its readers' sensibilities. She won third prize, not the striking success to which entrants must have aspired but still a clear indication of market preferences; her subsequent work endeavours to satisfy them without unduly compromising her own more severe standards. If Fothergill deserves attention today, it is not as a forgotten genius but rather as a passionate, perceptive, uneven writer, whose novels, enlivened by a sharply sarcastic wit, provide exceptional insights into some of the moral, social and literary dilemmas of her time, and whose literary career shows the fate of an author whose serious concerns clashed with the demands of the mass market for entertainment and excitement.

Fothergill was born in Manchester in 1851, the eldest child of Thomas Fothergill, a cotton manufacturer. His stories of his boyhood in Wensleydale, Yorkshire, in a farmhouse owned by his Quaker family since 1668, were part of what inspired her passionate interest in the countryside, while her pride in her yeoman descent helps to characterise the radicalism she espoused as an adult. She could in fact claim some distinguished forebears on her father's side, including, in the eighteenth century, a famous physician and botanist, a principal of St Edmund's Hall, Oxford, and a Quaker minister noted for his work in the United States. Henry Fothergill Chorley, music critic and writer for the *Athenæum* from 1834 to 1868, was a connection through his paternal grandmother. From her mother, Fothergill claimed chiefly to have inherited her sense of humour. Anne Coultate, the daughter of a medical man from Burnley, was a member of the Church of England and the marriage was blamed for Thomas Fothergill's ejection from the Society of Friends, though there were clearly deeper intellectual causes for the family's seemingly rapid shift into Nonconformity.[11] Fothergill defined herself as a 'free thinker' from an early age and the gleefully irreverent accounts of church-going in her early works read very much like personal experience, suggesting that the whole family held similarly unorthodox views. The fact that *The First Violin*, unlike her first two novels, initially appeared anonymously has been explained as a desire to protect her family's Quaker sensibilities;[12] it is equally likely that Bentley did not wish to associate it with her previous works. Fothergill's attitude to Quakers is ambivalent: her life and her writing make clear that she admired their simplicity and austerity and she invariably praises Quaker kindness and virtue but in *Healey* she initially wrote disparagingly of 'their small and narrow lives and notions, and their utter unconsciousness that there could be any other code of right and wrong than their own' (vol. 3, p. 201). By 1880, she was openly discussing agnosticism in her novels and must have been among the first to use the term approvingly in English fiction.[13]

Like many Victorian women, Fothergill owed her education mainly to her omnivorous reading, although she attended a small private school in Bowden, Cheshire, and later a boarding school in Harrogate for some years. Financial reverses following the early death of her father took the family from Manchester into the country, near a family-owned cotton mill in Littleborough (later to provide the location for *Healey* and *The Lasses of Leverhouse*). There, she explored the moors and the countryside she and her characters delight in, and studied the 'routine of the great cotton and flannel mills, the odd habits, the queer sayings and doings of the workpeople'.[14] Otherwise, she read 'all that [she] could get hold of', and 'wove romances, wrote them down, in an attic at the top of the house, dreamed dreams, and lived … far more intensely in the lives and loves of [her] imaginary characters, than even in the ambition of some day having name and fame'.[15] This was perhaps fortunate given the generally poor reception of *Healey* and *Aldyth*, with only a few encouraging reviews to counter the overtly hostile ones. After completing these two novels, she made the first of several trips to Germany, culminating in fifteen months in Düsseldorf, studying with her sister and two friends.[16] The experience exhilarated her, introducing her to a new artistic and social world, and to German music especially, the inspiration for *The First Violin* which she began there. Her movements for the rest of her life were generally dictated by her health, which was always extremely delicate and affected her output in her later years. She lived for the most part in or near Manchester except when chronic illness caused her to spend time abroad, in Europe and, for thirteen months in 1884–85, in the United States. In all Fothergill produced fourteen novels. (Three one-volume works are described as 'stories' rather than novels in some accounts of her life.) Two essays describing her experiences abroad and an enthusiastic appraisal of *Wuthering Heights* appeared in *Temple Bar*[17] and other articles and short fiction are now starting to be traced. She died shortly after her fortieth birthday in 1891, and her last novel was published posthumously two years later.

The literary market which Fothergill entered in 1875 was beginning a phase of accelerated change, one largely inimical to the interests of women authors aspiring to the realm of the high-culture novel. Although women continued to dominate the field of the best-seller at this time, their 'collective reputation', as Peter Keating points out, did not survive 'the advent of realism in the 1880s and the new self-consciousness of the Artist-Novelist',[18] with Mrs Humphry Ward, the novelist of Fothergill's generation thought likeliest to rival Eliot, suffering perhaps the most spectacular eclipse. Such 'edging out', which Gaye Tuchman attributes to men's 'control of major literary institutions', Keating and other scholars such as Norman Feltes and Graham Law see as a product of inter-linked cultural and material causes, related to the breakdown of older beliefs and systems of authority and to changing modes of literary production.[19] While Fothergill consciously grappled in her work with intellectual and social change, the wider historical processes are reflected in what is known of her relationships with publishers. Her first two novels were sold outright to Henry S. King, whose firm, always struggling, was taken over in 1877 by his reader, Charles Kegan Paul. As a former High Church clergyman turned Comtean Positivist, Kegan Paul may have had sympathies in common with Fothergill – both were far more politically radical than King[20] – but a sensational romance like *The First Violin* was unlikely to suit his determination to raise the firm's status. More significantly, though 1875, when *Healey* appeared, was a bumper year for novel production, the following decade saw a marked decline in annual averages, coinciding with waning fortunes among the lending libraries and a massive increase in periodical and newspaper publication of fiction.[21] It is clear from studies such as Law's that few authors could afford to ignore the commercial benefits of the newer forms of publication and also that the full implications for authors and for their writing have yet to be explored. After her early experience with King, Fothergill seems to have been well aware of the new publishing possibilities open to her. Her success in the *Bolton Weekly Journal's* fiction competition introduced her to the Tillotsons, who owned both the *Journal* and a Fiction Syndication Bureau, and thereafter, while four of her novels appeared first in *Temple Bar*, her contracts with Bentley normally reserved the rights for newspaper serialisation in India and Australia (as well as for Tauchnitz). She may also have had some contact with A. P. Watt, another syndicator who became the first major literary agent.[22] Hurst and Blackett rather than Bentley published *The Lasses of Leverhouse* in 1888 and *A March in the Ranks* in 1890, and the posthumous *Oriole's Daughter* was brought out by William Heinemann.

Some of the effects, for Fothergill, of the increasing divergence between 'serious' and 'popular' fiction in the 1870s and 1880s can be traced in the fate of *Healey*. Where *The First Violin* succeeded at least partly because it could be assimilated to the genre of sensational romance, *Healey*, initially subtitled 'A Romance', is defiantly anti-romantic and challenging in its conception of character and plot. Set against a background of strikes and industrial action in a small Lancashire town, it presents a cross-class love story between an aggressively plain heroine, who has 'all the trouble, and much of the responsibility of [managing her brother's] large business and property' (vol. 1, pp. 26–7), and a rising working-class overseer initially repelled by a woman who is conspicuously 'not feminine, not gracious, not "what a woman ought to be"' (vol. 1, p. 105). Katharine is instead, at least in her brother's eyes, an ideal worker – 'she understood his affairs; she managed his property and his business well; she never struck work; she wanted no wages; she never murmured or repined' (vol. 1, pp. 32–3) – and bitterly aware that this disbars her from conventional femininity: 'A

masculine person (I must be masculine, you know, I do a man's work),
one so strong-minded in appearance as I am, can never be liked, though
both [sic] her work, habits, and appearance may be sorely against her taste
and her will' (vol. 1, pp. 48–9). Though the heart of the story concerns her
emotional life, in particular her powerfully depicted relationship with her
brother, Wilfred, and her slowly growing dependence on the overseer, she
is shown working, writing letters, interviewing, making business decisions,
riding through the countryside to check the mills, actions rarely performed
by women characters in earlier Victorian fiction. Accompanying this is
the more conventional tale of her brother's betrayal of the beautiful factory
girl, her death, his involvement with and redemption by another woman,
and the revenge of the betrayed girl's former lover.

The novel was reprinted in one volume by Bentley in 1884, with the less
provocative subtitle of 'A Tale'[23] and an author's Preface which mentions
revision but is far from suggesting its extent. A great deal of what has so
far been quoted here has gone and much that might be considered
controversial, or even intellectual, has been excised or softened in 'A Tale'.
The overseer, Ughtred Earnshaw, a 'true Lancashire' name[24] ('Healey: A
Romance', vol. 1, p. 43), in 'A Tale' has annoyed a previous employer by his
different religious opinions, not by his rejection of orthodoxy. Katharine
is more 'womanly', the edge of sarcasm in her comments about herself
and other women muted. Ughtred's Quaker relations receive unqualified
praise and orthodox religion is more kindly treated. Wilfred's crime and
punishment come closer to a Christian tale of sin and repentance. Most
notably, much of the overt reference to other writers has gone. Almost all
the epigraphs have disappeared.[25] *Romola* is not mentioned. Ughtred reads
keenly, but not explicitly a work by 'the late John Stuart Mill'.[26] The
'Romance' carefully explains that he knows 'a great deal about human
understanding; [has] read much philosophy, and [is] acquainted with the
newest lights in the matter of Evolution, natural and social' and yet can
still 'only vaguely say that all women "ought" to be noble, pure, and true;
and that all men "ought" to be the same, and generous, tender, and long-
suffering as well' (vol. 1, p. 147). The 'Tale's' simple comment that he is not
destined to fall in love with Sara lessens both his historical and
psychological specificity. Sara's death-bed scenes vanish and with them
much evidence of the author's sarcastically anguished engagement with
the 'kind of philosophy which delights in abstractions, which would turn
us and our feelings into units of a whole, would tell us that suffering, in
the present state of humanity and "development," is inevitable, and would
kindly point out to us that our sufferings are but part of a universal

suffering' (vol. 3, p. 14). Reviewers in 1875 disliked what one described as the 'hasty reading of books, and hastier swallowing of formulas',[27] and some of their criticism is justified. The allusions and quotations can be excessive and intrusive, betraying the author's youth with their world-weary portentousness. They can also be witty, engrossing and intensely revealing about the impressions and connections Fothergill hoped to make. Omitting Sara's death deprives her of the dignity the author originally attributed to her intellectual growth, leaving just another 'ruined maid'. It deprives the reader of the chance to see an author grappling, as Thomas Hardy does, with the unwelcome aspects of a world which science and her intellect tell her she must accept. Losing its overt intertextuality thus transforms *Healey* from a novel which demands the reader's active involvement, whether positively or negatively, with the deeper issues of modern life into a much more comfortably distanced 'picture of certain phases of Lancashire life ... rendered with a certain fidelity' (as the author half-apologetically describes it in her Preface to 'A Tale').

Around 1890, Hardy was forced to modify *Tess of the D'Urbervilles* for serial production, famously eliminating, among other things, the rape and the baptism scenes, which he, as an established high-culture author and possibly (Tuchman might argue) as a male author, was able to restore for book publication. Fothergill was more rigidly confined by genre. Apart from their dislike of her views, the critics of the first version of *Healey* reveal their discomfort with a novel that does not conform to conventional formulas. The idea that this work deliberately set out to be discursive, to emphasise psychological situations rather than narrative, appears not to occur to them. That it was called a romance caused indignation. *Aldyth* gave them additional reasons for disapproval. Where *Healey* in some respects recalls *The Mill on the Floss*, *Aldyth* disconcertingly revises Charlotte Yonge, disturbing the expected patterns of response to what ought, in broad outline, to be a familiar story of renunciation and moral, if not worldly, reward. Witty irreverence where readers might expect solemn respect, the pervasive sadness of the heroine's plight, the cynicism and 'curious moral obliquity' (p. 321) of her ungrateful sister, and in particular the open discussion and acceptance of religious doubt made it no more likely than *Healey* to be popular.[28] Fothergill's subsequent works leave no doubt about her own views but show less open antagonism to established religions, emphasising instead other changes to the social and economic order caused by 'that huge breaker [i.e., wave] of the nineteenth century spirit which we call progress'.[29] The novel which followed *The First Violin*, as well as being one of her most uniformly successful works, demonstrates her strengths as a writer on social issues and also some of the difficulties she both presents for the modern reader and discovered for herself. *Probation* (1879), resisting any temptation to revisit romantic excess, returns to the industrial north to explore the plight of industrial workers, the position of women and Radical politics.

The novel opens, after a brief description of a cotton mill, with a tart comparison of the respective functions of a 'cut-looker', who checks the quality of the cloth, and a literary critic. (As well as venting the author's feelings, the equation of industrial labour and literary criticism can be read as an ironic commentary on contemporary concerns about the commodification of literature.) Both occupations, she writes,

> have a tendency to produce a turn of mind sceptical as to the merits of the work with which the cut-looker, or the critic, has to do. Incessant flaws, 'scamped' work, broken threads, ill-joined ends, an uneven weft, a rough warp – the parallel is certainly a striking one; and a long career of cut-looking, to say nothing of criticising, may tend to make the temper quick, and the tone just a little imperious.[30]

Probation, with a cross-class love affair, like *Healey*, and a growing friendship between the cut-looker and his employer, foregrounds work and the manufacturing industry more than the earlier novel. The action is set in Rochdale (renamed Thanshope) at the time of the cotton famine of the early 1860s, and relies on precise historical detail of the cotton trade to advance the plot. Myles Heywood, the upwardly mobile cut-looker, is a less idealised Ughtred Earnshaw, 'clever, honest, proud to excess, and self-opinionated' (vol. 1, p. 8). He initially mistrusts the heroine, Adrienne Blisset, believing her to be one of the fine ladies whom he despises, whereas 'for the women of his own class he had a hearty disrespect and admiration; they could earn wages; they could work; they did not meddle in things out of their sphere: they had a distinct use and purpose' (vol, 1, p. 62). Though well above Myles in class terms, Adrienne in fact works as her uncle's secretary and research assistant. Myles's employer, Sebastian Mallory, redeems his past life as an absentee mill owner by returning to become actively involved in the welfare of his workers when the trade is threatened and to enter politics as a Radical.[31] Helena Spenceley, the daughter of an industrialist, whom Sebastian eventually marries, tempers her overly-abstract views on 'the position of women' as she confronts first the realities of life for working women during the depression and then the need to work for her living after her father's failure and suicide.

Given her outspoken religious views, some of Fothergill's opinions on social issues now seem, at first glance, disappointingly conventional. Her insistence, in all her novels, on the value of work and her championing of industry over more genteel professions belong in a tradition traceable back to Thomas Carlyle, while her heroines' active working lives are often ultimately subordinated to their 'latent idolatry of [male] power'[32] and, especially in the earlier novels, to their destined role as the heroes' inspiration and moral guide. The radical aspect of her political views is today most evident in passing comments, such as the description, in *Peril* (1884), of an unruly crowd at a political meeting as 'Church of England Tory roughs';[33] her more formal accounts are often a reminder of how conservative much that was once considered highly progressive now appears. In *Probation*, an early exchange between Myles and Adrienne begins with his denunciation of employers, especially 'those lily-handed politicians who call themselves Radicals' – he excludes his idols such as Bright[34] and Cobden – who talk 'about "supply and demand" and how to improve the condition of the lower orders' without any real knowledge, and while living themselves on the fat of the land (vol. 1, pp. 212–13). Property, for Myles, is theft if it means some living in extreme wealth while workers remain in abject poverty. Adrienne effortlessly refutes his socialist arguments, advocating instead the standard liberal principles of self-advancement through independence and self-help, and urging him to avoid

'… blind submission to trade-union rules, and … obstinate resistance to your masters, just because they are your masters, or because your union bids you resist them. Don't be a tool; use your reason; consider the whys and wherefores of things. Be answerable to your conscience alone for all you say and do. Help to show your fellows that all improvement in their condition must arise actively from within, not be received passively from without – you know that, and own it, don't you?' (vol. 1, p. 219)

She never questions the adequacy of worker's wages and conditions or distinguishes moral from economic value and Myles is given no effective response. When Adrienne continues, however, by wishing that she were a working woman like Myles's sister, so she could show him 'how toil could be ennobled' (vol. 1, p. 220), he retaliates with a brutally unsentimental depiction of the life she would face as a working-class wife. 'What,' he concludes, 'about the ennobling of toil *then*?' (vol. 1, pp. 220–1, emphasis original). Her complaint that he has left out the crucial element of love does not stop his point hitting home.

In theory Adrienne wins the debate, since Myles is the one whose views change, but uncomfortable facts have been expressed and not negated. It is easier to find toil ennobling in the abstract than in practice; and love, that great Victorian solution to social conflict, cannot resolve all. Over-simple conclusions are further disrupted by the unacknowledged and socially inadmissible attraction each is beginning to feel towards the other. Typically, throughout Fothergill's work, intellectual discussions are charged with intense, unspoken emotions and assumptions, turning what could be mere set-pieces into real debates, part of the lived experience of the characters and capable of producing unexpected, and at times unwelcome, outcomes. The unintentional pun in the metaphor she chose proved all too meaningful: the wave of progress could 'break' the 'nineteenth century spirit' as well as embody it. So, contrary to Adrienne's beliefs and to familiar Victorian axioms, self-help is not always sufficient. Independence and integrity do little for men, like Paul Lawford in *Peril*, who lack patronage or money to buy preferment when trapped in dead-end, uncongenial occupations or by the vicissitudes of the wider commercial economy. No 'want of mental and moral backbone' initially prevents Godfrey Noble in *A March in the Ranks* (1890) from advancing in his medical career but rather 'a want of that nobly developed selfishness, ... the full and perfect flower of which may be seen any day flourishing like a green bay tree in the shape of the modern Practical Man'.[35] The tinge of sarcasm as usual marks Fothergill's reluctant acceptance that 'the present state of humanity' does not always accord with human desires.

Her most disheartening realisation is spelt out in *Probation*. Alongside the rise of its hero, this novel traces the cooperation of the employers, the civic authorities, and the workers to mitigate the effects of the depression caused by the American Civil War,[36] a war in which they wholeheartedly supported the cause of the North, against their own interests and the opinion of much of the country. A success story of this nature, testimony to the benefits of cross-class mutual aid and moral principle, might be expected to offer evidence of that 'growing good of the world' which Eliot envisages in the Finale of *Middlemarch*.[37] At the very least, it should support Elizabeth Gaskell's cautious optimism at the end of *North and South* that better industrial relations will 'render [future] strikes at least not the bitter, venomous sources of hatred they have hitherto been'.[38] Instead, Fothergill's account of the episode ends in extreme disappointment: 'sixteen years later [the time of writing], comes a strike almost without parallel for bitterness and unyielding stubbornness on either side ... and this on the identical ground where, during the cotton famine, the sore distress was most nobly borne and generously relieved. These things make a riddle hard to read' (vol. 2, pp. 230–1). Her bewilderment reflects a wider, secular 'crisis of faith', a declining confidence in the equation of 'development' with 'progress', which helps to explain why she never attempts, as Gaskell (with whom she has inevitably been compared) and Eliot both do, to demonstrate the potential influence of the individual on the wider social scene.

In her rejection of teleology, as in her readiness to interrogate her own assumptions and to face the possibility that she might be wrong, Fothergill's approach to social issues bears the distinctive imprint of her agnosticism, which for her always involves much more than religion.[39] For her, as for the heroine of *Kith and Kin*, 'it is a fatal fact that there are *almost always* two sides to a question' (p. 196, emphasis original). This belief colours her attitude to women's work, which draws some of her most impassioned pleas and strongest reservations. That women can and should work, she has no doubt. Mrs Spenceley in *Probation* looks 'better, happier, younger, and more contented' (vol. 2, p. 204) when busily poor after her husband's death than she ever did when idly rich. Katharine Healey regrets that a woman who 'shows the spirit of a petty tradesman' in her negotiations for a church bazaar has not 'been placed as the head of a small retail business! There … she might have been a useful and happy woman. In her present position she is clean thrown away' (vol. 1, pp. 250, 251). The Conisbrough sisters, in *Kith and Kin*, live a 'pinched, cramped, sordid life', because their mother's refusal to let them work leaves them dependent on a capricious and miserly uncle, 'and they were one and all girls of mind and spirit; girls who could not vegetate in inactivity without suffering from it, mentally and morally' (p. 80). The mother, whose own hopes for financial relief require the uncle's death, is shocked when Judith, the eldest, makes the familiar comparison of marriage for money with prostitution, and even more horrified when she threatens to write for advice about employment to 'some of the women's rights ladies' (p. 84). Judith's knowledge that things are different now, that 'the social law' against women working for money is 'no longer so stringent' (p. 81), gives urgency to her anguished echo of Jane Eyre and Caroline Helstone. For poor middle-class women like her leisure is a prison sentence:

'To be born, to vegetate through a term of years – to know that there is a great living world somewhere outside your dungeon, and to wish that you were in it. To eat your heart out in weariness; to consume your youth in bitterness; to grow sour and envious, and old and wretched, to find all one's little bits of enthusiasm gradually grow cold. To care only for the warmth of the fire, and the creature comforts that are left – to linger on, growing more tired and more fretful, and then to die. It is worse than the iron room which grew every day narrower, till it closed upon its inmate and crushed him to death, for that was over in a few weeks; this may last fifty, sixty years.' (p. 285)

The doctor who later offers her work confirms her pessimism: 'hundreds, if not thousands of young women annually die, or go mad, or sink into hopeless querulousness or hysteric invalidism, simply because they have nothing to do in the world' (p. 358).

Judith does become a nurse, rising to hospital matron, though this happens off-stage. Others of Fothergill's women work as governesses, teachers, singers, translators, research assistants, artists, a sculptor, and some, like Katharine Healey, work successfully in fields dominated by men. Margaret Hankinson, in *Peril*, unexpectedly finds herself caretaker head of a large firm, and learns to manage it with something like genius:

> So was carried on a sort of romance of commercial life … Anyone who knows anything about our manufacturing districts does not need to be told that they contain business women, women who conduct their factories, buy their yarn and their weft, attend the markets, and compete successfully enough with their rough rivals – and they are rough indeed, sometimes. Nor would it be a new thing to some people to hear of women who, whether their names figure as members of the London Stock Exchange or not, are virtually members of that august confraternity. (vol. 3, p. 180)

Emma Jane Worboise, a contemporary novelist who likewise insisted on the absolute need for girls to be trained to support themselves, also places a young woman in temporary charge of a large business but her character Anne Wreford, in *Robert Wreford's Daughter* (1877), is femininely diffident and all too ready to give it up. Margaret, by contrast, has very mixed feelings when she relinquishes control to the rightful owner, her long-lost fiancé, and he, the narrator comments at the end, never realises what their marriage has cost her.

Yet work is not a universal panacea for women's woes; almost all the heroines eventually marry and the costs – physical and emotional – of work are never under-estimated. Fothergill is aware that women have different interests, talents, and degrees of strength, and that there is a danger of imposing demands on them which are as repressive in their way as the restrictions of the older regime. Judith resists pressure to train as a doctor because she does not feel the vocation. Letty Noble, in *A March in the Ranks*, is sympathetically treated when she fears examinations and would rather be a servant or humble village schoolteacher than emulate her headmistress sister. In some cases, the reservations about women's work superficially resemble those found in authors like Charlotte Yonge. Alizon Blundell, who manages her invalid brother's property in *A March in the Ranks*, is too willing to assume she can therefore manage other people's lives. Hilda, the successful headmistress, finds her health broken by the demands of her busy social and professional life. For Fothergill, however, these are not automatic consequences but merely possible in some circumstances and for some personalities, part of her insistence on looking at all sides of a question: about women's capacity for work she is wholly positive. When she brings reservations to other aspects of women's rights her feminism shows its Victorian roots, in particular in her reluctance, like that of many otherwise 'advanced' contemporaries, to abandon the idea that women's best role is to be a wife. Helena and Sebastian, in *Probation*, finally reach a compromise whereby she admits that disagreeing with her feminist principles does not preclude good work in other areas, and he, having learned his own need for womanly 'help and sympathy', promises 'that "the *twain together* well might change the world." I shall never uplift my voice against those theories of yours, never' (vol. 3, pp. 239–40, emphasis original), but that is as far as Fothergill goes. *Probation* is the only novel in which the topic is prominent and, as the narrator notes, the '"Woman Question" had not been forced so far to the front in 1861 as in 1878' (vol. 2, p. 21).

Although she never abandons her social concerns, in the later novels Fothergill's emphasis shifts increasingly to the moral implications of finding '*almost always* two sides to a question'. Like George Eliot, she wrestles with the problem of evil and, rather more than Eliot, she progressively and surprisingly confronts the problems of virtue. For her 'bad' characters Fothergill usually asks, not so much sympathetic understanding of what made them as they are, as recognition that they too may have some right on their side. A canting hypocrite, who is also a hired agitator, thief and would-be murderer, might have made Sara a better husband than Wilfred Healey and has good reason to resent him. The worthy Bernard Aglionby's 'humiliating', 'painful', and 'saddening discovery' in *Kith and Kin* (p. 391), that his vulgar, frivolous fiancée fears and is oppressed by him transforms the reader's as well as his perception of their situation. In *A March in the Ranks*, a wife who is 'defiled morally' (p. 305) still deserves to have her opinions and desires considered. In *Peril* it is the eponymous heroine herself (named for the circumstances of her birth) whose 'wilfulness, hardness, sullenness and revengefulness' (vol. 1, p. 88) have some justice. Moral positions and judgements, which seem fixed and permanent when characters are introduced, can shift unsettlingly as the narratives proceed. For this reason the consistently villainous Jesuit priest, Father Pablo Somerville, in *The Wellfields* (1880), seems to have strayed from a polemical religious novel of the 1840s or 1850s when he schemes, with cold calculation, first to make Jerome Wellfield abandon his fiancée and marry for money, and then to destroy the marriage in the hope of bringing both Wellfield and a large fortune under the Catholic Church's control.[40] This, however, is the first novel in which Fothergill openly mentions agnosticism and Somerville, as the servant of absolute authority preaching absolute submission, rather too programmatically exemplifies agnosticism's exact opposite, the total refusal of open-mindedness.

Equally absolutist in its own way, the definition of agnosticism which Fothergill offers in *The Wellfields* displays a touch of the unwitting arrogance and self-satisfaction she had attributed to the Quakers. For 'many natures', she writes,

> some form of religion, of an infallible institution outside themselves, and yet within their reach, is an absolute necessity; and one begins to perceive more clearly why agnosticism has never been popular.
>   Wellfield could never have been an agnostic. He and such as he have not the mental and moral toughness of fibre which enables a man to contemplate the mystery of the heavens above and the earth beneath; of the life and the death, and the pain and the evil that are upon the earth, of his own feelings and speculations, and their origin, and the purpose and destiny of them – and then, while reverently owning 'I know nothing, and I will assert nothing, upon these things', has yet the courage to live up to an ethical code, as high, as pure, and as stern as that of St. John or of Jesus Christ – expecting nothing from a life to come, as to the existence of which he is in absolute ignorance. The more part of mankind want nothing of this; they want a religion, a thing that will let them sin, and prescribe to them how they must get forgiven.[41]

With characteristic rigour, however, Fothergill subjects her own creed to examination. In *Borderland* (1886) and *A March in the Ranks*, especially, the heroic characters, upholders of the strictest moral codes, are bewildered to find themselves rigid and unsympathetic, doing harm rather than good and being justifiably rebuked by their moral inferiors. The self-centred cad, Peregrine Blundell, rightly tells his implacably virtuous sister: 'You seem to think ... that there's only one kind of goodness, one kind of conduct – never to do wrong, and so be able to trample upon all who ever fall short of it'.[42] Similarly, when Eleanor Askam, in *Borderland*, regrets that her brother, Otho, is not marrying 'a woman of higher mind – one who would have roused him to better things', Gilbert Langstroth points out that '[g]ood people don't need half as much understanding as bad ones, and with due respect to you and to current notions on the subject, saints and people who never do wrong are not those who are the most sympathetic and comprehending'.[43] His point is amply demonstrated. Eleanor and the hero, Gilbert's brother Michael, rarely understand those less high-minded than themselves, with sometimes tragic results. Eleanor, trying to care for a severely depressed girl whom Otho has seduced and abandoned, has no way of grasping that '[i]t was not for moral and spiritual degradation that [Ada] mourned and refused to be comforted, but for material trouble – vanity crushed, great hopes of advancement and aggrandizement shattered; her social position, such as it was, gone forever, and humbler women who had been clever enough to take care of themselves, exalted above her' (pp. 455–6). Ada, a shopkeeper's daughter who has been given ideas above her station by a woman of higher class, follows the path that Jane Austen spares Harriet Smith in *Emma*.[44] She eventually commits suicide after giving birth to her illegitimate child not because she is cast out and friendless but because she does not want the future her virtuous friends have organised. Living is their choice for her: killing herself is her own. There is no suggestion that the good characters are hypocrites; their high ideals do far less damage than the lax morals of others and are substantially affirmed. They are simply 'children of the world' (a phrase adopted in *The First Violin* from the German novelist, Paul Heyse),[45] endeavouring to live as best they can in terms of this world, not a hypothetical future one, and discovering, like Fothergill herself, that the outcomes of their actions are not always predictable.

That there were technical as well as moral complications in this uncertainty was apparent to the novelist and her readers. When her characters 'sometimes unkindly refuse[d] to be disposed of according to her original intentions', reviewers complained about weak plotting[46] and their criticism cannot all be dismissed as the typical reaction to a woman writer who deviates from predictable fictional patterns. Fothergill's storylines are uncertainly stitched together in places, with loose ends left untied and promising leads not followed. The early novels, in particular, experiment with narration and most struggle with the rigid demands of the three-decker. There were few obvious literary models for the kinds of psychological understanding towards which she was groping[47] and the issues and emotional situations which interested her did not lend themselves to representation through the suspenseful or exciting incidents that suited serialisation. In any case, a novelist who does not believe in teleology is unlikely to produce plots which either conform to the moral determinism of mid-Victorian realism or fully satisfy popular fiction's simpler requirements for 'poetic justice'. The intensifying debate about romance and realism in the 1880s brought the added problem of dissociating her treatment of 'questions of the day' from 'what is often called realism now, the apotheosis of all that is ugly ... told in a minute, laborious way'; an 'impartial' depiction of life, she believed, would show 'romance' to be as prevalent as 'prose'.[48] What she meant by romance, at least when she first subtitled *Healey*, probably owed much to Nathaniel Hawthorne's ideas about inevitability and chance in life and to his interest in the 'mixture of good there may be in things evil',[49] but the marriage plots on which she frequently relies carry more conventional demands for happy endings which, however qualified or muted, can blur her insistence that virtue should be its own reward.

In the end, Olive Schreiner's *The Story of an African Farm*, rather than one of Fothergill's works, was acclaimed as 'An Agnostic Novel' in 1883,[50] while Mrs Humphry Ward's tale of religious doubt, *Robert Elsmere*, published in 1888, proved one of the century's best-sellers. Schreiner was four years younger than Fothergill and Ward (born Mary Augusta Arnold) exactly the same age. Leaving aside questions of natural talent, the three women form an illuminating comparison. Ward's background fitted her ideally to sum up the nineteenth century's spiritual crisis in fictional form. Born to one of England's leading intellectual families; raised amid religious controversy; encouraged in her education by leading Oxford academics; and accustomed as an adult to life in the intellectual and literary heart of London, she wrote *Robert Elsmere* at the height of her powers and when the issues it raised were already highly topical. Schreiner, in total contrast, was isolated in early life by her colonial birth, her precocious self-education, and her rejection of her parents' rigid religion. An unhappy affair at sixteen added bitter personal knowledge of the double sexual standard to the passionate feeling which informs her novel. Ward's magisterial survey looks back to the mid-century for its hero's intellectual history and its literary form; Schreiner's fragmented plotlines and rebellious, tormented heroine foreshadow the 'New Woman' writing of the 1890s. Yet despite these very different perspectives both novelists articulate the pain of loss of faith ('amputation of the soul' as George Orwell called it),[51] and thus offer vicarious emotional release, and both leave at least a glimmer of hope for believers, Ward through Elsmere's new sect and Schreiner through Waldo's transcendentalism. Fothergill, the sickly provincial who lamented her lack of wider contacts, allows no nostalgia and offers no consolations. Unlike Ward, or even Eliot, she cannot be easily assimilated into a tradition of feminine religious discourse. She begins from a position of uncompromising scepticism and assumes that readers will share her conviction that religious belief is at best a comprehensible error. If, in this, she expected too much of her audience, she was also perhaps ahead of her time.

There are, of course, two sides to her 'modernity'. On the one hand, Fothergill's explicit concern with living as an agnostic in a changing world contrasts with Ward's almost exclusive focus, in Bernard Lightman's words, on 'the effects of an individual's crisis of faith on his personal and family relationships' and her lack of interest in 'changes in social conditions, such as those accompanying the process of urbanisation [and] industrialisation'.[52] On the other, both women were deeply committed to older moral codes, sharing Eliot's unwavering belief that the one 'peremptory' and 'absolute' law in life was 'duty'.[53] Ultimately, then, agnosticism, an 'advanced' position when Fothergill was writing and one which marks her difference from her contemporaries, also marks her as essentially Victorian, while Schreiner's rejection of conventional morality strengthens her claim to be the first of the moderns.[54] Agnosticism as a separate movement, and as Fothergill advocated it, was already beginning to fade by the early 1890s as its major proponents grew old or died. It never became central to English literature: aestheticism, the 'New Woman', the new realism and romance, and later modernism would all take the novel down different paths. Whether, if Fothergill had lived longer and her health had allowed, her determined investigation of the relativity of good and evil might have taken her in new directions too is obviously unanswerable.[55] As it is, her fourteen novels help to chart a precise moment of English history through their vivid depiction of life in Lancashire and Yorkshire and especially through their exploration of the troubled borderlands between nineteenth-century religious certitudes and the twentieth-century secularism.

Notes

1 'So where was she going, Mademoiselle de Saint Geneix, in the middle of the night, in the middle of the mountains, in an unknown country?' Le Marquis de Villemer, *Oeuvres Complètes de George Sand* (Paris: Calmann-Lévy. n.d.), p. 231. The sentence correctly begins 'Où allait donc, ainsi'. Cited in Jessie Fothergill, *Aldyth; or, 'Let the End Try the Man'* (London: Richard Bentley and Son, 1891), p. 290. Subsequent page references are given in the text.
2 Helen C. Black, *Notable Women Authors of the Day, Biographical Sketches*

(Glasgow: D. Bryce and Son, 1893), p. 194. Black's essay, based on an interview with Fothergill, is the source of much of the published biographical information.

3   Jessie Fothergill, *Healey: A Romance* (London: Henry S. King and Co., 1875). This novel was written after *Aldyth* though published before it. Differences between the 1875 (three-volume) edition and the 1884 (one-volume) edition, published by Richard Bentley and Son, are discussed below. Unless otherwise specified, further page references given in the text are to the 1875 edition.

4   Jessie Fothergill, *Kith and Kin: A Novel* (London: Macmillan and Co., Ltd, 1899), p. 176. Subsequent page references are given in the text.

5   The quotation about life is from Herbert Spencer, first formulated in *The Principles of Biology* (1864–7) and recurrent in his writing thereafter. See *The Principles of Psychology* (New York: D. Appleton and Co., 1896), vol. 1, p. 293.

6   Fothergill, *Aldyth*, p. 117, emphasis original.

7   Black, *Notable Women Authors*, p. 190.

8   The £40 payment for copyright agreed on 26 March 1877 was raised to £200 by 30 May. Bentley Archive, Add. ms. 46619 fos 43, 56.

9   Mr Michael Turner, formerly of the Bodleian Library, Oxford, kindly showed me his private collection of thirty-six separate editions. I am indebted to him also for permission to read his thesis about Tillotsons' Fiction Bureau and to examine some of Tillotsons' account books in his possession.

10 Dee Garrison, 'Immoral Fiction in the Late Victorian Library', *American Quarterly*, 28:1 (1976), 71–89. Garrison, who cites only *The First Violin*, is the only modern scholar to pay detailed attention to any of Fothergill's work, though Graham Law (see note 19) and writers for recent biographical dictionaries speak highly of her. Jane Crisp's *Jessie Fothergill*, Victorian Research Guides, 2 (St Lucia: University of Queensland, 1980) is the first major bibliographical study.

11 Mr Ian Fell, former Director, Education and Interpretation, National Museums and Galleries of Wales, who is writing a biography of Jessie Fothergill, notes that Thomas Fothergill was criticised for non-attendance at Quaker meetings more than three years before the marriage. He has suggested in private correspondence that Fothergill either did not know about her father's long-term non-attendance or chose not to correct the more romantic implication that the marriage was the cause of the break. Mr Fell generously read a draft of this essay, correcting errors and providing additional information.

12 Phyllis Scherle, 'Jessie Fothergill', in Paul Schlueter and June Schlueter (eds), *An Encyclopedia of British Women Writers* (New Brunswick, NJ: Rutgers University Press, 1998), p. 255.

13 Invented by Thomas Huxley in 1869, the word's first recorded appearance in print was in the *Spectator* in that year. While the *Oxford English Dictionary* notes its appearance in various journals in the following years, the first time

'an important agnostic' used the term in print was Leslie Stephen's *An Agnostic's Apology*, 1876. See Bernard Lightman, *The Origins of Agnosticism: Victorian Unbelief and the Limits of Knowledge* (Baltimore, PA and London: Johns Hopkins University Press, 1987), p. 93 and p. 188 note 9. In 1884 Wilkie Collins joked about 'the last new name for a free-thinker' in *I Say No* (London: Chatto and Windus, 1891), p. 47.

14 Black, *Notable Women Authors*, p. 190.

15 Black, *Notable Women Authors*, p. 190.

16 Although Fothergill is quoted as saying that she first went to Germany after the publication of these two novels, returning later for the stay during which she began *The First Violin* (Black, *Notable Women Authors*, p. 190), this must be an error. Both *Aldyth* and *The First Violin* were published in 1877, so it is likely she first went abroad in 1874 or 1875.

17 Fothergill's *Temple Bar* essays from this period were 'Some American Recollections' (February 1886), 198–213; '*Wuthering Heights*' (December 1887), 562–8; 'Flowers and Fire' (August 1889), 518–26.

18 Peter Keating, *The Haunted Study: A Social History of the English Novel, 1875–1914* (London: Fontana Press, 1989), p. 176.

19 Gaye Tuchman, with Nina E. Fortin, *Edging Women Out: Victorian Novelists, Publishers, and Social Change* (London: Routledge, 1989), p. 4; N. N. Feltes, *Literary Capital and the Late Victorian Novel* (Madison, WI: University of Wisconsin Press, 1993), pp. 49–54; Graham Law, *Serializing Fiction in the Victorian Press* (Houndmills, Basingstoke and New York: Palgrave, 2000), p. 180.

20 For the relations between and opinions of King and Kegan Paul see Leslie Howsam, *Kegan Paul: a Victorian Imprint: Publishers, Books and Cultural History* (London: Kegan Paul International, 1998), pp. 1–75.

21 Keating, *Haunted Study*, p. 32.

22 Watt, in 1881, purchased (for £8) the right to publish *Aldyth* in one newspaper. See *Index of Authors and Titles, Kegan Paul, Trench, Trübner and Henry S. King, 1858–1912*: 14 November 1881.

23 In what follows, the subtitles are used to distinguish the two versions.

24 His name prompted reviewers to disparaging comparisons with *Wuthering Heights*.

25 In the 'Romance' Shelley, Spenser and the Brownings were favourites, while Thomas Woolner's *My Beautiful Lady* (1866) appeared several times and probably inspired Fothergill's 'Proem'.

26 Fothergill, 'Romance', vol. 1, p. 131; 'Tale', p. 82.

27 *The Academy*, 8 (1875), 245.

28 Though bought by Bentley with *Healey* in 1881, *Aldyth* was republished only in 1891 after Fothergill's death.

29 Fothergill, *Kith and Kin*, p. 85.

30 Jessie Fothergill, *Probation: A Novel* (London: Richard Bentley and Son, 1879), vol. 1, p. 5. Subsequent page references are given in the text.

31 Mrs Mallory's horror at her son's choice of political party is explicitly likened to that of George Eliot's Mrs Transome in *Felix Holt*. See *Probation*, vol. 2, p. 8.

32 Fothergill, *Kith and Kin*, p. 192.

33 Jessie Fothergill, *Peril: A Novel* (New York: Henry Holt and Company, 1884), p. 82.

34 Thomas Bright was married to Anne Coultate Fothergill's sister Caroline. I am grateful to Ian Fell for this information.

35 Jessie Fothergill, *A March in the Ranks* (New York: F. M. Lupton, n.d.), p. 373.

36 Fothergill apologises in a footnote 'to the Manchester Central Committee for putting into the mouth of a single individual their excellent proposal for the schools which were of so much benefit in the most distressed districts' (vol. 2, p. 136). She does not notice the political implications of this change.

37 George Eliot, *Middlemarch* [1871–2] (Oxford: Oxford University Press, 1997), p. 822.

38 Elizabeth Gaskell, *North and South* [1855] (Oxford: Oxford University Press, 1982), p. 432.

39 At the beginning of *Kith and Kin* the hero belongs to a group whose name, 'the Agnostics', is 'very much of a misnomer, since their confession of Agnosticism certainly went no further than matters religious; on all other topics – social, moral, and political – they professed to have the newest light, and to be capable of taking the lead at any moment' (p. 27).

40 In character Somerville resembles Charles Kingsley's caricature of J. H. Newman in Chapter 14 of *Yeast*. The English setting of *The Wellfields* is based on Stonyhurst and Whalley Abbey.

41 Jessie Fothergill, *The Wellfields: A Novel* (New York: United States Book Company, n.d.), pp. 299–300.

42 Fothergill, *March*, p. 336.

43 Jessie Fothergill, *Borderland: A Country Town Chronicle* [1886] (London: Macmillan and Co., Ltd., 1899), pp. 348–9. Subsequent page references are given in the text.

44 Austen is the favourite author of the young narrator of *The Lasses of Leverhouse*, a taste Fothergill shared.

45 Heyse's novel *Kinder der Welt: Roman in sechs Büchern* (1873) is enthusiastically read and discussed by Fothergill's characters.

46 Black, *Notable Women Authors*, p. 193.

47 Her work is occasionally reminiscent of that of Henry James but there is no evidence that she read him.

48 Black, *Notable Women Authors*, p. 194.

49 Nathaniel Hawthorne, *The Marble Faun: or, The Romance of Monte Beni* [1860] (Centenary Edition, Ohio State University Press, 1968), p. 383. A passage about inevitability and chance (p. 289) is cited, under the original English title, *Transformation*, in the epigraph to Healey, vol. 2, chapter 3.

50 Olive Schreiner, *The Story of an African Farm* (London: Chapman and Hall, 1883). The review quoted is cited first by Ruth First and Anne Scott, *Olive*

Schreiner (London: Deutsch, 1980), p. 122.

51 Cited in Lightman, *Origins of Agnosticism*, p. 177.

52 Bernard Lightman, 'Robert Elsmere and the Agnostic Crises of Faith', in Richard J. Helmstadter and Bernard Lightman (eds), *Victorian Faith in Crisis: Essays on Continuity and Change in Nineteenth-Century Belief* (Stanford, CA: Stanford University Press, 1990), pp. 291–2.

53 Gordon Haight, *George Eliot: A Biography* (Oxford: Oxford University Press, 1969), p. 464.

54 See Rachel Blau Du Plessis, *Writing Beyond the Ending: Narrative Strategies of Twentieth-Century Women Writers*, (Bloomington, IN: Indiana University Press, 1985), Chapter 2.

55 Fothergill's younger sister, Caroline, who published at least eight novels between 1883 and 1896, makes moral issues less prominent and seems for that reason closer to the 'New Women' writers of the 1890s. She was not as successful as Jessie.

Bibliography

Bentley Archive, Add. ms. 46619 fos 43, 56.

Black, Helen C., *Notable Women Authors of the Day, Biographical Sketches*, Glasgow: D. Bryce & Son, 1893.

Collins, Wilkie, *I Say No* [1883] London: Chatto and Windus, 1891.

Crisp, Jane, *Jessie Fothergill*, Victorian Research Guides, 2, St Lucia: University of Queensland, 1980.

Du Plessis, Rachel Blau, *Writing Beyond the Ending: Narrative Strategies of Twentieth-Century Women Writers*, Bloomington, IN: Indiana University Press, 1985.

Eliot, George, *Middlemarch* [1871–2] Oxford: Oxford University Press, 1997.

Feltes, N. N., *Literary Capital and the Late Victorian Novel*, Madison, WI: University of Wisconsin Press, 1993.

First, Ruth and Anne Scott, *Olive Schreiner*, London: Deutsch, 1980.

Fothergill, Caroline, Preface, in Jessie Fothergill, *Aldyth; or, 'Let the End Try the Man'*, London: Richard Bentley and Son, 1891.

Fothergill, Jessie, *Healey: A Romance*, 3 vols, London: Henry S. King and Co., 1875, reprinted as *Healey: A Tale*, 1 vol., Richard Bentley and Son, 1884.

—— *Aldyth; or, 'Let the End Try the Man'*, 2 vols [1877] London: Richard Bentley and Son, 1891.

—— *The First Violin: A Novel*, 3 vols, London: Richard Bentley and Son, 1877.

—— *Probation: A Novel*, 3 vols, by the Author of 'The First Violin', London: Richard Bentley and Son, 1879.

—— *The Wellfields: A Novel*, 3 vols [1880] New York: United States Book Company, n.d.

—— *Kith and Kin: A Novel*, 3 vols [1881] London: Macmillan and Co., Ltd., 1899.

—— *Made or Marred*, 1 vol., London: Richard Bentley and Son, 1881.

— *One of Three: A Fragment*, 1 vol., London: Richard Bentley and Son, 1881.
— *Peril: A Novel*, 3 vols, London: Richard Bentley and Son, 1884.
— *Borderland: A Country Town Chronicle*, 3 vols [1886] London: Macmillan and Co., Ltd., 1899.
‒ Some American Recollections', *Temple Bar*, 76 (February 1886), 198–213.
‒ Wuthering Heights', *Temple Bar*, 81 (December 1887), 562–8.
— *From Moor Isles: A Love Story*, 3 vols, London: Richard Bentley and Son, 1888.
— *The Lasses of Leverhouse: A Story*, 1 vol., London: Hurst and Blackett, 1888. First published in the *Bolton Weekly Journal*, 1878–79.
‒ Flowers and Fire', *Temple Bar*, 86 (August 1889), 518–26.
— *A March in the Ranks*, 3 vols [1890] New York: F. M. Lupton, n.d.
— *Oriole's Daughter: A Novel*, 3 vols, London: William Heinemann, 1893.
Garrison, Dee, 'Immoral Fiction in the Late Victorian Library', *American Quarterly*, 28:1 (1976), 71–89.
Gaskell, Elizabeth, *North and South* [1855] Oxford: Oxford University Press, 1982.
Haight, Gordon, *George Eliot: A Biography*, Oxford: Oxford University Press, 1969.
Hawthorne, Nathaniel, *The Marble Faun: or, The Romance of Monte Beni* [1860] Centenary Edition, Columbus, OH: Ohio State University Press, 1968.
Heyse, Paul, *Kinder der Welt: Roman in sechs Büchern*, Berlin: Wilhelm Hertz, 1873.
Howsam, Leslie, *Kegan Paul: A Victorian Imprint: Publishers, Books and Cultural History*, London: Kegan Paul International, 1998.
Index of Authors and Titles, Kegan Paul, Trench, Trübner and Henry S. King, 1858–1912.
Keating, Peter, *The Haunted Study: A Social History of the English Novel, 1875–1914*, London: Fontana Press, 1989.
Law, Graham, *Serializing Fiction in the Victorian Press*, Houndmills, Basingstoke and New York: Palgrave, 2000.
Lightman, Bernard, *The Origins of Agnosticism: Victorian Unbelief and the Limits of Knowledge*, Baltimore, PA and London: Johns Hopkins University Press, 1987.
‒ Robert Elsmere and the Agnostic Crises of Faith', in Richard J. Helmstadter and Bernard Lightman (eds), *Victorian Faith in Crisis: Essays on Continuity and Change in Nineteenth-Century Belief*, Stanford, CA: Stanford University Press, 1990, pp. 283–311.
Sand, George, *Le Marquis de Villemer*, Oeuvres Complètes de George Sand, Paris: Calmann-Lévy, n.d.
Scherle, Phyllis, 'Jessie Fothergill', in Paul Schlueter and June Schlueter (eds), *An Encyclopedia of British Women Writers* (Revised and expanded edition), New Brunswick, NJ: Rutgers University Press, 1998, pp. 254–5.
Schreiner, Olive, *The Story of an African Farm* [1883] Oxford: Oxford University Press, 1992.
Spencer, Herbert, *The Principles of Psychology*, vol. 1, New York: D. Appleton and Co., 1896.
Tillotsons' Fiction Bureau Records, private collection of Michael L. Turner, former

Head of Conservation, Bodleian Library, Oxford.

Tuchman, Gaye, with Nina E. Fortin, *Edging Women Out: Victorian Novelists, Publishers, and Social Change*, London: Routledge, 1989.

Turner, Michael L., 'The Syndication of Fiction in Provincial Newspapers, 1870–1939: The Example of the Tillotson "Fiction Bureau"', B.Litt. dissertation, Oxford University, 1968.

Ward, Mary Augusta [Mrs Humphry], *Robert Elsmere*, London: Smith Elder and Co., 1888.

Woolner, Thomas, *My Beautiful Lady*, London: Macmillan and Co., 1866.

Worboise, Emma Jane, *Robert Wreford's Daughter*, London: James Clarke and Co., 1877.

4

'All-sufficient to one another'? Charlotte Yonge and the family chronicle

Valerie Sanders

'Charlotte Yonge had an immature mind, an undistinguished style, and the values of a pious schoolgirl', Robert Liddell complained, as long ago as 1947;[1] even he, however, admitted that she had 'real literary gifts which anyone might envy', and critics before and since have tried, with some embarrassment, to account for her addictive effect.[2] Whatever her expectations about audience, men also read her, and famous men at that: Tennyson, Dante Gabriel Rossetti, William Morris, Lord Raglan, and the philosopher, Bernard Bosanquet, who believed she had 'expressed the motives and experiences through which great things are done in the world and great communities are strong and valuable'.[3] Those who enjoy her works surrender themselves wholeheartedly to her world of intense family bonds, emotional dependency, spiritual anxiety, and physical tribulation. With its long dialogues and detailed descriptions of daily activity – down to the doing of Compound Long Division, and the making of watch-guards for a bazaar – the intense realism of the writing assumes the reader's knowledge of the world it describes. Even the dense appearance of the print on the page, in the Macmillan reprints, somehow embodies the crowded, inward-looking lives it depicts.

Yet Yonge generates unease in the modern reader – even in those not immune to her appeal – because of her apparent endorsement of conservative, anti-feminist values, and her distrust of ambition. Talia Schaffer has recently argued that Yonge is essentially a repressive writer, who insists her characters 'learn to love their hampered lives'. They may initially resist the 'ideological vise [sic]' closing in on them, but ultimately her central project 'is to depict dissidence for the purpose of subduing it'.[4] On the other hand, her re-enactment of debates about aspiration is ambiguous; her novels, like Mrs Humphry Ward's and Eliza Lynn Linton's, are full of bright, eager young women longing to do something meaningful with their lives. Much of her appeal derives from her total empathy with this real-life adventure, as she fully involves her readers in the succession of moral dilemmas her characters undergo throughout her novels.

One of the most complex and fruitful areas of Yonge's writing in relation to her complex ideological position is her family chronicles. In a sense, much of her mature work falls into this category, with a projected readership that is both precisely defined and yet oddly nebulous. Yonge wrote primarily for teenage girls, but was widely read in the middle decades of the nineteenth century by men as well as women, adults as well as children. A brief biographical introduction will attempt to explain the principles on which she conducted her life and work.

Charlotte Mary Yonge, born on 11 August 1823, at Otterbourne, near Winchester, is always described as having lived a quiet life. No amount of biographical research has turned up any scandal or even many adventures. She went abroad only once (to France in 1869) – twice if we count Ireland – and despite her long editorship of the journal *The Monthly Packet* (1851–90) played no part in the metropolitan literary life of her time. Her experiences seem especially limited if compared with those of her boisterous near-contemporary, Eliza Lynn Linton, whose controversial career began with a year in London researching her first novel in the British Museum, progressed to a position as full-time journalist with the *Morning Chronicle,* and encompassed marriage, stepmotherhood, separation, and same-sex attachments, besides a reputation for virulent anti-feminism. Yonge's world, by contrast, was essentially the family and the church; her attachments were to her parents and brother, her cousins, neighbouring clergy, and (without Linton's sexual drama) her female friends. Family connections included minor titled gentry and the judiciary; she was also friendly with Elizabeth Wordsworth, the first Principal of Lady Margaret Hall, Oxford. Though she wrote about marriage in nearly all her novels, she never seems to have thought about it for herself; nor did her friendship with a Tractarian invalid, Marianne Dyson, nicknamed 'Driver' to Yonge's 'Slave', her main emotional outlet in early adulthood, prompt her to feature many strong female friendships in her novels. The really intense relationships are centred within the family itself, especially between brothers and sisters.

Yonge's father, William Crawley Yonge (1795–1854) was a former Etonian and army officer who had fought at Waterloo and in the Peninsular War; when he married her mother, Frances Mary Bargus (1795–1868), he left the army to placate his mother-in-law, and eventually became a magistrate. As their daughter grew up, both parents educated her at home, and when their only son Julian (1830–92) was old enough, Mr Yonge taught them Latin, Greek, and mathematics. Additionally, Sunday school became an integral part of her life, when, at the age of seven, she began teaching village children; then at fifteen, she was prepared for confirmation by John Keble, a leading churchman in the Tractarian movement of the 1830s and 1840s, which left her a staunch supporter not only of the High Church ethos and doctrines, but also of the practical reforms undertaken by the rural clergy to elevate the condition of their parishes: hence her characters' interest in church-building, teaching and missionary work. For hostile critics such as Q. D. Leavis (writing in 1944), Yonge's lack of first-hand experience outside this world of English village church life makes her inevitably a novelist of limited ability. The burden of Leavis's essay – surprising in view of her admiration for Oliphant's *Miss Marjoribanks*, which is set in a similar world – is that the absence of a 'lived' life was fatal to her writing: 'Charlotte Yonge,' she claims, 'was a day-dreamer with a writing itch that compensated her for a peculiarly starved life'.[5]

If Yonge herself ever thought of her life as 'starved' or limited, it was in the area of childhood companionship. What she longed for as a child were more brothers and sisters, like her extended family of cousins. Her unfinished autobiography shows that she was proud of her family history and fascinated by her ancestors: a lengthy genealogy precedes her own personal memoirs, which end suddenly at 1836 when she turned thirteen, and John Keble came to live in the neighbourhood. It was as if her adulthood was hardly worth recording (beginning her memoirs in 1877, when she was in her mid-fifties, she had plenty of time to complete them): all her emotional energy had gone into her childhood relationships, and Keble's arrival somehow marked the beginning of her taking mature religious responsibility for herself. What Yonge recalls most vividly is the riotous play in her sprawling households of cousins, occasionally overshadowed by sudden illness and death – very much as she records in her novels. 'I was the noisiest of all,' she admits, 'being very excitable, shrill-voiced, and with a great capacity of screaming'. One game, called 'Cats and Mice', was so noisy that the children of the house 'were always told beforehand not to play at it when I was there.'[6] For Yonge these family gatherings were probably the most important influence on her literary life.

Yonge's writing career began with the publication of stories in Anne Mozley's *Magazine for the Young*; her first novel, *Abbey Church* (1844), set the pattern for her later writing, which was usually about family groups of children and teenagers and their relationship with the neighbourhood and the church. Her parents, meanwhile, decided that her literary career should proceed only if she devoted her earnings to church and missionary activities. She discussed her work with them and with Keble, until their deaths: hence the frequent accusation that Charlotte Yonge never really grew up, but continued reliving her childhood in her writing, filling her family chronicles with the repartee and teasing, the picnics and school-talk of intelligent, lively families of children.

Yonge's whole life was spent writing: not just family chronicles, but historical tales, history books for young people, and a history of Christian names. Her books specifically written for younger children tend to be set in distant historical periods and are written in rather stilted English: the more realistic and psychologically more complex works are given contemporary settings, demonstrating her full empathetic engagement with the world she lived in. Her novels were published initially by firms who specialised in religious works: John W. Parker in London, and the Mozleys (John and Charles), who were John Henry Newman's brothers-in-law; later in her career, the first of the famous blue-cloth-covered collected editions of her works was published by Macmillan (1879–80), reproducing the small print of the original Parker editions. Tauchnitz editions and translations of her works ensured that in the heyday of her career her writing was known in Europe; she also received enthusiastic letters from readers in the United States. Many of her works were first published slowly and piecemeal, over several years in some cases, in *The Monthly Packet*, a journal designed for a young, churchgoing, female readership.

As she wrote her best-known novel, *The Daisy Chain* (1856), she was conscious of inventing something new: 'No one can be more sensible than is the Author that the present is an overgrown book of a nondescript class, neither the "tale" for the young, nor the novel for their elders, but a mixture of both', she confessed in her Preface.[7] In trying to categorise the work, she makes it sound like the body of an adolescent – neither one thing nor another, but 'overgrown', and a 'mixture'. Though many authors have written for a child audience and found popularity among adults, Charlotte Yonge stands out as devoting the bulk of her career to an age group she herself found it hard to define. In her introduction to *The Monthly Packet*, which she began editing in 1851, she regrets that 'the pretty old terms, maidens and damsels', have gone out of fashion, otherwise she would have used them to address her readers, whom she envisaged as aged fifteen to twenty-five: 'young girls, or maidens, or young ladies, whichever you like to be called, who are above the age of childhood, and who are either looking back on school-days with regret, or else pursuing the most important part of education, namely self-education'.[8] Alethea Hayter notes that the circulation of this journal was 'never much above 1500'; all the more surprising then is the immense popularity of the novels initially serialised in it, and then republished.[9]

Within this group, a more elite circle known as 'The Gosling Society' (Yonge was their 'Mother Goose') formed an essay-writing association between 1859–77. Research on this group by Charlotte Mitchell reveals them to have been initially cousins and neighbours of Yonge's, broadening out to include the daughters of rural clergymen and landowners. They all took nicknames, such as 'Kittiwake', 'Albatross' and 'Queen Bee', and for a few years ran a manuscript magazine called 'The Barnacle'. One of the most illustrious was Mary Arnold, the future Mrs Humphry Ward, who, for Gosling purposes, called herself 'Windermere'. According to Mitchell, these girls 'led isolated and monotonous lives', which were much enlivened by the stimulus of reading Yonge and writing essays for her.[10] What seems to have appealed to them, as well as to Yonge's other readers, was the reflection back to them of their own lives as a kind of domestic Christian romance, celebrated in novels such as *The Heir of Redclyffe* (1853), a modernising of Scott made relevant to their own times and conditions. Henry Sidgwick found *The Trial* (1864) more compelling than *Madame Bovary* because 'Miss Yonge makes one feel how full of interest the narrowest sphere of life is'.[11]

In many respects, the Goslings and their contemporaries were an awkward age group to write for, given their collective innocence on the brink of possible wifehood, but Yonge's favourite theme – the challenge of domestic management in a Christianised context – was astutely chosen. Unlike many Victorian novels (Oliphant's are a notable exception), the emphasis in her family chronicles is on how people (young women especially) cope with households full of demanding people, whether after marriage, or after the deaths of parents. *The Young Stepmother* (1861), for example, is essentially a saga of troublesome stepchildren gradually tamed, but with typical realism Yonge introduces a son of the new marriage who is just as unruly as the other, and admits that the stepchildren cannot be completely reformed. *Magnum Bonum* (1879) begins with echoes of Charlotte Brontë's *Villette*, as a dependent young woman is brought to stay with a bachelor doctor and his strong-minded mother: only unlike Lucy Snowe, Caroline Allen marries the doctor, has six children, and is then widowed. How she survives as a single parent of complicated children is the subject of the rest of the novel. Not much more than a child herself, she struggles to cope with a sulky eldest girl who wants to be a doctor, a frail younger son who nearly dies in a mountain-climbing accident, and then works himself to exhaustion in a parish, a decadent eldest son corrupted by what turns out to be a false inheritance, and a youngest daughter, nicknamed 'Babie', whose greatest pleasure is writing a crusading adventure for a family magazine. Nearly all find it hard to marry and to live conventional lives.

Of course Yonge did not invent the family chronicle. Stories of children's adventures within a family setting had been popular from at least Maria Edgeworth's *Harry and Lucy* (1801) onwards: Yonge comments in her 1886 Preface to *Scenes and Characters* that Maria Edgeworth's stories were 'chronicles, or more truly, illustrations of various truths worked out upon the same personages', which is the model she follows herself. Other examples were Mary Martha Sherwood's *History of the Fairchild Family* (1818–47), Catherine Sinclair's *Holiday House* (1839), Elizabeth Missing Sewell's *The Experience of Life* (1853), Dinah Mulock Craik's *The Head of the Family* (1852) and Harriett Mozley's *Family Adventures* (1852), based to some extent on the relationships of the Newman children. Interestingly, the children's father in Mozley's book at one point blames them for being unsociable, and only liking to be '*your own selves together*' – a warning of the exclusiveness and introversion to which large self-sufficient middle-class families such as Yonge's, and indeed many 'real life' families such as the Rossettis, Brontës, Bensons and Stephens, were liable.[12] Later family stories include E. Nesbit's tales of the Bastables (beginning with *The Treasure-Seekers*, 1899) and Eve Garnett's *The Family from One-End Street* (1937), which, like Yonge's novels, focuses alternately on the tribulations of different children while regularly returning to the collective family group. The best known American equivalent is clearly Louisa M. Alcott's *Little Women* (1868–69), with its sequels, *Little Men* (1871) and *Jo's Boys* (1886). Adult versions of the genre include Trollope's Palliser and Barchester series, and John Galsworthy's *Forsyte Saga* (1906–22), which explore more adult family problems related to marriage, money, property and politics.

The 'family chronicle' is perhaps best defined as an infinitely extendable story of family interaction and engagement with the outside world, written in a realist mode. It is both a 'history' and a 'story': recounting what happened chronologically, yet meandering at its own pace and digressing into side-stories, the connection with the main family history gradually becoming apparent. Structurally, the family chronicle can be as loose as the author wishes: by definition it is at least episodic. Yonge herself described the genre, in her Preface to *The Daisy Chain*, as 'a domestic record of home events, large and small, during those years of early life when the character is chiefly formed, and as an endeavour to trace the effects of those aspirations which are a part of every youthful nature'.[13]

Once she had invented popular characters such as the Mays of *The Daisy Chain*, Yonge introduced them to her other families, and even allowed them to inter-marry. She freely admitted to finding her own characters companionable: 'An almost solitary child, with periodical visits to the Elysium of a large family,' she described herself in the Preface to *Scenes and Characters* (1847), her second novel, 'it was natural to dream of other children and their ways and sports till they became almost realities'. Indeed, they were her 'companions in many a solitary walk'.[14] A large family of dolls had preceded this power of invention, as her autobiography recalls: 'My great world was indoors with my dolls, who were my children and my sisters; out of doors with an imaginary family of ten boys and eleven girls who lived in an arbour'.[15] Large families were therefore to Yonge – in theory at least – 'Elysium', as they seem to have been to her readers, wanting to lose themselves in following the fortunes of people like themselves, much as we do today in television soap operas. From Yonge's point of view at least, these large families were also there to serve a definable moral purpose. Her emphasis on aspiration is especially important, particularly given a pattern in many of her novels of apparent sympathy with her characters' ambitions, followed by a curbing of achievement as incompatible with proper submission to God, family and duty.

Most of Yonge's families regard themselves as being superior to their acquaintances: better educated, better bred, more intelligent and morally advanced. In *Magnum Bonum*, following the death of their doctor father, the widow and children move to an inferior town, where they miss the society of 'clever people', and their neighbouring cousins are markedly duller and more conventional. Albinia Kendall of *The Young Stepmother* sees her own family, the Ferrars, as both morally and physically superior to the listless Kendall family into which she marries; and the Mays lend a helping hand to several other families less fortunate than themselves. Within the family, however, this collective strength collapses, as individuals fail to reach the standards of the best. Later family novels for children, such as those by E. Nesbit and C. S. Lewis, regularly use the two-boy/two-girl structure which contrasts the heroic elder boy with the sly or mischievous younger, and the motherly elder girl with her emotionally volatile junior. In Yonge's families, the average size is nine, ten or eleven, allowing for far more variations, though her eldest children are usually in some way parent substitutes, while the youngest are undisciplined and troublesome. The *Literature Online* biography of Yonge uncompromisingly describes these large families as 'appalling, especially when there is usually a poverty-stricken tubercular father or mother at their head ... Her favorite theme is sacrifice, usually for others in the family, and submission to parental authority above all things'.[16] This has become the standard view of Yonge's morality in these novels. According to Q. D. Leavis, 'she has nothing to present but a moral ethos where everybody's first duty is to give up everything for everybody else':[17] a view shared by Talia Schaffer in her article on *Magnum Bonum*: 'I suggest that if we love the fantasy of winning approval from omnipotent parents, then we will adore Yonge's novels; if we resent this enforced capitulation to parental authority, then we will violently reject them'.[18] This is clearly a criticism to which any defender of Yonge must respond.

When Celia Brooke says of her sister Dorothea in *Middlemarch*, 'She likes giving up', she is not exactly expressing Yonge's philosophy (Celia is essentially an ironic speaker), but she is indicating an emotional vacuum in young women's lives that self-sacrifice filled.[19] Yonge is the chronicler of 'giving up', which is best exemplified in large jostling family groups where interests conflict and the head of the family is an older sibling rather than a parent with established authority. Her favourite plot device is to remove at least one parent, and often two, at an early stage in the story, throwing the children very much on their own resources. In later children's books, such as Nesbit's and Lewis's, the absence of parents is seen as an opportunity for the children to explore a wonderful, if morally demanding fantasy life in a parallel world. In Nesbit's case, the world is still largely the realist context of family life, only in stories such as *The Phoenix and the Carpet* (1904) or *Five Children and It* (1902), the children find themselves at odds with it – invisible, or temporarily powerful, or altered in some way, but only for the space of a day. Yonge, by contrast, sternly eschews magic or escapism of any kind, and makes her children face up to the harshest realities of illness, orphanhood, or poverty.

As Penny Brown has noted, the 'most impressive quality of her writing is undoubtedly the sensitivity and perceptiveness with which she explores the physical and psychological stresses, for girls and boys alike, of family life and learning to adapt to a gendered domestic and social identity'.[20] These 'physical' stresses include the sheer pressure on space in a family house, the constant noise of children wrangling, 'the confusion of voices' to which Yonge refers in *The Daisy Chain* (p. 107), and the risk of accidents. In *Scenes and Characters* (1847), Adeline is hurt by her brother Maurice's experimental gunpowder rocket inside the house, while in *The Daisy Chain*,

Ethel's inattention leads to her younger brother Aubrey's setting fire to himself. Physically weaker children go under, with too much schoolwork and pressure to win scholarships, or succeed musically: the casualties including Norman May, who exhausts himself with school preparation, Felix Underwood, whose health is undermined by a combination of work and care for his orphaned brothers and sisters, and Lance Underwood who is prostrated with sunstroke. Occasionally, she even shows what Ellen Moers has called 'the rough-and-tumble sexuality of the nursery', in the form of 'pinching, mauling, and scratching': for example, in the opening chapter of *The Daisy Chain*, 'the boys' (who include a girl) are seen in 'a tumultuous skirmish ... until Tom was suddenly pushed down, and tumbled over into Ethel's lap, thereby upsetting her and Norman together'; while in *The Pillars of the House*, Geraldine is rocked like a baby by her brothers.[21] The timing of Yonge's writing is all the more crucial in that it was preceded by two decades of advice manuals on family life (for example by Sarah Stickney Ellis) which stressed the importance of running a household on lines of order and propriety.[22]

Before fully establishing herself as a family chronicler in *The Daisy Chain*, Yonge experimented with family structures in *Scenes and Characters*, which traces the experiences of the motherless Mohun family after the eldest daughter, Eleanor, leaves to get married. In her absence, the remaining children debate whether they should be governed by a sense of love or duty (duty was Eleanor's guide), and soon find theory give way to the trials of experience. Yonge demonstrates at this early stage of her career that for her the family is a testing ground of moral probity and emotional resilience, where as many fail as succeed. Eleanor's deputy, for example, Emily, is formally 'deposed' as head of the household by their father, who comments: 'Your trial is over, and you have failed, merely because you would not exert yourself from wilful indolence and negligence' (p. 299). The girls collectively fail to manage the unruly younger boys, and the well-meaning Lilias learns not to take 'mere feeling for Christian charity' (p. 316). In other words, she learns to balance Eleanor's rigid sense of duty with her own compassion and humanity, while avoiding the dangers of mere sentimentality.

By the time she wrote *The Daisy Chain* nearly ten years later, retaining the structure of the motherless large family, with an absent (in this case invalid) eldest sister, Yonge was able to deal more subtly with the challenges of family life. Seventeen years later, in *The Pillars of the House* (1873), she intensified the challenges still further by removing both parents; while in *The Trial* (1864), an intervening novel about the Mays and their friendship with another orphaned family, the Wards, Yonge introduces the (for her) unlikely complication of a murder trial. With *Magnum Bonum* (1879) she retains a living mother, but one who is herself a rebel, and regarded by her implacably serene sister-in-law as an irresponsible tomboy. In her writing of family chronicles, therefore (and these are just a few representative examples of many more) she 'ups the stakes', as it were, subjecting her bands of semi-orphaned children to increasingly testing circumstances.

Yonge is particularly sympathetic to the dilemmas of the eldest children, who suddenly find themselves, at fifteen or sixteen, responsible for the welfare of crowds of juniors irresponsibly brought into the world by exhausted parents. One plot feature common to *The Daisy Chain* and *Pillars* is the birth, shortly before a parental death, of yet another child: Gertrude, in the earlier novel, and twins, Stella and Theodore, in the later. The latter are actually born on the day their father dies, and the handicapped boy twin especially commended to the eldest son Felix's care with the words: 'Take him as God's gift and mine – may he be a son of your right hand to you.'[23] Felix is therefore expressly commanded to take on his father's responsibilities – not just for the twins, but also for the rest of the children, who are shown at the start of the novel demanding he spends some of his birthday money on them: a scene repeated when he attains his majority, and his godfather leaves him a thousand pounds. 'Everybody regarded what belonged to Felix as common property', the narrative observes (vol. 1, p. 198). Yonge deflects the harshest criticism of Felix's situation away from the narrative voice and allows it to be expressed by the worldliest Underwood brother, Edgar: 'One could tear one's hair to see him tied down by this large family till his best days are gone' (vol. 1, p. 148). Edgar often says what we can imagine the modern reader saying about Felix's self-sacrifice. In *The Daisy Chain*, similar comments are made about Dr May by the grand London surgeon, Sir Matthew Fleet, who has no children himself: 'Poor May! I never saw a man so thrown away ... Of course he married early, and there he is, left a widower with a house full of children – screaming babies, and great tall sons growing up, and he without a notion what he shall do with them, as heedless as ever – ' (p. 131). Large families are associated for Yonge with the loss of worldly success. Because of his family duties, Felix abandons any thought of going to university, and works for the local bookseller and printer: work that entails loss of caste as well as freedom, until he is rewarded for his unselfishness with the inheritance of Vale Leston, the ancestral home – though not with a wife and children of his own.

Felix is a strong eldest child – morally, if not, as it turns out, physically. Edgar is not the only one to call him 'Blunderbore' (a giant tricked by Jack the Giantkiller into killing himself) and Atlas, the strong man holding up the world (vol. 1, p. 148); Chapter 12 mythologises him further with its title of 'Giant Despair's Castle'. In the earlier novel, *The Daisy Chain*, a natural leader is harder to find: the eldest son Richard being morally sound, but intellectually weak, and the eldest daughter Margaret injured in the same carriage accident that killed their mother. Though Margaret tries to 'bear the whole burthen of family cares alone', her real care is for her father, whose ease of mind she aims to protect; 'but, perhaps, she regarded him more as a charge of her own, than as, in very truth, the head of the family' (p. 159). Moreover, warns the narrative voice, even in her conscientiousness, Margaret is in danger of overstepping the mark: 'Nor had she yet detected her own satisfaction in being the first with every one in the family' (p. 160). Flora, the next daughter, is maternal and practical, but like Edgar Underwood and his other twin sister Alda, too worldly to be fully reliable. Ethel, who is neither worldly nor weak, lacks domestic abilities, while her brother Norman, though intelligent and decent, easily goes to pieces under pressure. The fabric of the family chronicles is essentially the mistakes made by each of the children as they develop towards maturity. Young readers, whatever their own strengths and weaknesses, were sure to find some familiar domestic dilemma or difficulty represented in the novels, from which they could implicitly learn.

Yonge is consistently interested in the difficulties faced by older children in gaining authority over the younger, who soon recognise that older siblings are not the same as real parents. She is less sympathetic, on the whole, to the younger children, whose role in the chronicles is mainly to provoke the older and provide new challenges for them. Early on in *The Trial*, we learn that Averil Ward's problems with her younger sisters following the deaths of both parents stem from her 'not having established her authority enough to keep them from growing too riotous' for the drawing-room where their convalescent brother is resting.[24] In *The Daisy Chain*, the older children have to deal with Tom's cheating at lessons, while in *Pillars*, Angela tells Felix she wants to join a Trappist order of nuns. This comes at a point when he is suffering from a scalded elbow after Angela and Lance accidentally tip a kettle of boiling water over him – symbolising the vulnerability of older children in Yonge's family chronicles at the hands of younger. It is also one of several points in this long chronicle where the characters reflect on what it means to be a parent who is really no parent at all but a sibling. 'I think you do just as well as most fathers', Angela tells him, 'You keep us all going…and you look after us and set us a good example, as people say; and isn't that all that fathers have to do?' (*Pillars*, vol. 2, p. 13). Yonge's allegiance is to those who set a good example, not to the subversives. On the other hand, some of her elder children are also subversives in their way, and present their families with even more testing problems.

In a Yonge family chronicle, no situation is static for long, and though the movement of the plot is towards greater stability, illness, death, accidents, marriage and economic factors supply an unpredictable threat to whatever has been achieved. In *Pillars,* the family are simply too numerous to be kept together in the early stages of their independence. Here again, the younger ones are seen as, if not superfluous, at least impossible to manage – boys and girls alike being sent away to school until they reach a degree of maturity. In an extreme move, the most troublesome boy, Fulbert, is packed off to Australia after becoming friendly with the son of a dissipated squire's household: 'for Fulbert had never accepted his eldest brother's authority, and could not brook interference' (vol. 1, p. 202). Edgar proves even more corruptible, though for different reasons. An artistic child and second son, he poses a new kind of problem to Felix: what to do with a brother who fails to fit the role mapped out for him by an affluent uncle willing to train him in a commercial enterprise. Indeed, a sub-theme of this novel is the disruption caused by musically or artistically talented children who need special treatment and opportunities: Lance the chorister and Geraldine the painter being two further challenges to Felix's authority as 'father'. Several of the children, Edgar and Geraldine among them, are easily bored with domestic routines, and the very youngest of the family become more outrageous still: Blanche of *The Daisy Chain,* for example, becomes a flirt, and like Gertrude and Stella, is all too aware of her sexual allure. Little 'Babie' in *Magnum Bonum* likes attracting clever men.

Any kind of achievement outside the family – whether academic (in Norman May's case) or artistic, tends to be viewed as a destabilising factor, as essentially, it distracts them from true devotion to the spiritual. Q. D. Leavis was especially angry with Yonge for dismissing all kinds of secular art as worthless, though I think the situation is more complicated than that.[25] Yonge fully acknowledges the allure of music, painting and writing – in their place, there is nothing wrong with them – but when they become ends in themselves, and the artist becomes an obsessive, she warns against a dangerous imbalance in her characters' outlook. For the boys, as much as the girls, ambition conflicts directly with their family relationships, as Norman's and Edgar's situations illustrate; while Geraldine, having sold a painting for fifteen shillings, finds it difficult to concentrate on the younger children's lessons: 'and she was forced to make it a rule never to touch a pencil till the lessons of Bernard and Stella were both over for the day' (vol. 1, p. 225). Though Geraldine exhibits at the Royal Academy, she remains mindful of the proper limitations to her talent, explaining what she feels in an anti-feminist pair of cartoons. The first picture ('a kind of parody of Rafaelle's School of Athens') shows a group of squabbling women watching an impossible demonstration of squaring a circle; while the second shows a harmonious scene in a cloister, the demonstration this time being 'the circle of eternity spanned by the Cross'. Geraldine interprets it for her family: '... I mean that while woman works merely for the sake of self-cultivation, the clever grow conceited and emulous, the practical harsh and rigid, the light or dull vain, frivolous, deceitful, by way of escape, and it all gets absurd. But the being handmaids of the Church brings all right.' (vol. 2, p. 363). Underlying Geraldine's anti-feminist argument, however, is a more subversive feminist point: that while married women have been kept 'in subjection' (p. 364) by men, they have not needed to consider their role in relation to self-cultivation and the community, whereas single women must now 'think it out'. Unmarried siblings in the family chronicles have an increasingly important role, as we see with Ethel May, and with Geraldine herself, in providing a home and education for younger children including nieces, nephews, friends and the poor. While this also looks like self-sacrifice, Yonge suggests that Ethel's role in life as her father's chief supporter and educator of his younger children is the noblest she could have chosen. Moreover, Yonge recognises that even the noblest self-sacrifices are an effort to keep up. Even the stalwart Ethel feels depressed after Margaret's death and Norman's engagement, 'and was so physically overcome with lassitude, that Richard insisted on her lying on the sofa, and leaving everything to him and Mary' (p. 650).

Whereas Geraldine's ambitions are necessarily limited by the fact of her being a girl and a lame one at that, Edgar is far freer to roam, and carries the more sensational features of the novel's plot. Before his death in exile, he has forged a cheque, killed a man in a duel, and fathered a child of his own. Yonge displaces the more terrifying temptations to which her village families are subject, on to the exotic exiles among her characters, especially the men. Those who are influenced by enervating or morally lax climates abroad seem to save their susceptible siblings from being similarly tainted. Lance, who is also dangerously talented, survives the equivalent of an enervating foreign climate when he suffers a bad bout of sunstroke; instead of becoming a professional musician, he joins Felix in the printing and newspaper business, his status as a gentleman safeguarded by his family's reputation. Nevertheless, Lance is subjected to one more temptation in volume 2 of *Pillars*, when, exhilarated by his involvement in a special celebrity concert, he is offered the chance to sing two nights a week in a London concert-room for a fee of five pounds. Yonge, interested as she is in the effects of aspiration, allows Lance several pages of debate about his career choice, first with his favourite sister Robina (destined for governessing, and then rescued by marriage), and then with Edgar the tempter. In conversation with the down-to-earth Robina, Lance is all for going to London; when he discusses it with Edgar, however, he has mysteriously decided against the plan. Yonge certainly understands the perverse dynamics of a talented young boy's ambition being challenged in a family context: '"Now, Robin, say in three words. Do you want me to be a mere counter-jumper all my life?" (vol. 2, p. 98). Yet two pages later, he has turned down the offer, and quotes Edgar some lines from the Communion service: 'And here we offer and present unto Thee ourselves, our souls and bodies, to be a reasonable, holy, and lively sacrifice.' (vol. 2, p. 101) – a phrase unrecognized by the wholly secular and worldly Edgar. For the benefit of her impressionable readers, Yonge stages a logical argument between the two brothers over the rights and wrongs of literal obedience to the Scriptures.

This is one of the most controversial and unpopular sections of *Pillars*, which is often seen as typical of Yonge's unimaginative and literal-minded adherence to a narrow religious viewpoint. How we read such passages today poses a real problem. We can, of course, just ignore them, and say they were part of the ethos in which she lived – much as the importance attached to chastity in Richardson's *Pamela* and *Clarissa* is hardly such an issue today, though the difference in cultural attitudes does not prevent our regarding these novels as canonical texts. Or, we can approach the issue of Lance's career – together with Geraldine's, Ethel's, Norman's, Felix's, Angela's and all the other major career decisions made in the family chronicles, and say that Yonge is in fact according them the seriousness they deserve in a way that belongs to the family chronicle as a genre, and involves her readers in a vicarious debate about the basis on which such career decisions should be made. Moreover, the family itself is made an attractive choice: a known, warm and supportive home, unlike the atomised commercial sphere, which is offered as the alternative.

Yonge is more aware of worldly temptation than one might expect. It occurs in all her major novels, and it always attracts at least one of the characters, usually an older girl. In the debate with Lance, Edgar is given some aggressive lines to shake his brother's confidence. Lance's quoted words from the Communion service are only 'a pious utterance that a *tête exaltée* takes literally'; why, if he takes them seriously, is he not 'living barefoot on bread and water in a hermitage?' (vol. 2, p. 102). In making her readers think about her characters' choices, Yonge, in other words, also makes them think about their own. As she suggests in her Preface to *The Daisy Chain*, 'That the young should take one hint, to think whether their hopes and upward-breathings are truly upwards, and founded in lowliness, may be called the moral of the tale' (pp. xi–xii).

Despite her emphasis on family values, the movement of these family chronicles is actually towards a splitting and scattering of families who were once crammed together in claustrophobic English houses: further evidence of Yonge's realism in acknowledging that the family home cannot be preserved for ever. The 'staircaseful of children' (vol. 1, p. 6) listed at the beginning of *Pillars* is soon dispersed, as are the Mays of *The Daisy Chain* and the Wards of *The Trial*. Missionary work and a career in the navy account for two May sons. Marriage also splits up the family, and removes the parent-substitutes, as does death. Perhaps the most surprising aspect of *Pillars* is Felix's death after many successful years of gaining control over his family. He is neither so lax, like Edgar, that he needs to be removed, nor a lingering invalid, like Margaret May. The other 'Pillar' of the family, Wilmet, does marry and have children, despite her unromantic briskness in the first half of the novel. In denying Felix the same happy ending, Yonge was perhaps refusing her readers the satisfaction of a too-simple moral reward. Significantly he collapses immediately after performing the fatherly act of giving away his baby sister Stella to her new husband: as if the role entrusted to him by his own dying father being now complete, he is himself free to die. The reader's assumption is that, like his father, he is simply worn out with years of caring for an enormous family.

As Penny Brown has noted, Yonge's characters move towards a 'gendered domestic and social identity'.[26] The gender issue is especially important in the family chronicles, where true and false notions of manliness and femininity are played off against each other. Her characters divide into those who are conventional stereotypes of their sex (for example Harry and Flora May) and those who are in some way at odds with it: for example, Mary May, who is a kind of honorary boy, and Clement Underwood, whose nickname 'Tina' derives from his unmanliness. In the course of her writing, Yonge explored what she understood by notions of femininity and masculinity, showing that she was aware of the limitations to which she felt each sex was prone. Wilmet Underwood may be an excellent mother-substitute, for example, but her rule is often stern and inflexible, like

Eleanor Mohun's in *Scenes and Characters*. The opposite kind of woman in Yonge's novels is frivolous and worldly: both Alda Underwood and Flora May are like this, and are easily seduced into inappropriate marriages with men who can offer them wealth and comfort, but none of the lively companionship they enjoyed with their siblings. Yonge punishes them by denying them the male issue needed to inherit the property. A third female type –Ethel May, Rachel Curtis (in *The Clever Woman of the Family*, 1865), Theodora Martindale (in *Heartsease*, 1854), Janet Brownlow (in *Magnum Bonum*) and to a lesser extent, Geraldine and Angela Underwood in *Pillars* – is too clever and restless to seek love and marriage, unlike the naturally marrying type, Violet Martindale, Blanche May, Jessie Brownlow and Stella Underwood: ultra-feminine girls who marry when they are scarcely grown up themselves. Yonge, in fact, has few truly exemplary characters in her novels who always know instinctively what to do. 'Mere' motherhood – in other words, motherhood without the extra dimension of moral effort – never impressed Yonge.

For men, too, she had more than clichéd ambitions. Though Yonge claimed that 'a woman cannot do a man truthfully from within', she often 'did' boys: indeed an article in the *Saturday Review* complained that there was too much 'schoolboy slang' in *Pillars*.[27] Weak men in her novels tend to be vain and self-absorbed, frequently the butt of their more manly brothers. In *The Young Stepmother* Albinia's husband Mr Kendal is repeatedly contrasted with her brother, the country clergyman Maurice Ferrars: he may be a man of the cloth, but he has the garden pond drained to make the air fresher for the children, and is often seen outdoors enjoying country pursuits. After a period of dissipation with the local idle youth, Kendal's son Gilbert makes a man of himself by fighting in the Crimean War and saving Albinia's virile cousin Fred. The daughter of a military man herself, Yonge has an unbounded admiration for the army and navy, but she acknowledges that not all men are suited to this kind of career. What she does endorse is the notion of an intellectual life buttressed in some way by more practical or athletic demands: hence the need for the scholarly and nervous Norman May to become a missionary, a 'soldier of God', if he cannot serve the country, like his brother Harry, as a sailor, or follow in his father's footsteps and become a doctor. In *Pillars*, however, Felix is unconvinced that his pious brother Clement 'could rough it as a missionary' (vol. 1, p. 210). When some loose-living boys get him drunk on brandy-and-water, Clement cringes with shame in a way that his brother Felix feels is 'unmanly': he believes Clement should know 'the difference between true and false manliness,' and that 'if one is not a man before one is a parson, one brings the ministry into contempt.' (I, p. 208).

One more character type is recurrent in the family chronicles, and that is the only child, usually an only daughter of an elderly father, whose situation is implicitly contrasted with those of the enormous family. In *The Daisy Chain*, the child is Margaret Rivers, the 'little hummingbird' Meta, whose daintiness enraptures Norman, and indeed his father Dr May. In *Pillars*, Mary Alda ('Marilda') Underwood, cousin of Felix's family, plays this role, but is more coarse and vulgar than Meta, if at least good-hearted. Warm and generous, Marilda even regrets having no mending to do for anyone; she loves small children, and with her father gives a home to two of her cousins, Alda and Edgar – with depressing results in both cases, as their simple home values are permanently corrupted. In each novel, the only child is wealthy but lonely, made emotionally vulnerable eventually by the death of her father. She looks to the large disorderly families for companionship and good cheer. There is never any suggestion in the text that it is better to be a Marilda or a Meta than it is to be an Ethel or a Wilmet.

In the Prelude to *Middlemarch* – another family chronicle in its way, though much else besides – the narrator refers to those who have lived 'no epic life … perhaps only a life of mistakes, the offering of a certain spiritual grandeur ill-matched with the meanness of opportunity'.[28] To a large extent, Yonge's family chronicles recount 'lives of mistakes' – successions of small accidents and major losses, turns of good fortune, and controversial opportunities. Maybe 'spiritual grandeur' is too elevated a term for Felix or Ethel, as compared with Dorothea Brooke, but Yonge's favourite characters are certainly somewhat at odds with the worldly societies in which they live. If we regard her novels as being intended only to teach religious principles, then, in my view, we overlook their wider remit. The Preface to *The Daisy Chain* admits that the tale 'outran both the original intention and the limits of the periodical [*The Monthly Packet*] in which it was commenced.' In fact the May family took on a life of their own, involving her teenage readers in a full and vicarious experience that was either a mirror of their own, or (as in her own case) a substitute for it, making them think extensively about their values and relationships. In her work as a whole, her frequently quarrelsome children need their brothers and sisters not only for companionship, but also as sounding-boards, good and bad moral guides, even as burdens to teach them patience and forbearance. They also need them to enable self-sacrifice. Without the large family, as we see with Marilda and Meta, life for the young adult has no real purpose in a Yonge novel. Even religious observance by itself is insufficient without a practical dimension; whereas self-sacrifice provides emotional thrills for those otherwise denied them.

Yonge never resolved her contradictory feelings about large families, which both hold people back and save them from loneliness. On the one hand, they supply all members with a strong sense of superiority and clannishness, a confidence derived from numbers, and a chance to make heroic sacrifices; on the other, the lack of space and time to pursue their own needs is conveyed by Yonge's descriptions of overcrowded houses and riotous noise. Though she thought of them as her own unobtainable 'Elysium' she in fact depicts in her mature tales families that are notably dysfunctional. Each family has its children with psychological or physical problems, and few emerge into adulthood without a crisis or a struggle of some kind. Even the conscientious are not necessarily rewarded, and the family house ends half emptied by death as well as marriage.

Yonge's is a realist world, in many ways, despite the romantic glow which has set around characters such as Guy Morville and Ethel May. Her best-seller status as a Victorian author seems to derive from her astuteness in identifying a class of readers for whom her type of novel was tailor-made: young girls whose romanticism needed to be grounded in the real life of the schoolroom and the family parlour. Amy Cruse suggests this romanticism enveloped their religion: Yonge's characters, she argues, 'had a real consciousness of unseen realms which were as truly theirs as their actual home on earth'.[29] Undoubtedly Yonge made religion sound meaningful, but perhaps her greatest claim to popularity lies in her increasingly complex exploration of family life, with its minute attention to individual characters' experiences. If Tennyson needed to read on, eager to know whether Mr Kendal is finally confirmed, so did many of his less sophisticated contemporaries.[30] Judging by their emotional responses, she left her readers, as she felt herself, feeling they had participated in a chronicle of compelling adventures without leaving home.

Notes

The phrase in the title refers to the close relationship between the twins, Stella and Theodore, in Yonge's novel, *The Pillars of the House*, 2 vols, 1873 (London: Macmillan, 1901), vol. 1, p. 311.

1 Robert Liddell, *A Treatise on the Novel* (London: Jonathan Cape, 1947), p. 24.
2 Barbara Dennis, for example, in her introduction to the Virago reprint of *The Daisy Chain*, having stressed the importance to Yonge of 'spiritual

perceptions,' admits that 'the novel is surprisingly more accomplished than all this might suggest' (p. x); while Elizabeth Jenkins begins her essay 'Charlotte Yonge as a Novelist,' which opens *A Chaplet for Charlotte Yonge* (London: Cresset Press, 1965), with the statement: 'The charm of Charlotte Yonge's novels is unique and impossible to convey to those who have not read them' (p. 3).

3 Bernard Bosanquet, *Some Suggestions in Ethics* (London: Macmillan and Co., 1918), p. 225. I am grateful to Noel O' Sullivan for giving me this reference. For Tennyson's enthusiasm, see Margaret Mare and Alicia C. Percival, *Victorian Best-Seller: The World of Charlotte M. Yonge* (London: George G. Harrap, 1947), p. 195. Other readers are listed by Amy Cruse in Chapter 3 of *The Victorians and Their Books* (London: George Allen and Unwin, 1935), and Nicola Diane Thompson in *Reviewing Sex: Gender and the Reception of Victorian Novels* (London and Basingstoke: Macmillan, 1996), p. 90.

4 Talia Schaffer, 'The Mysterious Magnum Bonum: Fighting to Read Charlotte Yonge', *Nineteenth-Century Literature*, 55:2 (2000), 245–7.

5 Q. D. Leavis, 'Charlotte Yonge and "Christian discrimination"' [1944] reprinted in G. Singh (ed.), *Collected Essays*, vol. 3 (Cambridge: Cambridge University Press, 1989), p. 235.

6 Charlotte Yonge's unfinished autobiography was originally published in Christabel Coleridge's *Charlotte Mary Yonge: Her Life and Letters* (London: Macmillan, 1903). Extracts are republished in Valerie Sanders (ed.), *Records of Girlhood: An Anthology of Nineteenth-Century Women's Childhoods* (Aldershot: Ashgate, 2000), p. 209.

7 Charlotte M. Yonge, *The Daisy Chain or Aspirations: A Family Chronicle* [1856] (London: Virago, 1988), p. xi.

8 Cited by Georgina Battiscombe in *Charlotte M Yonge: The Story of an Uneventful Life* (London: Constable and Co., 1943), p. 67.

9 Alethea Hayter, *Charlotte Yonge. Writers and Their Work* series (Plymouth: Northcote House, 1996), p. 21.

10 Charlotte Mitchell's fascinating research is to be found on the website of the Charlotte Mary Yonge Fellowship (www.cmyf.org.uk, accessed 16 December 2003).

11 Cruse, *The Victorians and Their Books,* p. 55.

12 Harriett Mozley, *Family Adventures, by the Author of 'The Fairy Bower'* etc. (London: John and Charles Mozley and Joseph Masters, 1852), pp. 177–8.

13 Yonge, *The Daisy Chain*, p. xi.

14 Charlotte M. Yonge, *Scenes and Characters: or Eighteen Months at Beechcroft* [1847] (fifth edn, London and New York: Macmillan, 1889), p. viii. Subsequent page references are given in the text.

15 Sanders, *Records of Girlhood,* p. 201.

16 *Literature Online Biography* of Charlotte Mary Yonge, adapted from data developed by the H. W. Wilson Company, Inc., p. 2. (http://lion.chadwyck.co.uk, accessed 6 September 2002).

17 Leavis, 'Charlotte Yonge', p. 238.
18 Schaffer, 'The Mysterious Magnum Bonum', p. 247.
19 George Eliot, *Middlemarch* [1871–72] (Harmondsworth: Penguin, 1965), p. 41.
20 Penny Brown, *The Captured World: The Child and Childhood in Nineteenth-Century Women's Writing in England* (Hemel Hempstead: Harvester Wheatsheaf,1993), p. 102.
21 Ellen Moers, *Literary Women* (London: The Women's Press, 1978), p. 105; Yonge, *The Daisy Chain*, p. 4; *Pillars*, vol. 1, p. 67. Subsequent page references are given in the text.
22 Brown, *The Captured World*, pp. 92–3.
23 Yonge, *Pillars*, vol. 1, p. 59.
24 Charlotte M. Yonge, *The Trial*, 1864 (Stroud: Alan Sutton, 1996), p. 35.
25 Leavis, 'Charlotte Yonge', p. 239.
26 Brown, *The Captured World*, p. 102.
27 Charlotte M. Yonge, 'Authorship', *The Monthly Packet* (September 1892), see the website of the Charlotte Yonge Fellowship, p. 6 (www.cmyf.org.uk, accessed 16 December 2003); *Saturday Review* (27 September 1873), p. 416.
28 Eliot, *Middlemarch*, p. 3.
29 Cruse, *The Victorians and Their Books*, p. 64.
30 This well-known anecdote of Tennyson's reading *The Young Stepmother* late into the night, told originally by Francis Palgrave, is summarised by Alethea Hayter, among others, *Charlotte Yonge*, p. 3.

Bibliography

Battiscombe, Georgina, *Charlotte M. Yonge: The Story of an Uneventful Life,* London: Constable and Co., 1943.
Bosanquet, Bernard, *Some Suggestions in Ethics,* London: Macmillan and Co, 1918.
Brown, Penny, *The Captured World: The Child and Childhood in Nineteenth-Century Women's Writing in England,* Hemel Hempstead: Harvester Wheatsheaf, 1993.
Coleridge, Christabel (ed.), *Charlotte Mary Yonge: Her Life and Letters*, London: Macmillan, 1903.
Cooper, Edward H., 'Charlotte Mary Yonge', *Fortnightly Review,* 75 (May 1901), 852–8.
Cruse, Amy, *The Victorians and Their Books*, London: George Allen and Unwin, 1935.
Dennis, Barbara, Introduction in Charlotte M. Yonge,*The Daisy Chain*, London: Virago, 1988.
Eliot, George, *Middlemarch* [1871–72] Harmondsworth: Penguin, 1965.
Hayter, Alethea, *Charlotte Yonge. Writers and Their Works* series. Plymouth: Northcote House, 1996.
Hunt, Peter, *An Introduction to Children's Literature,* Oxford: Oxford University

Press, 1994.

Leavis, Q. D., 'Charlotte Yonge and "Christian discrimination"' [1944] reprinted in G. Singh (ed.), *Collected Essays*, vol. 3, Cambridge: Cambridge University Press, 1989.

Liddell, Robert, *A Treatise on the Novel,* London: Jonathan Cape, 1947.

Mare, Margaret and Alicia C. Percival, *Victorian Best-Seller: The World of Charlotte M. Yonge,* London: George G. Harrap, 1947.

Moers, Ellen, *Literary Women*, London: The Women's Press, 1975.

Mozley, Harriett, *Family Adventures, by the Author of 'The Fairy Bower' etc.* London: John and Charles Mozley and Joseph Masters, 1852.

Sanders, Valerie (ed.), *Records of Girlhood: An Anthology of Nineteenth-Century Women's Childhoods,* Aldershot: Ashgate, 2000.

Schaffer, Talia, 'The Mysterious Magnum Bonum: Fighting to Read Charlotte Yonge', *Nineteenth-Century Literature*, 55:2 (2000), 244–75.

Thompson, Nicola Diane, *Reviewing Sex: Gender and the Reception of Victorian Novels*, London and Basingstoke: Macmillan, 1996.

Yonge, Charlotte Mary, *Abbey Church, or Self Control and Self Conceit*, London: James Burns, and Derby: Mozley, 1844.

——*Scenes and Characters: or Eighteen Months at Beechcroft* [1847], fifth edition, London and New York: Macmillan, 1889.

——*The Heir of Redclyffe* [1853] Oxford: Oxford World's Classics, 1988.

——*Heartsease* [1854] London: Macmillan, 1901.

——*The Daisy Chain or Aspirations: A Family Chronicle* [1856] London: Virago, 1988.

——*The Young Stepmother* [1861] London: Macmillan, 1889.

——*The Trial* [1864] Stroud: Alan Sutton, 1996.

——*The Clever Woman of the Family* [1865] London: Virago, 1985.

——*The Pillars of the House,* [1873] 2 vols, London: Macmillan, 1901.

——*Magnum Bonum, or Mother Carey's Brood* [1879] London: Macmillan, 1892.

—— 'Authorship,' *The Monthly Packet* (September 1892), website of the Charlotte Yonge Fellowship (www.cmyf.org.uk, accessed 16 December 2003).

5

'Worlds not realized': The work of Louisa Molesworth

Jane Darcy

Louisa Molesworth was both popular and highly regarded in her day but since her death in 1921 she has never quite attained the status of a classic 'golden age' children's writer and no single text has quite become canonical. Her work in many ways unsettles the boundaries of what might be construed as 'popular' on the one hand and 'canonical' on the other. She sits at the intersection between the two. Born Mary Louisa Stewart in Rotterdam in 1839, where her father was a merchant, she spent much of her life in various parts of Manchester and the surrounding area – though in later life she lived for some years in France and finally settled in London. Her background was that of the upwardly mobile middle class; that the family prospered during her young life can be gathered from their progression from a Manchester street house to the suburban area of Whalley Range. Louisa appears to have been a happy enough child though perhaps rather lonely on account of a large age gap between herself and her siblings. Certainly the isolation and loneliness of the child, even within a large household, is a recurring theme in her fiction. Something of this is captured in one of Molesworth's short stories for children, 'My Pink Pet' where the heroine tells us that she is the youngest of nine children and goes on:

> My eldest sister was married – she had always been married, I thought, for I could not remember her anything else. My other three sisters were all more or less grown up and the only brother at all near my own age was away at a boarding-school. So it came to pass that, though I had so many brothers and sisters, I was rather a solitary little girl.[1]

She also referred much later to the 'excessively Calvinistic surroundings' of her youth which had made her 'determined that no child with whom she was brought in contact should, if she could prevent it, be taught the religion of fear'.[2] Again her writings show that she distanced herself from the harshly didactic mode of much fiction for children in the generation before her. For example, in an article on her writing practice in *The Monthly Packet* in 1894 she remembers how she herself felt about the work of Maria Edgeworth: 'I was never *very* fond of Miss Edgeworth's stories – there was something hard and dry about them, and something wanting, which I could not define. They were too "sensible".'[3]

In the same article Molesworth makes it clear that her own literary preference was for something more romantic and fantastical. She says how much she enjoyed the fiction of Charlotte Yonge, Hawthorne's *Wonder Book* and Scott's Waverley novels and continues: 'Up to fourteen or fifteen however, I feel sure that my most perfect felicity was found in fairy tales, though the first taste of this delight was not given to me by books or reading, but by the story-*telling* of my already aged grandmother.'[4]

Her maternal grandmother, whose oral storytelling talents Molesworth often pays tribute to, seems to have been a pivotal figure in her own development as a writer and resurfaces in the fiction in a variety of guises: as the wise older woman, often a teller of tales; as an understanding older relative or friend; or as a fairy godmother whose magical powers allow the child or children access to alternative worlds. There are many examples of such women in her work and they play an important role in the lives of her child protagonists. Such a grandmother figure occurs in the character of Marcelline in *The Tapestry Room*. She has been nurse not only to the heroine, Jeanne, but also to her mother, and is described in the warm and affectionate way such figures always are in Molesworth's fiction:

> She was so old that for many years no one had seen much difference in her – she had reached a sort of settled oldness, like an arm-chair which may once have been covered with bright-coloured silk, but which, with time and wear, has got to have an all-over-old look which never seems to get any worse. Not that Marcelline was dull and grey to look at – she was bright and cheery, and when she had a new clean cap on, all beautifully frilled and crimped round her face, Jeanne used to tell her that she was beautiful, quite beautiful.[5]

Marcelline is a great storyteller and something of a mystical character who understands children's imaginative capacities. Later in the same book she appears thinly disguised, telling the story 'The Brown Bull of Norrowa' as the white lady who sits upstairs in the house spinning tales. Upon meeting her, one of the children remarks that he supposes sometimes the threads must get twisted and that's how stories get muddled. She replies:

'Just so,' said the white lady. 'My story threads need gentle handling, and sometimes people seize them roughly and tear and soil them, and then of course they are no longer pretty. But listen now. What will you have? The first in the wheel is a very, very old fairy story. I span it for your great-great-grandmothers; shall I spin it again for you?' (p. 140)

Throughout her life Molesworth herself loved to tell stories and it is from those that she told to her own children that her first children's book, a collection of tales, *Tell Me a Story* (1875), emerged. In many of her books, as in *The Tapestry Room*, the main narrative is interrupted by a tale of enchantment told to the child protagonists by a sympathetic adult. In this Molesworth draws upon and contributes to a female tradition of tale telling by women to children. Angela Carter has noted how in the nineteenth century the literary tradition of the fairy tale, as represented by the collections of male writers such as Perrault, the Grimms and Andersen, meant that the prominent position of women in the oral tradition was forgotten.[6] This oral tradition nevertheless continued, passed on by grandmothers and servants in the big houses, running parallel to the more public and official literary one. Molesworth captures something of this in her work, it is clear that she defined herself and can be defined as writing in a female context. Her fantasy worlds are also feminised and can be viewed as part of a recognisably female tradition which is complementary, even oppositional, not only to the literary fairy tale but also to the fantasy fiction of male writers like Kingsley, Carroll or MacDonald.

Molesworth was educated mainly at home by her mother, although she attended a school in Lausanne for a short time. In Manchester, Elizabeth and William Gaskell were neighbours and she attended classes held by William some time in the 1850s. After her marriage to Major Richard Molesworth in 1861 she gave birth to four daughters and three sons although her eldest daughter, Violet, died of scarlet fever in 1869, followed shortly after by the death of her first son at thirteen weeks. This was a sad time for Molesworth and something of a turning point in her life. The death of Violet affected her badly, although she had already begun writing by this time. Like Elizabeth Gaskell after the death of her son, she seems to have turned to writing with more determination and greater focus in her grief. Her letters to her friend, confidant and literary advisor at the time, the poet John Byrne Leicester Warren, hint that her marriage was not terribly happy either, though it was many years before she was to separate from her husband. For instance, she wrote of Violet's death: 'It seems to have utterly changed everything'.[7] Only a few days after the death occurred during the night of 3 April 1869, she writes to Warren about her manuscript:

You will think I am going out of my mind to speak of such a thing as the MS just now – but I have quite changed about it and am full of eagerness to have it published – I will tell you why. My darling knew about it & was so disappointed it was not 'made into a book'. She had read little bits of it – about the children – She even chose the titles of some chapters – I used not to like to tell even you about her precocity.[8]

Molesworth's biographer, Jane Cooper, does not think that she should be likened to Gaskell in turning to writing after the death of her eldest daughter as she was already writing her first book when it happened, but it is clear from the above quotation that her attitude to her work has changed and there is a new urgency about her commitment to writing.[9]

Unlike many of her contemporaries, there is no reason to suppose that Molesworth began writing for economic reasons, though later, when she and her husband had parted, money must have been more of a consideration. Molesworth separated from her husband finally in 1879, on account of his violent temper – allegedly the result of a head wound sustained in the Crimean War. Whether this was just an excuse for leaving an already failing marriage we do not know but it was certainly a bold step and one which had the approval of his family. After the split, Molesworth and her children moved with her mother to Northern France where they lived in various places until 1883 when, on the death of her mother, the family returned to live in London.

Molesworth's first four novels, written in the early 1870s and published under the pseudonym Ennis Graham, were for an adult market and, like her work for children, drew upon her own experience including unhappy marriages and childhood deaths. The first, *Lover and Husband* (1870), was published by Skeet and the three subsequent novels: *She was Young and he was Old* (1872), *Not Without Thorns* (1873) and *Cicely: A Story of Three Years* (1874) were published by Tinsley. Though they were obviously acceptable enough to be published and reviewed, they did not receive the acclaim of her work for children. There were further attempts to achieve success in the adult market with two three-volume novels, *Hathercourt Rectory* (1878) and *Miss Bouverie* (1880) and in 1888 Macmillan published a volume of four ghost stories by Molesworth which had previously appeared in magazines. The ghost stories are still in print as a group and individually appear in anthologies of Victorian supernatural tales; this is in contrast to her children's books, almost all of which are unavailable.[10]

In her earlier career, when she lacked confidence, Molesworth appears to have colluded with the idea of not being a serious writer. Her tone is very different from the confident discussions of children's literature she was capable of in the 1880s and 1890s. In the 1860s, she engaged in a very close friendship with the poet John Byrne Leicester Warren, later third Lord de Tabley. She and her husband, Richard, met him in the mid–1860s when they rented Tabley Grange on his family estate in Cheshire. Warren spent much of the year in London but he and Louisa corresponded regularly and intimately for a number of years. The exact nature of their relationship is difficult to determine since only Louisa's letters to him have survived but it is possible to glimpse in the letters her yearning for something more than what confinements of respectable middle-class family life had to offer. She perhaps enjoyed the thrill of a clandestine friendship, addressing him sometimes by the pseudonyms 'Mr Redrose' and 'Mr Bentley' as a cover and reminding him often at the end of a letter to remember to burn it – which of course he obviously did not. Her tone is emotional; she veers from the accusatory to the apologetic in the course of a single letter, and is often self-deprecating. Whatever his feelings, it is certainly the case that Warren helped and advised Molesworth with her early attempts at writing fiction and provided much needed support in her endeavours to get into print. Cooper notes of the earliest long letter from Louisa to Warren in the collection that 'The bulk of it is taken up with a discussion of her own writing'.[11] He had apparently been asked to read and criticise a short story she had sent him (never published) with a view to his telling her how to improve her writing. Many of the subsequent letters are also taken up with discussion of her writing and with her doubts about its quality. She refers to it as 'rubbish' on more than one occasion. In a letter of 1 March 1868 Molesworth thanks Warren for 'marking the rubbish' and goes on, 'Do you know I had not the *least* idea you would have found so much good to say – were you quite honest? I hope so.'[12] In the same letter she talks of her 'real ignorance and inexperience', adding that she is 'not afraid of work' but is afraid that anything she undertakes will be 'worthless when done'. 'How am I to improve myself?' she asks Warren, and continues:

> Would it be better to go on at little things for some time or can I set myself any particular course of reading? I really do not see how I am to improve unless I had the chance of someone like you to act as 'friendly critic' close at hand, *wh.* I have not. I am not ambitious but even if all my M.S.S remain such always, I *wd* like them to be better.[13]

On another occasion in 1868 she writes to him from Pau in Southern France, where she was then staying. The letter discusses how wonderful she feels being in the sun and how much she has enjoyed reading Dickens's

Our Mutual Friend and refers to her own literary endeavours, 'I have just written my first chapter for the fourth time. It reads more twaddley than ever, & I am consequently in a state of depressed disgust or disgusted depression whichever you think the prettier expression'. However, the next sentence in the letter reads, 'There are such pretty Spanish things here. Don't you want any present for your sisters or anyone?'[14] This is significant, I think, if only because it puts writing in another perspective and shows how for Molesworth, as for many writers, their writing is part of a wider matrix which could involve such frivolous touristy thoughts as sun and presents for relatives.

Warren appears to have been encouraging about her work and she did eventually finish what was to be the first of her adult novels, *Lover and Husband*. She then took it to London and handed it over to Warren who placed it with his publisher, Bentley, though in the end it was Skeet, not Bentley, who published it in December 1869. It was not a runaway success but sold moderately well and had reasonable if unenthusiastic 'notices'. In one letter to Warren, Molesworth remarks upon the mildness of some of the comments in the notices, saying that rather than kind protectiveness she would prefer more brutally honest criticism to help her improve. The lukewarm reception of her early work and its failure to make any money did not deter Molesworth from starting a new book. In securing Warren's help, Molesworth had set up a pattern which was to continue throughout her long writing career. She relied much upon various male business contacts and friends to give her sound advice and to provide support. As in the letters to Warren, surviving letters to Macmillan and other publishers show how firmly she could stand her own ground while remaining on close personal terms with those she was negotiating with.

The book that made Molesworth famous was *Carrots: Just a Little Boy*, written in 1876, near the start of her long career. From a current perspective *Carrots* seems perhaps too stereotypically Victorian. Carrots is the youngest of six children and much cosseted by his slightly older sister, Floss, of whom we are told, 'She had the most motherly heart in the world, though she was such a quiet little girl that very few people knew anything about what she was thinking, and the big ones laughed at her for being so outrageously fond of dolls'.[15]

Once Carrots is born, however, Floss has a focus for her motherly instincts. The plot revolves around Carrots being wrongly accused of stealing a half-sovereign because he has misunderstood some of the things people have said to him. Molesworth represents Carrots' immaturity by having him speak in a 'baby' language, which as Cooper has argued is grammatically accurate and which was obviously popular with many Victorian readers but which has irritated many subsequent critics of Molesworth.[16] Here is a typical example from *Hoodie* (1882), one of Molesworth's most loved books in her day. According to Peter Hunt, her representation of the language of a small child 'severely mars' *Hoodie*.[17] The context is that Hoodie, who is generally a naughty child, has been wrongly accused by the servant, Martin, of meddling with the basket of their newly acquired greenfinch. Hoodie rounds on her, saying, '"It's very nasty of you to say that, Martin," she exclaimed violently. "*Vezzy* nasty. You always think I'm naughty. I daresay I did look funny, 'cos I was temptationed, awful temptationed to touch the bird, but I wouldn't, no I *wouldn't*, 'cos I p'omised"'.[18] Similarly, in *A Christmas Child* (1880), an unusually sentimental tale for Molesworth in which the child, Ted, dies, he is characterised by his baby language. He thinks, for instance that his mother's friend is a 'diant' (giant) who lives on the nearby mountain and is a bit frightened of him. His cousin Percy remarks on how much he likes mountains and Ted replies, 'But it wouldn't be nice to be alone, kite alone, on the top of one of zem, would it?'.[19]

Ted, like Carrots and other Molesworth boys, is gentle and feminised. He hates violence and bullying (as Carrots hates cruelty and killing) and is a bit too good to be true. This is not the case with many of Molesworth's child characters, especially as her work matures; some of her children behave badly – often through loneliness or misunderstanding – but all show sensitivity, imagination and a love of birds and animals. The ages of Carrots and his sister Floss, their relationship, as well as the way they are idealised in the text lead one to think Molesworth may have been writing into their characters a projection of the relationship her dead daughter and baby son never had. Almost all her books thereafter announce her as the author of *Carrots* on the flyleaf.

From 1870 to her last publication in 1911, Molesworth produced over 100 novels and stories for children, many of them with Macmillan for whom she produced a new book each Christmas for her entire career. Even when she had stopped producing her own work she acted as a reader for them. She was introduced to the firm by Sir Noel Paton, artist and illustrator of *The Water Babies* whom she met while living in Edinburgh and who is alleged to have advised her to try her hand at children's books after hearing her tell stories to her own children. Macmillan recognised her talent immediately when she sent them the manuscript of her first children's book, *Tell Me a Story*, in 1875. This was as well known and respected a publishing house in these years as it is today; much information exists about its dealings with what were to become famous writers such as Carroll and Kipling and, of course, Thomas Hardy. Hardy's relationship with the firm was as long, and as productive and as satisfactory as Molesworth's, though given his rather different background, he did not have the benefit of an introduction by someone as influential as Sir Noel Paton. From the outset, the person Molesworth dealt with most frequently at Macmillan was George Craik, husband of the novelist Dinah Mulock, and a partner in the firm. They got on well and very quickly became close. In a letter to Warren Molesworth says 'I am on very intimate terms with some of the firm and have received the greatest kindness from them'.[20] The tone of her early correspondence with the firm is helpful, polite and unassuming. She refers to her manuscript as 'a little book of children's stories' and offers to add more if it is not long enough, even asking what kind of stories they would want.[21]

Molesworth's relationship with Craik as her main contact at the firm lasted until his death in 1906. The only real tension that appears to have arisen was in the early 1890s because Molesworth was attempting to place her work with too many other publishers at the same time. For, although her primary loyalty was to Macmillan, Molesworth had work published with an astonishing array of other firms, among them Chambers, Nisbit, Nelson, Nister, Routledge, Longmans, Cassell, Hatchards, Unwin and the SPCK. In addition her work was serialised in many magazines including *Little Folks, The Monthly Packet,* and *Aunt Judy's* – though she did not use the latter as often as she might have because they did not pay very well. Her letters to Macmillan show her professionalism and business sense and how aware she was of her books as a marketable commodity. She often asks Craik for advice about quite complex publishing and commercial issues and there was evidently a good deal of trust and mutual respect in their relationship. An example of this is where she writes in 1889 to tell him that a French reader she has been persuaded to work on is not a good financial proposition. There is much detail about royalties and so on and she goes on, 'I have so much the habit of frankness with you that sooner or later my feeling *wd* have shown itself, so I think I will take the bull by the horns and tell it to you *right out*'.[22]

Later on in her career she writes regularly asking him to send some of her novels to worthy causes to raise funds. He always obliges as can be seen by the pencilled instructions at the top of the letters in the Macmillan archive. For instance in 1891 she writes asking if he will take an interest 'in the Reading Room for women students about to be started in Bloomsbury'. She explains how much it is needed and adds of the women, 'Many of them lead pitifully isolated lives, especially artists – and almost fall out of track with refinement becoming complete Bohemians'.[23] All of this provides an interesting complement to the homely persona projected by the title 'Mrs Molesworth'.

Another long and close association which began in these early days was with Walter Crane, Macmillans' chief illustrator, who was commissioned to illustrate *Tell Me a Story* and who illustrated all her work for Macmillan until 1890. Molesworth was fortunate to be given the services of so talented and dedicated an illustrator. It must be assumed that in accepting her manuscript so quickly and employing Crane to illustrate the work, Macmillan recognised her talent. Crane was not only an illustrator but also an important figure in the Arts and Crafts movement, an early socialist and a friend of William Morris. He loved illustrating fantasy and fairy tale, for reasons he explains, 'They are attractive to designers of an imaginative tendency, for in a sober and matter-of-fact age they afford perhaps the only outlet for unrestrained flights of fancy open to the modern illustrator, who likes to revolt against the despotism of facts.'[24] It could also be argued that for similar reasons many writers were also drawn to working on children's books.

Comments in the Macmillan correspondence show that Molesworth had respect for Crane's work, appreciating the care he showed in reading the story and producing illustrations to complement it exactly. In a letter to Craik returning Crane's first illustrations for her she comments:

> I am very much pleased with them, and though less than nothing of a judge I can appreciate better than anyone the extreme care and thoughtfulness Mr.Crane has shown in his treatment of the subjects – for he has forgotten no trifles mentioned in the stories and must really have read them – even to the slipper beside 'Winny's Cot'.[25]

Crane was forward-looking in his recognition of the importance of story and illustration complementing one another. It is interesting that up to now Molesworth's books have often been preserved in special library collections more for Crane's illustrations than for her writing. There does not seem to have been much recognition so far that Molesworth herself was as thoughtful, sensitive and talented as her illustrator. For example, this comment of Molesworth's from an article 'On the Art of Writing Fiction for Children' is in a similar vein to Crane's, 'And yet you must be true to nature. Save in an occasional flight to fairyland (and is true fairyland unreal after all?)'.[26] She also considers that the best writers for children are those 'who while not closing their eyes to the dark and sad side of things, yet have faith in the sunlight behind and beyond' (p. 342). There are moments in many of her books when we get some sense of this 'faith', which is more mystical than conventionally religious.

Molesworth's belief in fairyland, in the power of storytelling to create other worlds which can inspire and provide hope, is well represented in a typical scene from *Christmas Tree Land* (1884). Here Silva, the children's godmother is telling them tales:

> Oh, the wonderful tales that were told round the bright little fire in Silva's dainty kitchen! Oh, the wood fairies, and water-sprites, and dwarfs, and gnomes that they learnt about! Oh, the lovely songs that godmother sang in that witching voice of hers – that voice that was like none other that the children had ever heard. It was a true fairy-land into which she led them – a fairy-land where entered nothing ugly or cruel or mean or false, though the dwellers in it were of strange and fantastic shape and speech, children of the rainbow and the mist unreal and yet real, like the cloud castles that build themselves for us in the sky, or the music that weaves itself in the voice of the murmuring stream.[27]

From early in her writing career and certainly after the publication of *Carrots,* Molesworth was considered to be one of the foremost children's writers of her generation and was best known for her books for and about very young children. She had many admirers, among them Swinburne, who she corresponded with and occasionally met; he was a great lover of children and a devotee of her work. In the course of an article on Charles Reade, he had this to say of her:

> It seems to me not at all easier to draw a life-like child than to draw a life-like man or woman … since the death of George Eliot, there is none left whose touch is so exquisite and masterly, whose love is so thoroughly according to knowledge, whose bright and sweet invention is so fruitful, so truthful or so delightful as Mrs Molesworth's. [28]

In 1887, another contemporary and commentator on literature for children, Edward Salmon, was equally complimentary, 'I have left till the last any mention of the lady, who by right of all-round merit, should stand first. Mrs Molesworth is, in my opinion, considering the quality and quantity of her labours, the best storyteller for children England has yet known'. He bases his judgement upon the realism of many of her stories, 'realism, that is, in the purest and highest sense'.[29] In this he presumably intends that his readers should not associate the term realism with the much-detested earthiness and naturalism of the French novelists of this period. He considers her 'stories of everyday child life' to be more original than her fairy stories and it becomes clear in the course of the discussion that by realism he means close knowledge of and psychological insight into a child's world: 'she knows their characters, she understands their wants, and she desires to help them'. He adds that she is 'never sentimental, but writes common sense in a straightforward manner'.[30] She herself thought clarity of expression to be important, as we can see from this advice to would-be writers for children:

> Your language should of course be the very best you can use. Good English, terse and clear, with perhaps a little more repetition, a little more *making sure you are understood* than is allowable in ordinary fiction. Keep to the rule of never using a long word where a short one will express your meaning as well.[31]

But she also suggests it is appropriate to use longer words as long as they are placed in a comprehensible context: 'In such a case you can often skilfully lead up to the meaning, and children must learn new words' (p. 344).

Since her death in 1921, Molesworth has been known only as the author of a few highly regarded novels for the older child such as *The Cuckoo Clock* (1877), *The Tapestry Room* (1879), or *The Carved Lions* (1895). With hindsight, her strength as a writer does seem to lie in her work for the older child, particularly where, as in these books, she combines realism and fantasy. However, there are many more of her children's books, apart from the those few cited above for which she is still known, that are worth revisiting. It is only by reading a wider spectrum of Molesworth's work that a fair assessment of her distinctive qualities and her considerable contribution to writing for children is possible.

When Molesworth died her reputation, like that of many other Victorian writers, was at a low ebb and no one thought to collect correspondence or recollections for a biography or even a memoir. However, in 1936 G. M. Young's *Victorian England: Portrait of an Age*, assesses Molesworth as one of a new generation of writers for children who emerged in the 1870s. He talks of 'the new unpietistic handling of childhood by Lewis Carroll, Mrs Ewing, Mrs Molesworth' and remarks that 'a whole world of pious, homiletic convention has passed away'.[32] A little later, in 1944, Charles Morgan, commenting on the authors publishing fiction with Macmillan in the 1870s and 1880s notes that, 'Fiction, so far as the Macmillans were concerned, though kindly enough to them at the time, seems a trifle bleak to us. William Black, George Fleming, Mrs Oliphant, Frances Hodgson Burnett, Mrs Molesworth and Charlotte M. Yonge – the two last have at any rate survived'.[33] A similar account written in more recent years would have been much more likely to place Burnett or Oliphant before Molesworth. In his monograph on Molesworth, Roger Lancelyn Green mentions a Ruth Robertson who, in 1938, was collecting material for a biography but whose work had been interrupted by the war.[34] Although Green acknowledges Ruth Robertson's help in his work her biography never appeared. Her research, however, has been incorporated into the newly published biographical study by Jane Cooper. Green, and to some extent Marghanita Laski in her appraisal of the work of Molesworth, Ewing and Burnett, tried to revive interest in Molesworth's work in the late 1950s and 1960s but this led to nothing. Until at least the late 1980s *The Cuckoo Clock* was available in a Puffin edition; it then went out of print but became available again in 2002.[35] It is symptomatic of the recent state of Molesworth's reputation that Cooper has had to publish her biography at her own expense. There are signs, however, of which the biography is one, of a little more interest in Molesworth's work. This is partly because of the increased attention being paid to women's and more middlebrow writing but also because literature for children is now taken more seriously as an object of academic study. There have always been canonical children's writers as there have been canonical writers for adults but in both spheres there is an attempt to be more inclusive – to look further than the obviously exceptional and privileged individual works which have long constituted the children's literature canon. Part of the problem of Molesworth's reputation has been that in addition to being a popular writer for children, Molesworth was, of course, a woman writing in a patriarchal society. Peter Hunt encapsulates the problem in his introduction to an extract from *The Cuckoo Clock* in *Children's Literature, An Anthology 1801–1902* when he comments, 'Mrs Molesworth's literary reputation has suffered from two things. The first is that the most invisible class of writing to modern critics has been (at least until very recently) the mainstream, the female and the children's author: Molesworth was all three'.[36]

In fact recent interest in Molesworth's writing has not come so much from those who teach and research children's literature. With certain exceptions,[37] there has not been a tremendous amount of research or criticism on popular writing for children by Victorian women writers, by children's literature scholars and certainly not much on Molesworth; articles in the children's literature journals have tended to concentrate on single classic texts from the nineteenth century like *The Secret Garden* or on contemporary writers and texts. Most of the work in this area has been done by those interested in women's writing. Perhaps this is about to change. In a recent edition of *The Guardian Review*,[38] the highly regarded and extremely popular children's novelist Jacqueline Wilson wrote of her enthusiasm and respect for Molesworth's books, and how she has become an avid collector of early editions. So far as she is concerned, Molesworth's books are well worth reading. Describing her chance discovery of *The Carved Lions* as an adult she says, 'I thought it one of the best books I'd ever read' (p. 37). It is clear from Wilson's article that she does not mean that it is one of the best *children's* books but simply what she says – one of the best books. She talks about Molesworth's huge popularity in her own time but suggests her work might still appeal to children today, not least because of the clarity of her expression. Echoing Edward Salmon's view of over a century earlier and Molesworth's own advice, Wilson says: 'She writes in a clear, simple style that still reads easily nowadays.' She also thinks her child characters would still have appeal, adding 'She's uncannily accurate at portraying nineteenth century children in her books, bringing them alive for us now' (p. 37). As a novelist who specialises in evoking reader sympathy for unsympathetic and lonely child characters, Jacqueline Wilson is well placed to recognise this characteristic feature in Molesworth's writing.

In an article of hers of 1898 in *Chambers's Journal* on writing children's books, Molesworth notes the contrast in attitude to books between her own childhood and that of the present generation. Whereas in her childhood days there were so few books that each book was a treasured friend, intimately known and loved, now they are read and cast off without a thought, 'in scores of nurseries and school-rooms, a book, once hurried through, practically ceases to exist save as an ornament on the shelves'.[39] So we can see from this that Molesworth knew her culture and recognised her role in the marketplace. Molesworth typifies the professional popular writer not only in the volume of material she produced for consumption but also in drawing from and working in a variety of different forms. As noted, she started her career by writing three-volume novels for the adult market, and in her writing for children she ranges quite widely, producing different material for all different age groups up to adult. There are full-length novels, as well as what might be termed story-books, and then short tales and articles which appeared in magazines and were often collected into a book later. This variety is also evident within the texts themselves. Molesworth writes in the modes of fairy tale and fantasy but is just as happy with domestic realism and the family story. Like much children's writing, her work is characterised by its being something of a hybrid form.

Lynne Vallone[40] has noted the tendency of nineteenth-century children's books by women to draw upon many different forms of writing but particularly varieties of the realist and moralist tradition and in this Molesworth is no exception. Far from making the finished products into something of a rag-bag, this hybridity was a kind of experimentation that helped the genre to grow and thrive into the twentieth century and beyond. I would argue that one of Molesworth's distinctive qualities is her reworking of fantasy to bring together domestic realism and the supernatural and mystical worlds of fantasy. Being perceived as a popular genre and not being treated seriously as literature probably served the development of children's literature well. Because there were then no firm literary expectations (although of course there were moral ones) there was more freedom for individual development.

So far as the didactic function of children's literature goes, there is an emphasis in Molesworth's writing upon children – usually girls – learning to control and monitor their behaviour. Selfishness, outspokenness, hasty temper and jealousy are all shown to be destructive – even unacceptable – although Molesworth understands how difficult such self-control can be and shows sympathy with the child's anger, indignation and pain. Jacqueline Wilson recognises this. Speaking of *The Cuckoo Clock,* Wilson notes that although the story is old-fashioned in many ways Griselda is an appealing heroine, 'Griselda isn't a milk and water goody-goody Victorian miss. There's a real, sparky, flesh-and-blood child underneath the frilly pinafore. She gets bored, she gets angry, she gets irritable, she even throws things. We understand why she feels the way she does.'[41]

Molesworth's texts move beyond mere endorsement of conventional behaviour and morality and adult expectations of children. In *Rosy* (1882), for example, the heroine is an interestingly 'difficult' child not unlike Mary Lennox in *The Secret Garden*. Rosy is jealous and cross much of the time. She has good intentions of being better behaved but even at the end of the novel hasn't entirely reformed. Yet we sympathise with her because she is good-natured at heart but has been over-indulged by the well-meaning aunt she has lived with while her parents are abroad. We are told that, 'Rosy had stayed altogether with her aunt, who had loved her dearly, but in wishing to make her perfectly happy had made the mistake of letting her have her own way in everything'.[42] She is also often lonely and insecure which we see affects her behaviour and she does not undergo any miraculous transformation at the end of the book. Even in *Carrots,* which is more sentimental, Molesworth questions the concept of 'spoiling' the child. Cousin Sybil has had everything she wants in life but is not spoiled; the narrator comments, 'Perhaps after all there is a kind of spoiling that isn't spoiling – love and kindness, and even indulgence, do not spoil when there is perfect trust and openness'.[43] In *Four Winds Farm* (1887) the hero Gratian is a dreamy boy who loves to be outdoors; in many ways he epitomises the Romantic child. We are told that, 'He had been at church and at the Sunday School; but I am afraid he could not have told you much about the sermon, and in his class he had been mildly reproved for inattention.[44] But this is all right for he is told by one of the winds that 'dreaming is no harm in its right place' (p. 4). Gratian is an early version of Dickon in *The Secret Garden* and his sickly friend, Fergus, reminiscent of Colin in the same book. As well as being dreamy he is an imaginative boy who wishes 'there were no lessons in the world. I wish there were only birds, and lambs and hills, and moors and the wind – most of all the wind' (p. 4).

Other children in Molesworth's books run away from an unhappy situation and are not condemned for doing so. In *The Carved Lions* (1895) Geraldine is sent to school when her parents go abroad; it is not a good school and she is wrongly accused by an insensitive (but not thoroughly evil) teacher of stubbornly refusing to learn some verses when in fact she has merely frozen up with fear at having to recite them in public. She runs away and luckily is found and taken in by a sympathetic family who are acquainted with her parents. It is clear from the narrative that she was right to run away and that no child should be treated in such a harsh and unsympathetic manner. Similarly, in *My New Home* (1894), Helena lives alone with her grandmother because her parents are dead; they are poor but happy. A rich but stern relative, Mr Cosmo Vandaleur, then offers a much better home to both of them in return for grandmother acting as housekeeper as his wife is seriously ill. Helena hates it in her new home; whereas in their old home grandmother had always spent a lot of time with her and they had been great friends, she now seems to Helena to be completely ignoring her and she and the rich cousin want to send her away to school. She feels rejected and miserable, and in desperation runs away back to her old home. The denouement makes clear that Helena is not really to blame. The adults in the story have not explained things to her and have not considered her feelings enough. Her cousin arrives to take her back; she is terrified and expects to be punished but what happens is rather different:

> I heard a sort of sigh or a deep breath, and then a voice, which it almost seemed to me I had never heard before, said, very, very gently – 'My poor little girl – poor little Helena. Have I been such an ogre to you?' I could *scarcely* believe my ears – to think that it was Cousin Cosmo speaking to me in that way! He goes on, 'Tell me more about it all,' said Mr. Vandaleur. 'I

want to understand from yourself all about the fancies and mistakes there have been in your head'.[46]

It is important to Molesworth, and something that was characteristic of her own mother, that adults are able to admit when they have been wrong, that they too can learn lessons. In *Grandmother Dear* (1878), the child Molly is reprimanded for something her grandmother has misinterpreted. Later the grandmother is sorry for her actions, "'Poor little soul," said grandmother. "I wish I had not been so hasty with her. It will be a lesson to me".[46] As a 'popular' writer we might assume not only that Molesworth wrote for the sake of money and fame but also that she courted the public, writing what she thought her audience would want and adopting unthinkingly the social norms and conventional morality of her time. As we have seen, this is not quite the case. Although Molesworth always had a keen sense of the business side of writing, she was also a thoughtful and an innovative writer whose work developed as she went on. She successfully treads a fine and difficult line between satisfying the expectations of the market and expressing something more individual and personal.

Molesworth herself recognised that writing for children was considered a lesser literary activity and increasingly challenged this view in her later career. She argued persuasively for its being taken more seriously on more than one occasion but this is her most articulate and memorable statement of the case:

> so many young writers, too modest to aspire very high, think they can 'write for children'. And often this is a mistake. Writing for children calls for a peculiar gift. It is not so much a question of taking up one's stand on the lower rungs of the literary ladder, as of standing on another ladder altogether – one which has its own steps, its higher and lower positions of excellence.[47]

A fuller picture of Molesworth as a writer must include not only a re-reading of her many books and stories for children, but also a (re)consideration of her non-fictional writing and an investigation of her writing practices. She did not survive her forty-year writing career through luck (although she was fortunate in her dealings with publishers) but through determination, negotiation and regular hard work. It is worth paying attention to her journalism, particularly her essays on the art of writing for children. In the absence of any kind of diary, and as there is relatively little of her correspondence remaining, this work is particularly helpful in understanding her working practices and attitudes. Molesworth deals with a range of issues relating to her writing, some of which have already been touched on. As already indicated, she was at pains to distance herself from the overtly didactic method in children's writing, considering that teaching and guidance must be handled 'so skilfully, so unobtrusively, that the presence of the teacher is never suspected'.[48] This sets her apart from an earlier generation of children's writers and puts her in a tradition of children's writing that includes her near contemporary, Juliana Ewing and her successors, Edith Nesbit and Frances Hodgson Burnett. A study of Molesworth's work makes it clear how much these writers owe to her – whether they drew on her writings consciously or unconsciously.

One very powerful aspect of her writing, which can be found later in Burnett and others, is her sensitivity to the natural world and her use of animals and birds to link the natural with the mystical. In *The Wood Pigeons and Mary* (1901) the lonely child makes friends with and talks to two pigeons in the city. They leave to go to the country and later, when she too moves to the country she re-encounters them. Most adults think her odd and fanciful when she says she talks to the birds but her older cousin Michael believes her, saying, "'I have heard of some people who have a kind of power over animals, and perhaps you are one of them". "Perhaps I am", said Mary'.[49] The old godmother she goes to live with understands her too; she has a special insight and gives her a beautiful cloak made of feathers which has magical qualities. Her home is in a forest and Mary has a lovely little room with a corner window that juts out right into the forest and makes her feel she is actually in it. Here the lonely and misunderstood child finds happiness.

Even more extravagant is the chariot that takes the children on a magical journey in *Christmas Tree Land* (1884):

> The sails were made of an immense collection of birds all somehow or other holding together. Afterwards Silva explained to her that they were all clinging by their claws to a great frame, round which they were arranged in order according to their size, and all flapping their wings in perfect time, so as to have much the same effect in propelling the vessel through the air as the regular motion of several pairs of oars in rowing a boat over the sea.[50]

This is Molesworth at her best – inventive and fantastical. But what is different about her fantasy from a work like *Alice in Wonderland* for example, is that there is always a sympathetic and protective maternal presence with the child adventurers. This is never the children's real mother, who is a kindly but distant figure but an intuitive female helper who possesses special powers.

As was illustrated earlier, however, the power and moral ascendancy is not all with the adults in Molesworth's fiction. We are given to understand that there are sensitive and insensitive *people* regardless of age and in this sense her work challenges earlier Victorian convention and stereotype which held that the child should obey the adult. Nanni, who looks after the children in *Christmas Tree Land* is represented as someone who should not be told about their adventures because she is of limited imagination. She is described as, 'one of those people that did not like anything she did not understand'.[51] Molesworth pays lip-service to adult authority in her narrative voice and in general exhortations to her child readers to behave themselves but, as with her successors Nesbit and Burnett, we never quite take this seriously and know that she is often on the side of the child against arbitrary adult authority. In *The Narrator's Voice: the Dilemma of Children's Fiction,* Barbara Wall claims that, 'in stories like Nesbit's and Potter's and Burnett's, a new children's literature had begun. Children were now to have a literature that was wholly for them'.[52] Her argument for this is that these writers began to write *to* the child rather than writing '*down*'; the narrator's voice is child-centred, rather than adult and distant. I would argue that Molesworth also writes in a child-centred way. A classic example of this is in *The Cuckoo Clock* (1877), a book which precedes the work of those other authors by at least twenty years. The heroine, Griselda, has been sent to live with two maiden aunts in a large gloomy old house after her mother has died. They employ an arithmetic tutor for Griselda; the narrator tells us that her earlier experience of being taught has been rather different: 'Griselda had never been partial to sums, and her rather easy-going governess at home had not, to tell the truth, been partial to them either'.[53] Thus we realise that the narrator perhaps agrees that sums are dull and this is confirmed when Griselda complains to her aunt about the difficulties she experiences with sums. The aunt replies:

> 'Hush!' said her aunt gravely. That is not the way for a little girl to speak. Improve these golden hours of youth, Griselda; they will never return.'
> 'I hope not,' muttered Griselda, 'if it means doing sums.'
> Miss Grizzel fortunately was a little deaf; she did not hear this remark.
> (pp. 19–20)

Later in the book Griselda gets angry and throws a book at the cuckoo in the clock but we understand that her temper (and the fantasy woven around the cuckoo clock) is a result of loneliness, misery and frustration.

Molesworth herself expresses a view that children's books should be positive in outlook and show belief in 'goodness, happiness, and beauty'.[54]

I do not think by this she means some kind of facile optimism should prevail but, to use more contemporary terminology, that writing for children should be 'life-enhancing' rather than 'life-denying'. She considers that, 'anyone who does not feel down in the bottom of their hearts that this "optimism" is well founded, had better leave writing for children alone'.[55] I do not think it is unreasonable to claim that Molesworth made an important contribution to the development of writing for children, paving the way for her successors such as Nesbit and Burnett. In an obituary of Juliana Horatia Ewing, whom she drew much from and greatly admired, she gives the clearest expression of the high aims she had for her children's writing:

> Books for children should be written in such a style and in such language that the full attention and interest of the young readers should be at once enlisted and maintained to the end without any demand for mental straining or undue intellectual effort. But that everything in a child's book should be of a nature to be at once fully understood by the child would surely be an unnecessary lowering of the art of writing for children to a mere catering for their amusement or the whiling away of an idle hour.[56]

She goes on to add that children should not learn of what they are not ready for but that this is different from 'tales with a visible purpose of instruction, intellectual or moral, which are happily a bygone fashion'. Most important in writing for children she says is, '*suggestion* ... of the infinity of "worlds not realized"; of beauty; of poetry; of scientific achievements; of, even, the moral and spiritual problems which sooner or later in its career each soul must disentangle for itself'.[57] Furthermore, she concludes, 'this is one of the most powerful levers for good which we can use with our ever and rapidly changing audience' (pp. 505–6).

Notes

1 Louisa Molesworth, 'My Pink Pet', in *A Christmas Posy*, 1888 (London: Macmillan, 1902), pp. 30–1.
2 Roger Lancelyn Green, *Mrs Molesworth* (London: The Bodley Head, 1961), p. 24.
3 Louisa Molesworth, 'Story-writing', *The Monthly Packet* (1894), 162.
4 Molesworth, 'Story-writing', p. 163.
5 Louisa Molesworth, *The Tapestry Room: A Child's Romance* [1879] (London: Macmillan, 1920), p. 4. Subsequent page references are given in the text.
6 Angela Carter, *The Virago Book of Fairy Tales* (London: Virago, 1990), Introduction, p. xxii.

7 Louisa Molesworth, Letter to John Byrne Leicester Warren, later Lord de Tabley, 30 April 1869, Tabley Muniments, John Rylands Library, University of Manchester.

8 Louisa Molesworth, Letter to Warren, 7 April 1869, Tabley Muniments.

9 Jane Cooper, *Mrs Molesworth* (Sussex: Pratts Folly Press, 2002), p. 135.

10 Louisa Molesworth, *Four Ghost Stories* (London: Macmillan, 1888). One of these stories 'The Story of the Rippling Train' is, for example, included in Michael Cox and R. A. Gilbert (eds), *Victorian Ghost Stories, an Oxford Anthology* (Oxford: Oxford University Press, 1991). The other three stories are: 'Lady Farquar's Old Lady', 'Witnessed by Two' and 'Unexplained'.

11 Cooper, *Mrs Molesworth*, p. 99.

12 Louisa Molesworth, Letter to Warren, 1 March 1868, Tabley Muniments.

13 Louisa Molesworth, Letter to Warren, 1 March 1868, Tabley Muniments.

14 Louisa Molesworth, Letter to Warren, 16 March 1868, Tabley Muniments.

15 Louisa Molesworth, *Carrots: Just a Little Boy*, (London: Macmillan, 1876), p. 5.

16 As well as Carpenter and Pritchard's comment (see note 17), Peter Hunt remarks on Molesworth 'making her small children speak in lisping (not to say nauseatingly "cute") language', Peter Hunt, *Children's Literature: An Anthology 1800–1901*, (Oxford: Blackwell, 2001), p. 286.

17 Humphrey Carpenter and Mari Pritchard, *The Oxford Companion to Children's Literature* [1984] (Oxford: Oxford University Press, 1991), p. 355.

18 Louisa Molesworth, *Hoodie* (London: Routledge, 1882), p. 200.

19 Louisa Molesworth, *A Christmas Child* [1880] (London: Macmillan, 1900), p. 67.

20 Louisa Molesworth, Letter to Warren from Ulverston, 1877, Tabley Muniments.

21 Louisa Molesworth, Letter to Macmillan, 2 March 1875. Macmillan Archive, British Library.

22 Louisa Molesworth, Letter to George Craik, 5 July 1889, Macmillan Archive.

23 Louisa Molesworth, Letter to George Craik, 13 April 1991, Macmillan Archive.

24 Walter Crane, cited in Carpenter and Pritchard, *The Oxford Companion to Children's Literature*, p. 133. (Original source unknown).

25 Louisa Molesworth, Letter to George Craik, 21 August 1875, Macmillan Archive.

26 Louisa Molesworth, 'On the Art of Writing Fiction for children', *Atalanta*, 6 (1893), 583–6, in Lance Salway (ed.), *A Peculiar Gift* (London: Kestrel Books, 1976), pp. 340–6. Subsequent page references are given in the text.

27 Louisa Molesworth, *Christmas Tree Land* [1884] (London: Macmillan, 1981), p. 204.

28 Algernon Charles Swinburne, 'Charles Reade', *The Nineteenth Century*, 17 (October 1884), 563.

29 Edward Salmon, 'Literature for the Little Ones', *The Nineteenth Century*, 22 (October 1887), 563–80, in Lance Salway (ed.), *A Peculiar Gift*, p. 59.

30 Salmon, 'Literature for the Little Ones' in Salway (ed.), *A Peculiar Gift*, p. 60.

31 Molesworth, 'On the Art of Writing Fiction for Children', in Salway (ed.), *A Peculiar Gift*, p. 343.
32 G. M. Young, *Victorian England: Portrait of an Age* (Oxford: Oxford University Press, 1936), p. 154.
33 Charles Morgan, *The House of Macmillan* (London: Macmillan, 1944), p. 105.
34 Green, *Mrs Molesworth*, pp. 9–10.
35 Louisa Molesworth, *The Cuckoo Clock* [1877] (London: Jane Nissen Books, 2002).
36 Hunt, *Children's Literature*, p. 286.
37 The exceptions I am thinking of are Gillian Avery, *Nineteenth-Century Children, Heroes and Heroines in English Children's Stories, 1780–1900* (London: Hodder and Stoughton, 1965), Jacqueline Bratton, *The Impact of Victorian Children's Fiction*, (London: Croom Helm, 1981) and Julia Briggs and Dennis Butts, 'The Emergence of Form', in Peter Hunt (ed.), *Children's Literature: an Illustrated History* (Oxford: Oxford University Press, 1995), pp. 130–66, although the work of the latter two scholars is broad in scope.
38 Jacqueline Wilson, 'Griselda's Big Adventures', *The Guardian Review* (21 December 2002), 37. Subsequent page references are given in the text.
39 Louisa Molesworth, 'Story-reading and Story-writing', *Chambers's Journal* (5 November 1898), 773.
40 Lynne Vallone, 'Women Writing for Children', in Joanne Shattock (ed.), *Women and Literature in Britain 1800–1900*, (Cambridge: Cambridge University Press 2001), pp. 275–300.
41 Wilson, 'Griselda's Big Adventures', p. 37.
42 Louisa Molesworth, *Rosy* [1882] (London: Macmillan, 1893), p. 10.
43 Molesworth, *Carrots*, p. 141.
44 Louisa Molesworth, *Four Winds Farm* [1887] (London: Macmillan, 1920), p. 4. Subsequent page references are given in the text.
45 Louisa Molesworth, *My New Home* [1894] (London: Macmillan 1968), p. 155.
46 Louisa Molesworth, *Grandmother Dear* [1878] (London: Macmillan, 1918), p. 72.
47 Molesworth, 'On the Art of Writing Fiction' in Salway (ed.), *A Peculiar Gift*, p. 341.
48 Salway (ed.), *A Peculiar Gift*, p. 341
49 Louisa Molesworth, *The Wood Pigeons and Mary*, (London: Macmillan, 1901), p. 47.
50 Molesworth, *Christmas Tree Land*, p. 181.
51 Molesworth, *Christmas Tree Land*, p. 173.
52 Barbara Wall, *The Narrator's Voice: the Dilemma of Children's Fiction*, (London: Macmillan, 1991), p. 177.
53 Molesworth, *The Cuckoo Clock*, p. 18
54 Molesworth, 'On the Art of Writing Fiction' in Salway (ed.), *A Peculiar Gift*,

p. 342.

55 Molesworth, 'On the Art of Writing Fiction' in Salway (ed.), *A Peculiar Gift*, p. 342.

56 Salway (ed.), *A Peculiar Gift*, p. 342.

57 Louisa Molesworth, 'Juliana Horatia Ewing', *The Contemporary Review*, 49 (1886), 675–86 in Salway (ed.), *A Peculiar Gift*, p. 505. Subsequent page references are given in the text.

Bibliography

Avery, Gillian, *Nineteenth-Century Children, Heroes and Heroines in English Children's Stories, 1780–1900*, London: Hodder and Stoughton, 1965.

Bratton, Jacqueline, *The Impact of Victorian Children's Fiction*, London: Croom Helm, 1981.

Briggs, Julia and Dennis Butts, 'The Emergence of Form', in Peter Hunt (ed.), *Children's Literature: an Illustrated History*, Oxford: Oxford University Press, 1995, pp. 130–66.

Carpenter, Humphrey and Mari Pritchard, *The Oxford Companion to Children's Literature* [1984] Oxford: Oxford University Press, 1991.

Carter, Angela, *The Virago Book of Fairy Tales*, London: Virago, 1990.

Cooper, Jane, *Mrs Molesworth*, Sussex: Pratts Folly Press, 2002.

Cox, Michael and R. A. Gilbert (eds), *Victorian Ghost Stories: An Oxford Anthology*, Oxford: Oxford University Press, 1991.

Dusinberre, Juliet, *Alice to the Lighthouse: Children's Books and Radical Experiments in Art*, London: Macmillan, 1987.

Green, Roger Lancelyn, *Mrs Molesworth*, London: The Bodley Head, 1961.

—— *Tellers of Tales, Children's Books and their Authors from 1800–1964* [1946] London: Edmund Ward, 1965.

Hodgson-Burnett, Frances, *The Secret Garden* [1911] Oxford: Oxford World's Classics, 2001.

Hunt, Peter, *Children's Literature: An Anthology, 1800–1902*, Oxford: Blackwell, 2001.

—— (ed.), *Children's Literature: An Illustrated History*, Oxford: Oxford University Press, 1995.

Molesworth, Louisa, Letters to Macmillan, The Macmillan Archive, The British Library, London.

—— Letters to John Byrne Leicester Warren, Tabley Muniments, John Rylands Library, The University of Manchester.

—— *Lover and Husband*, London: Skeet, 1870.

—— *She was Young and He was Old*, London: Tinsley, 1872.

—— *Not Without Thorns*, London: Tinsley, 1873.

—— *Cicely: A Story of Three Years*, London: Tinsley, 1874.

—— *Tell me a Story*, London: Tinsley, 1875.

—— *Carrots – Just a Little Boy*, London: Macmillan, 1876.

—— *The Cuckoo Clock* [1877] London: Macmillan, 1931.

—— *Grandmother Dear* [1878] London: Macmillan, 1918.

—— *Hathercourt Rectory*, London: Macmillan, 1878.

—— *The Tapestry Room: A Child's Romance* [1879] London: Macmillan, 1920.

—— *A Christmas Child: A Sketch of Boy-Life* [1880] London: Macmillan, 1900.

—— *Miss Bouverie*, London: Macmillan, 1880.

—— *Hoodie,* London: Routledge, 1882.

—— *Rosy* [1882] London: Macmillan, 1893.

—— *Christmas Tree Land* [1884] London: Macmillan, 1981.

—— 'Juliana Horatia Ewing', *The Contemporary Review* 49 (May 1886), 675–86.

—— 'The Best Books for Children', *Pall Mall Gazette* (29 October 1887), 5.

—— *Four Winds Farm* [1887] London: Macmillan, 1920.

—— *A Christmas Posy* [1888] London: Macmillan, 1902.

—— *Four Ghost Stories,* London: Macmillan, 1888.

—— 'On the Art of Writing Fiction for Children', Atalanta, 6 (May 1893), 583–6.

—— *My New Home* [1894] London: Macmillan, 1968.

—— How I Write my Children's Stories', *Little Folks*, 40 (July 1894), 16–19.

—— Story-writing', *Monthly Packet* (August 1894), 162.

—— *The Carved Lions* [1895] London: Macmillan, 1964.

—— Story-reading and Story-writing', *Chambers's Journal* (5 November, 1898), 773.

—— *The Wood Pigeons and Mary,* London: Macmillan,1901.

Morgan, Charles, *The House of Macmillan,* London: Macmillan, 1944.

Salmon, Edward, 'Literature for the Little Ones', *The Nineteenth Century,* 22 (October 1887), 563–80, in Lance Salway (ed.), *A Peculiar Gift*, London: Kestrel Books, 1976.

Salway, Lance (ed.), *A Peculiar Gift: Nineteenth-Century Writings on Books for Children*, London: Kestrel Books, 1976.

Shattock, Joanne (ed.), *Women and Literature in Britain 1800–1900,* Cambridge: Cambridge University Press, 2001.

Swinburne, Algernon Charles, 'Charles Reade', *The Nineteenth Century,* 17 (October 1884), 563.

Thompson, Nicola (ed.), *Victorian Women Writers and the Woman Question,* Cambridge: Cambridge University Press, 1999.

Tuchman, Gaye with Nina Fortin, *Edging Women Out: Victorian Novelists, Publishers and Social Change*, London: Routledge, 1989.

Vallone, Lynne, 'Women Writing for Children', in Joanne Shattock (ed.), *Women and Literature in Britain 1800–1900*, Cambridge: Cambridge University Press, 2001, pp. 275–300.

Wall, Barbara, *The Narrator's Voice: The Dilemma of Children's Fiction,* London: Macmillan, 1991.

Wilson, Jacqueline, 'Griselda's Big Adventures', *Guardian Review* (21 December

2002), 37.

Young, G. M., *Victorian England: Portrait of an Age,* Oxford: Oxford University Press, 1936.

6

'One wing clipped': the imaginative flights of Juliana Horatia Ewing

Jennifer H. Litster

If I have any gift for writing, it really *ought* to improve under circumstances so much more favourable than the narrowing influence of a small horizon – such as prevents Miss Yonge from improving as time goes on. I only wish my gift were a little nearer *real* genius!! As it is, I do hope to improve gradually; and as I *do* work slowly and conscientiously, I may honestly look forward with satisfaction to the hope of being able to turn a few honest pennies to help us out … I only wish I could please myself better! However, small writers are wanted as well as big ones, and there is no reason why donkey-carts shouldn't drive even if there are coaches on the road!

Juliana Horatia Ewing, Letter to her mother Mrs Gatty, January 1868.[1]

'I do not think praise really hurts me,' Juliana Horatia Ewing told her elder sister, 'because, when I read my own writings over again they often seem to me such "bosh"'.[2] If by 'bosh' she meant worthless then Mrs Ewing did her work a great disservice. The children's stories that brought her widespread acclaim in the 1870s and 1880s, tales like 'Amelia and the Dwarfs', 'Our Field', 'Mary's Meadow' and 'Benjy in Beastland', still retain their original charm and vitality. In her twenty-four year career, Ewing wrote poems that Louisa Molesworth thought were treasured 'in every nursery';[3] she wrote books for boys and books for girls; she wrote fables, short stories, novellas, and longer works in the style of Victorian three-deckers; she wrote hints for amateur theatricals and constructed new mumming plays from old;[4] she turned her hand to factual nature pieces. Far from being 'bosh', then, Ewing's literary output is diverse, and also intriguing, exciting and potentially as appealing to modern readers as it was to her contemporaries.

This said, with these inventive fantasies and playful tales, Juliana Ewing often presented youngsters with more 'bosh' – more nonsense and fewer lessons – than sterner quarters thought appropriate for juvenile readers.

However, by the time of her death on 13 May 1885, such ground-breaking achievements had been superseded by the popular success of Mrs Ewing's more conventional soldiering stories. Not only did 'Jackanapes' (1879) and 'Lætus Sorte Mêa' (1882) seal Mrs Ewing's fame by striking a chord with adult readers sympathetic to the business of army and Empire, the pathos of these two novellas became particularly resonant in light of their author's fate. When 'Lætus Sorte Mêa' was reprinted as *The Story of a Short Life* by the Society for the Propagation of Christian Knowledge only four days before Ewing died at the age of forty-three, 'most of the reviewers spoke of it as being the last work that she wrote, and commented on the title as a singularly appropriate one'.[5] With an original Latin title meaning 'happy in my fate', readers could also be consoled by trusting that Ewing's short life was as contented as that of the crippled child she wrote of in a work Gillian Avery describes as her 'sole major lapse' in fiction.[6]

Born Juliana Horatia Gatty on 3 August 1841, Ewing was the second of eight children raised in the Ecclesfield vicarage by the Rev. Alfred Gatty and his wife Margaret Scott. (Two others died in infancy.) Gatty was the Eton and Oxford-educated son of a London solicitor; Margaret, four years his senior, the daughter of another Yorkshire parson, Dr Alexander Scott of Catterick. To ease the hardships of living on a vicar's salary and offset the cost of educating their four sons at public school, the couple embarked on a series of literary projects. By the 1860s Margaret Gatty achieved a degree of renown, both as a natural scientist, producing an authoritative *History of British Seaweeds* (2 vols, 1863), and as a children's writer, with her instructive *Parables from Nature* (5 vols, 1855–71). Mrs Gatty's success was cemented in *Aunt Judy's Tales* (1859) and *Aunt Judy's Letters* (1862), two volumes of nursery life in which an elder sister entertains the 'little ones' with stories.

A taxonomist by temperament, Mrs Gatty's numerous literary endeavours owed more to financial need than imagination, and in the domestic scenery of these books she catalogued the antics of her own children. Dubbed 'Aunt Judy' by her brothers, Ewing was, as her sister Horatia Eden recalled, 'at once the projector and manager of all our nursery doings. Even if she tyrannised over us by always arranging things according to her own fancy, we did not rebel, we relied so habitually and entirely on her to originate every fresh plan and idea' (p. 6). Mrs Gatty was fortunate to be surrounded by children whose gumption and creativity supplied ample literary material, although her enthusiasm and eccentricity did much to foster this imaginative world of 'theatricals' and manuscript magazines. In time her home-educated daughters were conscripted into the parish work, and did their bit for 'the common cause' on the literary production line, working as amanuenses for the missionary Josiah Wolff, whose autobiography their parents prepared for publication.

This companionable and stimulating childhood would in turn be rich fodder for Ewing's pen. Moreover, her power of invention proved the greater for, as she was to concede, her mother's 'fancy played with very delicate hues, and was deficient in chiaroscuro and colour' and was disadvantaged by 'the narrowness of the lines in which her lot in life was cast'.[7] In 1861 three of Juliana Gatty's stories were published in Charlotte M. Yonge's *The Monthly Packet*.[8] Bell and Daldy of London reprinted these, with two others, as *Melchior's Dream, and other Tales* in 1862.[9] The title story, which in Eden's words demonstrates her sister's talent for 'teaching deep religious lessons without disgusting her readers by any approach to cant or goody-goodyism' (p. 16), is an early example of Ewing's fondness for adding supernatural elements to a domestic tale. Although her literary offerings were sparse initially – and included 'The Mystery of the Bloody Hand' (1865), a sensational story in the Wilkie Collins vein – new impetus to write for children came in 1866 when the publisher George Bell, whose bookseller father was a friend of the Gattys in Yorkshire, invited Margaret Gatty to collaborate on a new juvenile periodical, *Aunt Judy's Magazine*. In its pages almost all Juliana Ewing's stories debuted.

In 1866 the Gatty family also renewed their acquaintance with Major Alexander 'Rex' Ewing, an Aberdonian army paymaster who enjoyed a certain artistic cachet as composer of the hymn, 'Jerusalem the Golden', but had abandoned his musical ambitions for the security of the military after his father's death. Although her parents were initially reluctant to consent – something of a family tradition, for Dr Scott objected to Alfred Gatty, and Scott himself was rejected by his wife's parents – Juliana and Rex were married on 1 June 1867, leaving England one week later for Fredericton, New Brunswick. Here Mrs Ewing produced the final sections of *Mrs Overtheway's Remembrances* (1869), five stories written in a 'chatty' style that developed from her fascination with oral storytelling.[10] This interest now matured into the beginnings of two literary experiments: in the new Dominion of Canada Ewing began to write new folktales that conformed to conventional properties, afterwards gathered as *Old-Fashioned Fairy Tales* (1882), and to create literary fairytales, collected as *The Brownies, and other Tales* (1870) and *Lob Lie-by-the-Fire, and other Tales* (1873), that, unlike her folktales, twisted tradition and 'told afresh'.[11]

In 1869 the Ewings returned to England and lived until 1877 at Aldershot. On the army base Ewing embarked on her most productive phase, perhaps, as Avery suggests, because she was free of parish work, but also because the temperate climate suited her precarious health. She wrote more fairytales, and the four stories of *A Great Emergency* (1877), and also concentrated her efforts on three longer, domestic serials that follow child protagonists to adulthood: *A Flat-Iron for a Farthing* (1872), *Six to Sixteen* (1875), and *Jan of the Windmill* (1876). From 1874 to 1876 Ewing shared the editorship of *Aunt Judy's Magazine* with her sister Horatia for, after several years of debilitating illness, Margaret Gatty died on 4 October 1873.

Juliana Ewing's life after Aldershot was nomadic. The Ewings lived in Boston, Lincolnshire for a year, then at Fulford near York, but Juliana's delicacy aborted her attempts to follow Rex overseas to Malta in 1879 and prevented her travel to his posting in Ceylon altogether. Instead she relied on the hospitality of friends and relatives, and occasionally chaperoned the younger daughters of General Smyth, father of composer Dame Ethel Smyth, at Frimley. When Rex came home in 1883 the couple settled at Taunton, where Mrs Ewing continued to write, albeit less prolifically as her health and mobility deteriorated. She produced only one longer work, *We and the World* (1881), before her death in 1885, possibly from spinal cancer.

New book editions of *Jackanapes* (1883), *Daddy Darwin's Dovecot* (1884) and *Lob Lie-by-the-Fire* (1885), were illustrated, at Ewing's request, by the acclaimed artist, Randolph Caldecott, an indication of the regard in which her work had come to be held. Although out of print now for many years, Mrs Ewing's children's books sold quickly in their day, in print runs of ten thousand, their verisimilitude, humour, sincerity, and stylistic economy making them popular also with adult readers. (*Daddy Darwin's Dovecot*, described in the *Daily Telegraph* as 'a manifest work of consummate genius', sold 400 copies a day.)[12] She did not, however, make her fortune. Ewing's earnings remained small despite the increased circulation she gained when she began to publish with the SPCK. As her correspondence demonstrates, authors, who negotiated terms with illustrators and printers and used publishers as distribution agents, were exposed to a considerable degree of financial risk for limited returns. Additionally, Ewing often found her needs sidelined and received, for example, only a halfpenny per shilling copy of *Jackanapes* sold whereas Caldecott netted a penny. Publishers seemed bent on exploiting authors, even if they were Christian houses or family friends like Bell.

Acquaintances like Jean Ingelow, who wanted Ewing's work for the highly regarded periodical *Good Words*, and John Ruskin, who personally safeguarded *Aunt Judy's* cover price, confirmed to Ewing that she was lacking due remuneration and recognition. In her dissatisfied spells, and when her ill health caused particular frustrations, Ewing wrote of her desire for 'a *larger public*' and for vistas beyond her 'small horizon' to lend her work 'new local colour'.[13] She felt the weight of Mrs Gatty's reputation and shortcomings and thought it 'worth sacrificing something to emerge from the small way in which mother's work was kept *to the end*'.[14] That Juliana Ewing never fully left Margaret Gatty's 'old groove' to write for 'the higher flight' – that is, for adults – is partly a consequence of her premature death.[15] Furthermore, although Ewing had no children, she was not free from the money problems her mother experienced: new ventures were financially hazardous when one had obligations to family, to charity and to an 'erratic husband' (p. 219).

As this last description of Major Ewing, written by the author's biographer, and niece, Christabel Maxwell, suggests, Mrs Ewing possibly faced personal as well as professional discontent. Maxwell rings some discord in the Ewings' domestic harmony, revealing the altercations that ensued when General Smyth discovered an intimate and apparently atheistic letter from Rex to Ethel, his music student. (Juliana, it seems, was Ethel's real 'passion'.) Her readers are left to dwell on the distaste Maxwell feels that her aunt was not buried at Ecclesfield, but in Trull near Bath, later resting not only with Rex, but also his second wife. Such whispers of unquiet slumbers hint that future biographers may unearth something more than happiness in Juliana Horatia Ewing's short life.

Unquestionably, Juliana Horatia Ewing wrote her children's stories in unquiet times. Her first book was published in 1862, the year that serialisation of Charles Kingsley's *The Water Babies* began in *Macmillan's Magazine* and 'Lewis Carroll' dreamt up *Alice's Adventures in Wonderland*. When her final volume appeared in 1885, many children's books bore the imprint of these pioneering works. By the later Victorian period, the better parts of British juvenile literature valued entertaining youngsters over inculcating morals, and privileged the imagination and fancy over didacticism and piety. Thus Mrs Ewing emerged as a children's author at a critical moment in the genre's development: furthermore, she pursued her career during three decades of uncommon transformation, not just in artistic terms, but also in the book trade, as advances in production and diversified house lists kept pace with increased literacy and the demands of an expanding and leisured middle class.

The SPCK for one recognised that this sector was unlikely to be satisfied with doctrinal texts and answered demands for cheap and varied fiction by establishing a new publications branch in 1832. Although the religious vetting procedure and a lack of imagination meant their authors initially produced more dreary tract-like stories for working-class children, by the late 1860s the Society put out a 'considerable range of children's story-books and classroom works and competed very successfully with commercial publishers through its network of agencies'.[16] Mrs Ewing would become one of the SPCK's more critically acclaimed authors. Similar trends lay behind the dramatic growth of juvenile periodicals, with over one hundred titles launched in the 1860s and 1870s.

For any new author these conditions must have been stimulating, liberating even, and not a little daunting. For the daughter of a children's writer whose books were widely praised and read by Queen Victoria and Gladstone among others, there were additional, and conflicting, pressures. Juliana Gatty was initiated into the family business, so to speak, with *Melchior's Dream*: indeed, her mother's preface encouraged those who had 'listened kindly and favourably to me for several years' to be 'no less well disposed toward my daughter's writings' (p. viii). The spectre of *Aunt Judy* linked the two still further. Contemporaries often confused their identities.[17] For many 'Mrs Alfred Gatty' was synonymous with 'Aunt Judy' – Bell's periodical relied on this association – yet Juliana was 'Aunt Judy' to new acquaintances, including the Smyths, and her mother's fame was cushioned on her childhood alter ego.[18]

If by following in her mother's footsteps Juliana Ewing aimed to emulate her success, her own artistic autonomy could obviously be jeopardised by adhering to Mrs Gatty's literary style. Margaret Gatty, with her eclectic curiosity in chloroform and sundials, seaweeds and mowing, came late to children's books. Her 1851 debut, *The Fairy Godmothers*, is novel in that it harnesses supernatural elements 'to illustrate some favourite and long cherished convictions',[19] but in truth Gatty handles this blend of fantasy and instruction 'rather awkwardly'.[20] She was on surer ground with *Parables from Nature*, vignettes written 'in an outburst of excessive admiration of Hans Andersen's *Fairy Tales*, coupled with a regret that … he had so often left his charming stories without an object or moral at all'.[21] As Ewing wrote of her mother's creative talents, 'Whatever genius she may have had, her industry was far more remarkable – the pen of a ready writer is not grasped by all fingers, and gifts are gifts, not earnings'.[22]

As an editor, however, Margaret Gatty did much to embrace the changing tastes in children's literature and, amid the maelstrom of sensational 'blood-and-thunders', *Aunt Judy's Magazine* fast became 'the darling of the critics'.[23] Her 'honest endeavour and wish', Gatty announced, was 'to provide the best of mental food for all ages of young people, and for many varieties of taste'.[24] This diet was fiction in the main, occasionally 'an emblem or allegorical picture, typifying some moral truth'. Parents shrinking from 'an overflowing of mere amusement' were promised 'facts and anecdotes, historical, biographical, or otherwise, deserving a niche in the brain temple of the young' (p. 2), in Brian Alderson's words, a 'dignified balance between the pi and the rumbustious, a balance typical of Victorian children's literature at its best'.[25]

This periodical is perhaps 'more pietistic in tone than most memories, unrefreshed, would probably believe', but Harvey Darton also concedes that, '"Aunt Judy" was on the side of the fairies as well as the angels'.[26] Hans Christian Andersen's tales, which 'even in their wildest flights, appeal to the good feelings of their readers', were praised in *Aunt Judy's* first review section.[27] Better still was 'the exquisitely wild, fantastic, impossible, yet most natural history' (p. 123) of *Alice's Adventures in Wonderland*. Given that Gatty thought Andersen's tales flawed, and was a little po-faced about *The Water Babies*, we might wonder which 'Aunt Judy' was the reviewer here; this said, Carroll's 'Fairy Sylvie' and 'Bruno's Revenge' were written for *Aunt Judy's* in 1867 at Mrs Gatty's request.[28]

In Mrs Ewing's hands this review section expanded to meet the new profusion of children's books. Acknowledging that adults with neither time nor inclination to preview purchases might be tempted to choose 'the smartest volume at the smallest cost', she assessed a wide range of books, old and new, on behalf of parents and parish librarians. She also tried to protect her field from an invasion of cheap and nasty writing that publishers would distribute should adults seem to demand it:

> It is a great responsibility to give children bad grammar, incorrect information, vulgar slang, clap-trap sentiment, morbid twaddle, and narrow and feeble teaching on high and holy subjects to 'instruct and amuse' them; and yet how much is written and bought of which this is no harsh account, and which would never be printed at all if thousands of parents were not so ready to buy it?[29]

Thus Ewing ridiculed one author for believing 'in field officers with daggers in their socks' and chastised another for permitting child characters to tote guns as toys. This sounds rather humourless, but her reviews, especially of religious books, are lifted by the same wit and 'delicate irony' her fiction employs:[30] the Rev. F. O. Morris's versifications of the Ten Commandments seemed 'so very comical that we sincerely hope we may forget them before next Sunday!'[31]

As editors of a sixpenny monthly, Gatty and Ewing were ideally placed to advocate quality juvenile literature. As the magazine made a profit in only one of its nineteen years, they also had first-hand experience of the obstacles impeding the production and sale of good writing. Gatty's insistence on 'excellence, both in art and literature' may in fact have sounded a death knell for, as Edward Salmon reflected in 1888, *Aunt Judy's Magazine* 'frequently took up a position far above the nursery',[32] and coupled this stance with a refusal, in Margery Lang's analysis, to 'adopt the popular formulae that earned huge sales' (p. 52). As the periodical's publisher conceded, 'its appeal was to a rather select class, and it never gained the wider popularity which can only be attained by consulting the tastes of various social levels'.[33]

Unlike her ailing mother, Juliana Horatia Ewing had the opportunity to embrace new trends as an author as well as a critic. Her first offering to *Aunt Judy's* was the opening story in *Mrs Overtheway's Remembrances*, which Humphrey Carpenter praises as 'a pioneer book in its portrayal of childhood as a state of perception, a special way of observing and reacting to ordinary surroundings'.[34] Like Mrs Overtheway, Ewing 'remembered distinctly many of the unrecognised vexations, longings, and disappointments of childhood' (p. 32), and in this lay the foundation of her literary achievement. Her stories for young readers are unaffected, authentic and in them, Gillian Avery argues, 'we probably get as near to what the real mid-Victorian child was like as it is possible to get in children's fiction'.[35] In the welter of little prigs and saints, sinful boys and sentimental girls, Ewing's fresh approach carried her writing to an audience beyond nursery walls.

Mrs Ewing's willingness to experiment creatively and to seek new audiences, coupled with her reluctance to abide by staid mid-Victorian literary conventions, brought difficulties similar to those *Aunt Judy's Magazine* encountered. In an age when respected commentators like Miss Yonge differentiated readers by social class, Ewing's sophisticated stories were deemed suitable for upper middle-class nurseries only. Yonge found her 'country stories' especially problematic, 'too delicately worked for the ordinary style of children or the poor' who were traditionally presumed to respond to rural subjects.[36] Although Gillian Avery argues from this that books like *Lob Lie-by-the-Fire*, *Jan of the Windmill* and *Daddy Darwin's Dovecot* are Ewing's 'unique contribution to children's literature', other critics have partially supported the tenor of Yonge's view.[37] In a market where country tales 'were specifically intended for the cottager's child, and were usually designed to point a simple moral',[38] Ewing's complex tales show 'touches of *Silas Marner* and *Cranford*, and seem to be addressed chiefly to a grown-up audience'.[39] They sit more easily with rural literature produced for a general readership by the North American 'local color' or the Scottish Kailyard schools, than they do with children's books.

In this respect, these country books betray Ewing's literary anxiety. Mrs Gatty's status and success opened doors for her literary daughter, and *Aunt Judy's Magazine* was a convenient repository, but working for the family firm bound her to a readership and a remit that could be restrictive. For example, *Daddy Darwin's Dovecot*, which Ewing considered her 'best and tersest and most finished writing', had the potential to put her on the map as a Yorkshire novelist to rival the Brontës, but only if her adult readers supplanted juvenile ones.[40] Whether Ewing's ambition was clipped by convention, by illness, by fear or by finance, the 'sacrifice' needed to 'emerge' from her mother's nest seems one she was ultimately unable to make. Nonetheless, it would be a mistake to see Ewing as a one trick pony. While she never believed herself to be greater than a 'small writer', Mrs Ewing did not stand still in her literary groove and, as she set about 'improving as time goes on', the changes she made, in subject, in theme and in style, offer insights into the craft of a popular writer.

The Dickensian Christmas nightmare central to 'Melchior's Dream' is an early indication that this 'Aunt Judy' could find moral worth in a story that was 'not too true' (p. 18). In January 1869, possibly wishing for motherhood, though invalidism probably proscribed this, Ewing's thoughts turned to 'household stories' and she began to write fairy tales consistent with her own theories on archetypes and style. These were to be tested on *Aunt Judy's* 'nursery critics' and were published anonymously to encourage unbiased criticism. The eighteen stories published by the SPCK as *Old-Fashioned Fairy Tales* first appeared between 1869 and 1876, the majority before 1873. These tales of weavers and princes, fools and knaves, wise women and grasping farmers, magicians and angels were, Ewing later explained in her preface, 'a scrupulous endeavour to conform to tradition in local colour and detail' through employing 'ideas and types, occurring in the myths of all countries' (p. vii). With origins in oral tradition, she took care to write them as 'tales that are told' and to avoid 'a discursive or descriptive style of writing' (p. viii).

The folktales of the Grimms, of Andersen and of Ludwig Bechstein in particular, inspired Ewing, although her anthology alternated tales of a continental antecedence with those grounded in British folk beliefs. 'The Laird and the Man of Peace', for example, combines Celtic fairy lore with the traditional motif of three wishes squandered foolishly. When lost in a mist, the Laird of Brockburn finds his incredulity exploited by a fairy who grants wishes which see the Laird's home transported to the bleak hillside, then back to its original situation, where, finding his fabulous story dismissed, the final wish is wasted in making the fairy reappear. 'The Magic Jar' is markedly European: the hero's appreciation of beauty and lack of anti-Semitism (a Bechstein influence) is rewarded with a jar that bestows riches and flowers and, by chance, kingship. In 'The Widows and the Strangers', a covetous woman reaps as she sows and the message is Christian. In the less conventional 'The Ogre Courting', the spirited 'Managing Molly' outwits a giant with a predilection for marrying notable, short women.

Despite Christian lessons in generosity, patience, thoughtfulness, tolerance and resourcefulness, Mrs Ewing detected enough resistance to traditional tales, even in 1882, to considered it prudent to outline her motives. She insisted in her preface that fairy tales were valuable reading that did not 'confuse children's ideas of truth' for 'in childhood we appreciate the distinction [between fancy and falsehood] with a vivacity which, as elders, our care-clogged memories fail to recall' (p. viii). In fact, she believed folktales taught the 'first principles' of morality, and did so in wider settings than the narrow confines of the nursery. Fairy tales could 'foster sympathy with nature' and 'love of animals' and, most importantly, 'cultivate the Imagination' (p. ix).

Mrs Ewing's scheme may have had a nostalgic tint that harked back to her own nursery days. The children in 'Friedrich's Ballad' in *Melchior's Dream* are so attached to their only 'Märchen-Frau' collection that they hide the book for a time in the hope of refreshing their excitement in the old stories. More pertinently, Ewing was returning to the basics of storytelling. But her desire for anonymity may have been intended to distance these stories from her mother's whimsical and moralising fairies. With these folktales Mrs Ewing starts establishing her independent existence as a children's writer and as commentator on what juvenile literature should do. Her contention that children's imaginations were better served by tales of sprites and giants than they were by either out-dated didacticism or the fashionable 'real life' sensations that give Reginald Dacre nightmares 'like the columns of a provincial newspaper' is not entirely original but not entirely Mrs Gatty either.[41]

This is supported by the fact that Juliana Ewing next began to break and bend the principles of folktales in fantasies that innovate around tradition and invent new 'properties' for contemporary settings. The genesis of this belongs also to Canada where separation from Gatty seems to have stimulated Ewing's creativity. Although Carolyn Sigler selects 'Amelia and the Dwarfs' for her collection of *Alternative Alices* (1997), the superficial links are stronger between Carroll and the first of Ewing's fancies, 'The Land of Lost Toys' (1869). In the central lesson, told to a boy who smashes his sister's toys in a pretending earthquake, Aunt Penelope recalls her adventures when she disappears down a hole in a tree where in childhood she believed the fairies lived. In this entomological *Alice*, a talking beetle leads Penelope to the land toys go to when broken or forgotten, where her own discarded playthings, presided over by judge Jack-in-the-Box, try her for misuse under the 'strict law of tit for tat'.[42] She escapes the nonsense court, and the threat of gruesome punishments, under the care of a doll she treasured. After Penelope falls asleep she wakes back in the woods, the episode, like Alice's journey to Wonderland, revealed to be a dream.

Although intended to teach Sam to respect his own and Dot's possessions, the dream story is more complex, chilling and thoughtful than this simple moral suggests. Penelope herself is a puzzling character. A favourite (and childless) aunt with a bag of gifts, a repertoire of stories and a mania for toyshops, she belongs neither in youth nor in adulthood, like the ghostly childhood toys that never entirely disappear. If toys are the props of children's fancies – and the lost toys have all perished in inventive ways, making them as frightening as Christina Rossetti's 'Speaking Likenesses' – then Penelope's story urges the reader to treasure the imagination but warns about its fragility, even its possible corruption and excess. 'Christmas Crackers' (1869–70) shares this menacing edge: an uncanny tutor mesmerises Christmas guests with incense and firecrackers, releasing their secret longings and fears and leaving them bewildered and unsettled by their imaginative journeys.

Amelia in 'Amelia and the Dwarfs' (1870) is another reluctant traveller. Amelia is a 'peevish, selfish, wilful, useless, and ill-mannered little miss' with little hope of maturing into anything other than a selfish, ill-mannered woman until she steals out to the hay fields one night and disappears.[43] With roots firmly in folk tradition – as Ulrich Knoepflmacher identifies, it derives from an Irish source, 'Wee Meg Barnileg' – Amelia's story is told as an oral tale handed down through female generations. Ewing also employs archetypal motifs such as dwarfs, full moons and four-leafed clovers, and juxtaposes the extremes of south and north, drawing-room and countryside, humans and animals, masters and servants. Captured by dwarfs and taken underground, Amelia is forced to make amends for her brattish behaviour by washing and darning the clothes she has ruined, mending the objects she has smashed and picking up the threads of all the conversations she has broken. Unfortunately the reformed Amelia becomes too useful for the dwarfs to take her back, but she engineers her own escape, aided by the dwarfs' ageing housemaid, through distracting her captors with her dancing.

'Amelia' is interesting on several levels. Unlike 'The Land of Lost Toys', the 'real' scenes are as intriguing as the fantasy ones, so much so, indeed, that Mrs Gatty thought her daughter had found a 'vocation' in merging the domestic with 'supernatural machinery'.[44] The tale is a witty social satire: on the fluttering mother and her hysteria when Amelia is, deservedly, bitten by the sensible bulldog; on the hypocrisy of those who ostensibly tolerate Amelia's misbehaviour; on drawing-room culture in general and its harm to women in particular. The tale has surprising sexual undercurrents. Like the little men in Rossetti's *Goblin Market*, Ewing's dwarfs are predatory and salacious, none more so than Amelia's dancing partner, whose 'shoe-points were very much in the way' when they waltzed closely (p. 226). Snatched and returned at full moon in a place where courting couples tryst, Amelia is initially powerless but learns how to be desirable and manipulate the little men with her feminine ways. As this suggests, Amelia herself is captivating. She may be 'the most tiresome girl in that or any other neighbourhood' (p. 198) but it is as difficult for readers not to like her as it is for Ewing not to form a 'tacit alliance' with her fellow 'ironist'.[45] As readers we sympathise with Amelia when, known now by the diminutive 'Amy', she re-enters her mother's tiresome orbit and shut the pages hoping for some future rebellion, imagining Amelia, like Amabel in *Jan of the Windmill*, embarking on adulthood with 'her energetic, straight-forward spirit … in continual revolt' (p. 379).

As her parents accept a sickly changeling and are unaware of her disappearance, Amelia's adventures are dismissed by adults as feverish delusion, as is a boy's story of a journey to the moon in 'Benjy in Beastland' (1870). ('Beastland', like 'the land of lost toys', is a reformatory and tribunal, where Benjy is cured of torturing animals.) Indeed, only 'Timothy's Shoes' (1870–71) does not have the fantastic undermined in this fashion, although this boy's trials with magic shoes designed to keep him on the straight and narrow betrays its cynical side in the form of a pedestrian fairy godmother who declares, 'the experience of many centuries has almost convinced us poor fairies that extraordinary gifts are not necessarily blessings'.[46] This world-weariness, where fairies verge on the point of disappearing but never quite go, is a touchstone of fairy belief, and not necessarily, as Knoepflmacher concludes when the shoes leave the family, Ewing bidding 'farewell to the genre she helped to revitalize'.[47]

Nevertheless, except for a handful of old-fashioned tales, Mrs Ewing stopped writing this kind of story after 1873. Her motives are unclear.

Margaret Gatty died in October of that year, and lacking her support while facing Rex's resistance, perhaps, for he disliked 'Lost Toys', Ewing may just have abandoned the project. Gatty's death must have thrown the future of *Aunt Judy's Magazine* into the balance, potentially removing an easy channel to publication, yet releasing Ewing from her obligations to its subscribers. Mrs Ewing's fantastic tales were intricate and witty enough to carry her work to the adult readers she sought. Yet, paradoxically, this crossover unsettled her. Ewing thought 'Christmas Crackers' had 'gone quite near the wind' where ideas of children's stories were concerned,[48] and had to 'soften Benjy down a bit' to 'make him less repulsive'.[49] Mrs Ewing seems unsure that 'honest pennies' could be brought from such imaginings and from the threatening lands she had journeyed to.

There is one other possibility. Gillian Avery argues that 'the book that has the most magic in it, that one tends to think of as one of the fairy stories, is a book that is purely domestic – *Mrs Overtheway's Remembrances*'.[50] The opening chapter is explicitly set in a world restricted to real possibilities, for although Ida reads fairy tales she understands that 'a travelling companion who expands into a bridge on an Emergency is not to be met with everyday' (p. 17). The magic here springs from imaginative journeys, not to lands of dancing dwarfs or talking toys, but to other homes. Literally a 'domestic' tale, the first four stories visit houses over which romance has grown like ivy: the home of the old woman 'over the way'; of Mrs Overtheway's neighbour, Mrs Moss; the strange bedroom at a friend's home; 'Reka Dom', the Russian river house. The final, and weakest, episode follows Ida's father, who is presumed drowned, home from foreign lands.

While these stories enter the homes that get 'almost bound with one's life' (p. 200) they also break their spell. A young beauty ages into a grotesque with a 'hooked nose, black eyes that smouldered in their sockets, and a distinct growth of beard upon her chin (p. 59), like the fairy-tale characters grown old in Mrs Gaskell's 'Curious, if True' (1860). In 'The Snoring Ghosts' the hosts prove patronising and the ghosts are owls up the spout. Enchanting Mrs Overtheway is really called Mary Smith. If the book has a lesson it comes with the reappearance of Ida's father from 'Kerguelen's Land': things we are told are true can be false, and sometimes the true things must be told fancifully if we are to understand them. So popular were these stories with adults that there were complaints when a gap appeared in their serialisation. Ewing never wrote a second series, although she wanted to, but it seems that this style of book – which Louisa Molesworth thought ideal for that 'indefinite age ... when maidens begin to look down upon "regular children's stories," and novels are as yet forbidden' (p. 506) – came closer to a safe formula for wider success than her experimental fantasies did.[51]

Certainly Mrs Ewing's fiction began to tread a more realistic path. As her upbringing in rural Ecclesfield had been somewhat unconventional, however, it inspired something distinctive in domestic and nursery fiction. Ewing confessed herself 'an absolute, hopeless, unredeemable stick at mere middle class modern life' and, when requesting an illustration for *Jackanapes*, cautioned Caldecott against sending scenes of a 'rising young family in sandboots and frilled trousers with an overfed mercantile mamma'.[52] For all Juliana Ewing's religious and social conservatism, her days in literary circles, army camps and other people's homes, supplemented her instinct for the unusual with a degree of detachment from bourgeois conventions and frills.

Ewing's portraits of childhood also acknowledged their debt to Wordsworthian philosophy and are anchored in the Romantic belief that children were blessed with uncommon insight, that the incidents of childhood were precious and vital in themselves, and that adults should be guided by remembrance of earlier days. The narrator of *Jan of the Windmill* upbraids grown-ups who esteem 'bluff, hearty, charmingly naughty, enviably happy, utterly simple and unsentimental' children and disapprove of those with an artistic nature: 'It is probably from an imperfect remembrance of their nursery lives that some people believe that the griefs of one's childhood are light, its joys uncomplicated, and its tastes simple', when 'simple tastes are rather a result of culture and experience than natural gifts of infancy'. Although 'crude tastes' and 'romance' are 'affectations of nursery days' they are accompanied by 'a very real love of nature', 'a living romance' that creates 'a world apart, peopled with invisible company … or with the beasts and flowers, to which love has given a personality' (pp. 179–80).

This 'world apart', where children were neither genteel miniature adults or incorrigible embodiments of original sin, was recreated by Ewing in two distinct kinds of 'family' tales: short stories written from a child's perspective, and longer *bildungsromans* that recall 'the simple and truthful history of a single mind from childhood'.[53] Two of these longer works are narrated in the first person: in *A Flat-Iron for a Farthing*, Reginald Dacre reflects on his life from infancy to marriage; in *Six to Sixteen* Margery Vandaleur gives an account of her childhood after her parents' death from cholera in India. A third, *Jan of the Windmill*, is a *kunstlerroman* that records the rise of a painter abandoned in babyhood to the care of a poor miller's family. These three books are chiefly episodic, describing formative 'spots of time', but not always successful. Ewing finds it hard to keep her own voice out of Reginald Dacre's narrative, which, in any case, is composed from other people's recollections as much as his own. Additionally, as the only son of a wealthy man, his story is punctuated by cloying social lessons. Reggie's pompous benevolence toward his father's cottagers is absurd and amusing, but Ewing largely supports his view that 'uneducated people and servants have not – as a class – strict ideas on absolute truthfulness and honourable trustworthiness in all matters' (p. 135). The first half of *A Flat-Iron* is not uninteresting, but Reggie is nearer a boy in sandboots and frilled trousers than Ewing might allow.

That Jan Lake is raised at the opposite end of the social spectrum is shown when his foster family are wiped out by cholera, partly because they are too ignorant to accept medical advice. Damning in its indictment of 'the village [childrearing] system of bawling, banging, threatening, cuddling, stuffing, smacking and coarse language' (pp. 90–1), *Jan of the Windmill* adds a confused identity to *A Flat-Iron*'s awkward class-consciousness, for Ewing seems unsure whether the book is a portrait of an artist or, with its foundlings, mysterious parentage, kidnap and rogues, a rural counterpart to *Oliver Twist*. Ultimately, these two books are imperfect companion pieces to Wordsworth's 'Intimations of Immortality', for although Ewing's foot was on her native heath when describing 'the visionary gleam' that Wordsworth wrote of, *A Flat-Iron* and *Jan* are marred by too few childish dreams and too many adult realities, especially when the 'shades of the prison-house begin to close' upon the growing heroes.

Sandwiched between these books, *Six to Sixteen* is superior to both, and more thoughtful and open-minded. Returned to England by a troop of social-climbing army wives, and handed to the guardianship of an equally snobbish aunt, Margery learns to contest the accepted thinking that 'certain vulgar vices, such as cheating, lying, gluttony, petty gossip, malicious mischief-making, etc., are confined to the lower orders ... I have heard polished gentlemen lie, at a pinch, like the proverbial pickpocket, and pretty ladies fib as well as servant-girls' (p. 43). If *Six to Sixteen* is therefore too realistic to 'divide people neatly into the good and the bad' (p. 121), it also has a purpose that prevents cosy reinforcement of the status quo. Although Ewing claims in her preface not to offer 'any complete theory on the vexed question of the upbringing of girls' (p. v), Margery's story extols the benefits of home-education over boarding schools, the out-of-doors over the classroom, sensible shoes over silly footwear, and demonstrates 'that girls' heads not being jam-pots – which if you do not fill them will remain empty – the best way to keep folly out was to put something less foolish in' (p. 169). As well as being a pivotal fictional treatment of female education, *Six to Sixteen* was a highly influential work, inspiring E. Nesbit (the Arkwrights have a dog called Pincher, as do the Bastables), Frances Hodgson Burnett – *The Secret Garden* follows to the Yorkshire moors a girl orphaned in an Indian cholera epidemic – and especially Kipling, who thought it 'a history of real people and real things' which he owed 'more in circuitous ways to … than I can tell'.[54]

Mrs Ewing's shorter family stories chart different territory by introducing ordinary children who are made extraordinary by their 'world apart', 'where their games are of paramount importance'.[55] In this respect, 'A Great Emergency' (1874) is typically named as the most influential on Nesbit of all Ewing's stories, and there may be something of its plot in *The Treasure Seekers*. Rather than restore their family's fallen fortunes, Charlie, Rupert, Henrietta (and Baby Cecil) teach themselves 'how to act with presence of mind in any emergency' such as 'a fire in the house, an epidemic in the neighbourhood, a bite from a mad dog, a chase by a mad bull, broken limbs, runaway horses, a chimney on fire, or a young lady burning to death' (p. 18–19). However, only the opening and closing chapters, especially Rupert's lectures and their reception, are truly reminiscent of Nesbit. As the story's strength lies in the exchanges between domineering Rupert, muffish Charlie and Henrietta the tomboy – and Charlie's communication of these – it ironically becomes rather commonplace when Charlie runs away in search of bigger emergencies.

'A Happy Family' (1883), by contrast, has a vitality that is wholly original, and a narrator who assumes the 'flexible, informal, colloquial' tone Nesbit later uses for that 'complacent Victorian patriarch in embryo', Oswald Bastable.[56] Bayard has assured ideas of his own merit – 'I am the eldest, as I remind my brothers; and of the more worthy gender, which my sisters sometimes forget' – and his siblings' humiliating deficiencies: 'It is not pleasant for a fellow to have a sister who grows up peculiar, as I believe Lettice will'.[57] These children enjoy inspired and reckless play, horrifying a rich relative with their near-naked game of 'Ancient Britons' in an incident reminiscent of the 'Jungle Book' fiasco in *The Wouldbegoods* – 'We had doormats on, as well as powder-blue, but the old lady was terribly shocked, and drove straight away and did not return' (p. 267) – and recreating, with calamitous results, a tableau from a painting of an 'immovable cat, with sparrows on her back, sitting between an owl and a magpie' (p. 267). This tale is plain good fun, with no hard lessons for its children to learn; indeed, by ridiculing the sentimental Victorian painting 'A Happy Family', Ewing's message for young readers may be a radical one.

The moral in 'A Very Ill-Tempered Family'(included in the 1877 collection, *A Great Emergency*) is relatively intrusive, yet this story of an irritable brother and sister is still refreshing, for Philip and Isobel rebuff the many didactic warnings about people who have lost their tempers and regretted it and learn instead from a strange combination of faith and nursery theatricals. 'Our Field' (1876), a dainty and delightful piece where three siblings find a sheltered playground, is a memorable example of Ewing's empathy for children's relationships with their pets, in this case Perronet, the 'nicest possible kind' of dog, whom they count as a fourth sibling.[58] 'Mary's Meadow' (1883–84), Ewing's last serial story, is probably the most successful. Five children – Mary (the narrator), Arthur, Adela, Harry and Chris, whose 'head is rather large for his body, with some water having got into his brain when he was very little' (p. 23) – have little contact with adults (apart from helpful servants) and plenty of freedom in which to befriend the Squire's dog, Saxon, and invent a game that combines dressing-up and role-playing with gardening. In the course of this play, they teach grown-ups about charity, selfishness and pettiness, and learn that children can be in the right: 'We don't believe that Saxon ever was savage; but I daren't say so to the old Squire, for he does not like you to think you know better than he does about anything' (p. 112).

By seeing the world though a child's eyes, and interpreting the world with a child's voice, Mrs Ewing was not only a literary pioneer, she questioned a society that would see but not hear its youngest members. These stories of real children, then, have messages for Victorian adults. The major's wife could be forthright on matters of discipline: in *The Story of a Short Life*, parental reluctance to enforce rules indirectly causes Leonard's death. Yet children are shown to suffer from austerity as much as indulgence, rather unpleasantly in *We and the World*, where a dogmatic father sends brothers Jem and Jack to a schoolmaster who routinely terrifies and abuses them. Outside make-believe like 'Amelia', Mrs Ewing's adult targets are rarely satirised, but receive forceful sideswipes nonetheless, like the Skratdjs in 'Snap-Dragons' (1870): 'I doubt if the parents were ever cured ... bad habits are not easily cured when one is old'.[59] Like Ewing's portraits of 'childhood as a state of perception', the way in which she exposed parental fallibilities was a landmark in children's literature.

The difference between Mrs Ewing's longer 'family' books and her shorter tales is akin to the difference between Kenneth Grahame's *The Golden Age* and *Dream Days* and E. Nesbit's *The Treasure Seekers*. Ewing's novels like *Jan of the Windmill* view childhood from adulthood and, though they exhibit a child's understanding, seem primarily aimed at adult readers. The stories where an authentic child narrator relays the action are fun for children and funny for grown-ups. Why Mrs Ewing's novels of childhood should be unsuccessful overall, and Grahame's widely-acclaimed, is partly a consequence of Ewing's artistic limitations in matters of plot and construction but also her over-reliance on mid-Victorian literary devices and on social mores that fetter her innovative flights. Although written only marginally later in her career, 'A Happy Family' and 'Mary's Meadow', with their energetic, imaginative child-heroes, pre-empt the ground-breaking books of Edwardian writers by giving children a voice and acknowledging that the world of play, the world of experience, was lesson enough and a credible literary subject in its own right.

Yet it was not these tales, but rather Juliana Horatia Ewing's two 'army' books, that made the greater impact on the Victorian popular consciousness. Her sentimental stories of brave 'soldier' heroes are also the most problematic to read today. This is less squeamishness at outmoded jingoism, although Ewing can make us squirm – her poem, 'A Soldier's Children', includes the prayer, 'if the black men kill our men, send down white angels to take their poor dear souls to heaven' – than difficulty in imagining *Aunt Judy's* young readers gaining any enjoyment from *The Story of a Short Life*. (*Jackanapes* has a more obvious attraction in the gypsy fair that offsets the military action.) In fact such reservations were voiced nearer Ewing's own time. An 1897 article in *Parents' Review* concluded that 'there are many little girls quivering with sensibility and too keenly responsive to all sadness and pathos, to whom [*The Story of a Short Life*] ought to be a closed book': a later review judged it and *Jackanapes* 'good for parents and not good for children'.[61]

Judith Plotz develops this conclusion in reading *The Story of a Short Life* as a Victorian 'comfort book' implicitly intended for parents seeking consolations from losses of their own. By granting the dying Leonard immortality in a number of 'families' (nuclear, extended, ancestral, military and spiritual) Ewing dignifies and sanctifies the life of a child, no matter how brief.[62] But 'Lætus Sorte Mêâ' was explicitly intended for juvenile reading and illustrates another side of Ewing's understanding of child nature. The passage in *Jan of the Windmill* that pleads the cause of the artistic child, avows that 'the strongest taste for tragedy comes before one's teens, and inclines to the melodramatic' (p. 179). Reginald Dacre, for instance, comforts himself during a severe illness by play-acting 'like a poor person' in giving 'from time to time, directions as to my wishes in the events of my death' (p. 87). In 'Lætus' this morbid capacity finds expression in the Tiresias-like 'Blind Baby', chief-mourner at pretend funerals around the army camp.

With this in mind, *The Story of a Short Life* is not so much an indulgence calculated to profit on adult tastes for lachrymose works in the 'Little Nell tradition'[63] – the grounds on which the story is usually criticised – than it is an attempt to cater for the mawkish sentimentality Ewing supposed thriving in her child audience. (*Aunt Judy Magazine* contained morbid 'progress' reports on the occupants of the Great Ormond Street cots it sponsored.) Nor does the fact that the story ultimately fails to engender much sympathy for the little cripple's fate – except, ironically, when his crutches become 'ready instruments of his impatience to thump the floor with one end, and not infrequently to strike those who offended him with the other' – mean that its lessons on the consequences of not doing as you are told fall on deaf ears.[64] Furthermore, bravery in meeting the challenges of a restricted life is not merely the redemptive act of evangelical literary tradition, but a stirring act of patriotism: children are not too small or powerless to be soldiers for Queen and Country as well as soldiers for Christ.

Jackanapes takes both patriotism and piety from peacetime to the battlefield. As Horatia Eden points out, this novella was written when her sister's time was 'chiefly spent amongst civilian friends and relations' (p. 107) and designed specifically to challenge civilian reaction to the Prince Imperial's death in the Zulu Wars, by demonstrating that 'it was better to die in combat than not to rescue a stricken comrade'.[65] Civilian incomprehension of military life had been part of Ewing's work as long as soldiers themselves. In 'The Peace Egg' (1871) the country people inhabit a time when soldiers seem 'here today and gone to-morrow, you "never know where you have them"; they are probably in debt, possibly married to several women in several countries, and, though they are very courteous in society, who knows how they treat their wives when they drag them off from their natural friends and protectors to distant lands where no one can call them to account' (p. 12). Ewing battles this prejudice with a fictional version of Rex, who shows that 'when a soldier is kind-hearted, he is often a much more helpful and thoughtful and handy husband than any equally well-meaning citizen' (p. 13).

The opening chapter of *Jackanapes* – set some twenty years before the main plot – introduces 'the Black Captain', who flees with Little Miss Jessamine from Goose Green to Gretna Green. (The Captain is no Wickham in truth, but 'the unnecessary incident of the elopement' was enough to shock Miss Yonge.)[66] Although he is sanctified by death at Waterloo, some locals hold to their opinion that 'a soldier ... is a bloodthirsty, unsettled sort of a rascal; that the peaceable, home-loving, bread-winning citizen can never conscientiously look on as a brother, till he has beaten his sword into a ploughshare, and his spear into a pruning-hook' (p. 14). This thinking is gradually undermined in the story of two little boys, Theodore ('Jackanapes', the Black Captain's son) and Tony Johnson, who grow up to be soldiers. Hapless Tony is unseated in battle, but rather than leave him dying, Jackanapes and Lollo his horse return to save him. When Jackanapes is fatally wounded during the rescue, their fellow soldiers, Goose Green, and Ewing's readers ask, was the life of a mediocre soldier worth the sacrifice of a superior man? Yet the question is itself a blind: Jackanapes' actions are not so much the work of a brother officer, or Christ-like figure, but a friend who remains faithful to the comrade who enlisted with him.

Jackanapes is a more satisfying read than 'Lætus Sorte Mêa', not because the death-scene is less lachrymose, although it is, and not because Jackanapes is a more appealing hero than Leonard, although this is also true. It is not even that the battlefield can provide more dramatic tension than the army camp. Although Salmon links Ewing to Louisa May Alcott, arguing each is 'strongest when tempering her domesticity with the arbitrament of war' (p. 132), the reverse seems to be true here; the soldier is domesticated, and this is *Jackanapes*'s merit. It is not military codes that make Jackanapes a hero, or army discipline, or having the example of a brave 'V.C.' to emulate as Leonard does. The values that make him a hero are learned from the Postman, his grandfather the General, and especially his great-aunt Miss Jessamine, for 'Jackanapes (who had a boy's full share of the little beast and the young monkey in his natural composition) was none the worse, at his tender years, for learning some maidenliness – so far as maidenliness means decency, pity, unselfishness, and pretty behaviour' (p. 25).

The story was bound in Union Jack book covers, but its patriotism celebrates, not a soldier who dies for his country, but a peaceable, home-loving woman who raises a man brave enough to die for a friend. Writing of *Six to Sixteen*, Judith Rowbotham argues that Mrs Ewing tried 'to reconcile her readers to the conventional view of the role that women could play' in 'the continuance of Empire' despite her 'personal experience of the darker side of involvement' in being a soldier's wife.[67] *Jackanapes*, too, might seem to promote this conservative message, were it not that Miss Jessamine stands outside conventional womanhood (and society) as represented by Mrs Johnston or the dim-witted Grey Goose who 'had a very small head, and when one idea got into it there was no room for another' (p. 12). That Jackanapes has not been spoiled by Miss Jessamine's care is an alternative view of the manliness so prized in Victorian society.

Because these tales were Mrs Ewing's most famous and the last that she wrote, to the public mind at least, she was presumed to have found her literary niche in army life. Horatia Eden contested this, concluding that 'whatever class of men she was mixed with, she could not help throwing herself into their interests, and weaving romances about them' (p. 125). Mrs Ewing certainly loved soldiers – the Royal Engineers in particular according to green-eyed Dame Ethel – but wrote of them only when she was outside soldiering life: her army stories are more elegiac than imperialist in tone. At their heart *Jackanapes* and *The Story of a Short Life* promote the thinking that the army camp, 'military life in epitome ... represents, as no other phase of society represents, the human pilgrimage in brief'.[68]

In the final analysis, this was, perhaps, the army's main attraction to a writer who valued brevity above all else. Mrs Ewing 'clipped, condensed and pruned her style', Maxwell writes, 'like the complete miniaturist'.[69] 'Word-painting is such a pleasure,' Ewing explained, 'like playing a game of skill – to me – and I take such minute pains, and cut and polish, that no praise is so pleasant as the flattery that the word-painting has fallen artistically on the reader's ears!'[70] Although these values are not universal in her serials, partly because 'she wrote from month to month, and had no opportunity of correcting the composition as a *whole*',[71] she always prized condensation and doubted 'if one should ever leave less than fifty per cent of a situation to one's readers' own imagination, if one aims to the highest class of readers'.[72]

Children, or young girls anyhow, still have one way to Mrs Ewing. Her story, 'The Brownies', of two brothers who learn from a wise old owl to be useful in the home was adopted by Lord Baden Powell for the junior branch of the Girl Guides and became to Brownie Guides what Kipling's *Jungle Books* are to the Cub Scouts.[73] But this is an exception. Juliana Horatia Ewing's longer works have disappeared from children's bookshelves. A number of her fantasies have been anthologised more recently and included on university syllabi, strengthening their claim to being Ewing's most original, and subversive, work: this also suggests, conversely, that her domestic, country and army books – the forgotten books – cannot easily be resurrected for modern tastes.

Thus twentieth-century critics have been obliged to account for Mrs Ewing's decline in popularity. Harvey Darton concludes that her very strength, her realism of detail and character, 'automatically reduces the breadth of her appeal to later generations'.[74] Writing in the early 1950s, Anne Eaton finds Ewing's books too 'slow and uneventful' for the tastes of post-war children.[75] John Townsend considers that, despite a 'varied and respectable output' none of her stories 'have the vitality that will carry a book on through changing times and tastes'.[76] The *Oxford Companion to Children's Literature* highlights the 'thinness of plot' in Ewing's longer works, with their 'stock devices' of 'foundlings, orphans, and early deaths'. Importantly, Carpenter and Pritchard also point out that 'none of her books has become a classic'.[77] This last explanation may be the most convincing, for children's books can endure as classics even if their appeal to young readers wanes. No one Ewing book was vastly more popular than the others, nor vastly better received. The stories that sold the most were the army tales, and the country tales that date most easily and are hardest to classify as books for children, even in the context of their own day. And finally, for all that Mrs Ewing's fictional children are 'real', no individual child leaps off her page as the heroes and heroines of children's classics do.

Of course many once-acclaimed and influential authors go unread today. One problem in assessing Juliana Ewing's legacy, however, comes when differentiating between critical and popular success. Reviewers considered Mrs Ewing above the common herd, but children did not write reviews and such evidence as exists casts doubt on her popularity with children. Edward Salmon's snapshot of juvenile reading habits drew conclusions from an 1884 survey of some one thousand girls, aged eleven to nineteen, on their favourite books and authors. Salmon is not one to take results at face value – he judges that girls, but, curiously, not boys, were prone to list the authors they felt they *should* like – but in concluding that Mrs Ewing's name was 'among the most popular on the tongues and in the hearts of young people' when only one girl named Ewing – and a hundred named Miss Yonge – Salmon argued against the evidence entirely.[78]

Roger Lancelyn Green is correct to write of Ewing's books that 'critics of the seventies must have looked on amazed to see children's stories turned out that were works of literature'.[79] But faced with of a good deal of bad writing were these opinions projected onto children, conferring on Ewing a mantle that she did not have, either in sales or juvenile estimation? In an 1886 appreciation for *The Contemporary Review*, Mrs Molesworth sets *Jackanapes* and *The Story of a Short Life* aside as 'so well known, so universally loved, that they may indeed be spoken of as "household words" (p. 504), and turns to less familiar stories, a suggestion that the popularity of Ewing's earlier books had dipped in her own lifetime. To this end, Gillian Avery contends that Ewing's books, along with Elizabeth Sewell's and

Louisa Molesworth's, were never 'truly popular'.[80] Although bought and read in thousands, Ewing's stories were neither true best-sellers nor, in their erudition, could they be of universal appeal. Ewing acknowledged these limitations. She worried that her volumes were more highly priced than other children's books. Her letters to Caldecott resound with what he called her 'warfare with publishers and book producers',[81] yet her eagerness to publish her stories for the Christmas market, say, and with a minimum of 'detail worry' to herself, meant she often acquiesced to publishers or let her printer 'fleece [her] a little':[82] she did not wield the power a more popular author would.

Juliana Horatia Ewing's writing life is a story of experimentation, in improving gradually, in achieving popular success, in writing for 'the higher flight', where Ewing fluctuates between dissatisfaction and contentment with her literary 'donkey-cart'. She was not as small a writer as she thought, but she could be a frustrated big writer, and her works for children gave her most happiness when they moved adults. Like the hero of *Lob Lie-By-The-Fire* she had to learn that it was 'not cockatoos only who have sometimes to live and be happy in this unfinished life with one wing clipped' (p. 101). Paradoxically, with this literary fate, Mrs Ewing achieved a reputation as an outstanding author and innovator in juvenile fiction. In their realism, their originality and their magic, Juliana Ewing's stories hold kernels of inspiration for readers and other children's writers that make them impossible to ignore. In this sense her legacy has indeed proved to be the 'fifty per cent' she aspired to leave to her 'readers' own imagination'; as Horatia Eden perceived, the 'lights she "left out"' were 'some of the most striking points in her work' (pp. 17–18).

Notes

Citations from Juliana Horatia Ewing's works are taken from the eighteen-volume *Complete Works of Juliana Horatia Ewing* published by the SPCK between 1894 and 1896. The eighteenth volume, H. K. F. Eden's *Juliana Horatia Ewing and Her Books*, includes the fullest published bibliography of Ewing's stories, novels and poems.

1   Margaret Howard Blom and Thomas E. Blom (eds), *Canada Home: Juliana Horatia Ewing's Fredericton Letters 1867–1869* (Vancouver, BC: University of British Columbia Press, 1983), p. 98.
2   Cited in Horatia. K. F. Eden, *Juliana Horatia Ewing and her Books*, *Complete Works of Juliana Horatia Ewing*, vol. 18 [1885] (London: SPCK, 1896), p. 133. Subsequent page references are given in the text.

3   Mrs Molesworth, 'Juliana Horatia Ewing', *The Contemporary Review*, 49 (May 1886), pp. 675–86 in Lance Salway (ed.), *A Peculiar Gift: Nineteenth-Century Writings on Books for Children* (London: Kestrel Books, 1976), pp. 503–16, p. 505.
4   See Peter Millington, 'Mrs Ewing and the Textual Origin of the St Kitt's Mummies' Play', *Folklore*, 107 (1996), 77–89.
5   Eden, *Juliana Horatia Ewing*, p. 118.
6   Gillian Avery, *Nineteenth-Century Children: Heroes and Heroines in English Children's Stories, 1780–1900* (London: Hodder & Stoughton, 1965), p. 157.
7   Juliana Horatia Ewing, 'Margaret Gatty' in Margaret Gatty, *Parables from Nature, By Margaret Gatty, With a Memoir by her Daughter, Juliana Horatia Ewing*, First Series (London: George Bell and Sons, 1885), p. xxi.
8   'A Bit of Green', (July 1861); 'A Blackbird's Nest', (August 1861); 'Melchior's Dream', *Monthly Packet* (December 1861).
9   'Friedrich's Ballad' and 'The Viscount's Friend' were added: a new edition published by George Bell and Sons in 1885 – the partnership of Bell and Daldy lasted only from 1854–72 – also included 'The Yew Lane Ghosts', 'A Bad Habit' and 'A Happy Family'.
10 Juliana Horatia Ewing, Letter to Margaret Gatty, 2 March 1869, Blom and Blom (eds), *Canada Home*, p. 270.
11 Juliana Horatia Ewing, Preface to *Old-Fashioned Fairy Tales*, *Complete Works*, vol. 3, p. vii.
12 Juliana Horatia Ewing, Letter to Edward Bell, 3 December 1884, cited in Edward Bell, *George Bell Publisher, A Brief Memoir* (London: Chiswick Press, 1924), p. 89.
13 Bell, *George Bell Publisher*, p. 89.
14 Cited in Christabel Maxwell, *Mrs Gatty and Mrs Ewing* (London: Constable, 1949), pp. 222–3.
15 Gillian Avery, *Mrs Ewing* (London: Bodley Head, 1961), p. 21.
16 Brian Alderson, 'Tracts, Rewards and Fairies: The Victorian contribution to children's literature', in Asa Briggs (ed.), *Essays in the History of Publishing* (London: Longman, 1974), p. 266.
17 U. C. Knoepflmacher, *Ventures into Childland: Victorians, Fairy Tales and Femininity* (Chicago, IL: University of Chicago Press, 1998), p. 381.
18 George Bell's son later decided this tactic was counter-productive as the publication 'had to depend for its existence on a continuous accession of new supporters who were not necessarily familiar with its original', Bell, *George Bell Publisher*, p. 54.
19 Mrs Alfred Gatty, *The Fairy Godmothers, and other tales* (London: George Bell, 1851), Preface.
20 Knoepflmacher, *Ventures into Childland*, p. 381.
21 Mrs Alfred Gatty, *Parables from Nature* (London: Bell and Daldy, 1855), pp. x–xi.
22 Juliana Horatia Ewing, 'In Memoriam Margaret Gatty', *Miscellanea, Complete*

Works, vol. 17, p. 186.

23 Marjory Lang, 'Childhood's Champions: mid-Victorian Children's Periodicals and their Critics', *Victorian Periodicals Review*, 13:1 and 2 (Spring and Summer 1980), 17–31, 24. Subsequent page references are given in the text.

24 *Aunt Judy's Magazine*, 1:1 (May 1866), 1–2.

25 Alderson, 'Tracts, Rewards and Fairies', p. 255, p. 257

26 F. J. Harvey Darton, *Children's Books in England: Five Centuries of Social Life*, 1932 (London: British Library and Oak Knoll Press, 1999), p. 268, p. 269.

27 *Aunt Judy's Magazine*, 1:2 (June 1866), 123. Subsequent page references are given in the text.

28 Gatty praised *The Water Babies* but criticised Kingsley's scientific inaccuracies.

29 *Aunt Judy's Magazine*, 13:104 (1875), 123.

30 Avery, *Nineteenth-Century Children*, p. 152.

31 *Aunt Judy's Magazine*, 13:105 (1875), 187–8; no. 110 (1875), 509.

32 Edward Salmon, *Juvenile Literature as it is* (London: Henry J. Drane, 1888), p. 201.

33 Bell, *George Bell Publisher*, p. 54.

34 Humphrey Carpenter, *Secret Gardens: A Study of the Golden Age of Children's Literature* [1985] (London: Unwin Hyman, 1987), p. 104.

35 Avery, *Nineteenth-Century Children*, p. 150.

36 Charlotte M. Yonge, *What Books to Lend and What to Give* (London: National Society's Depository, 1887), p. 38.

37 Avery, *Mrs Ewing*, p. 57.

38 Avery, *Mrs Ewing*, p. 57.

39 Carpenter, *Secret Gardens*, p. 104.

40 Carpenter, *Secret Gardens*, p. 60. (*Daddy Darwin's Dovecot* is included in *Jackanapes and Other Tales*.)

41 Juliana Horatia Ewing, *A Flat-Iron for a Farthing, Complete Works*, vol. 4, p. 14. Subsequent page references are given in the text.

42 Juliana Horatia Ewing, 'The Land of Lost Toys', *The Brownies and other Tales*, *Complete Works*, vol. 5, p. 111.

43 Juliana Horatia Ewing, 'Amelia and the Dwarfs', *The Brownies and other Tales*, p. 220. Subsequent page references are given in the text.

44 Maxwell, *Mrs Gatty and Mrs Ewing*, p. 185.

45 Knoepflmacher, *Ventures into Childland*, p. 401.

46 Juliana Horatia Ewing, 'Timothy's Shoes', *Lob Lie-By-The-Fire and other Tales*, *Complete Works*, vol. 7, p. 112.

47 Knoepflmacher, *Ventures into Childland*, p. 415.

48 Maxwell, *Mrs Gatty and Mrs Ewing*, p. 185.

49 Juliana Horatia Ewing, Letter to Margaret Gatty, 22 March 1870, Eden, *Juliana Horatia Ewing*, p. 186.

50 Avery, *Mrs Ewing*, p. 75.

51 Juliana Horatia Ewing, Letter to Margaret Gatty, 2 March 1869, *Canada Home*, p. 270.

52 Juliana Horatia Ewing, Letter to R. Caldecott, 4 August 1879, in Michael Hutchins (ed.), *Yours Pictorially: Illustrated Letters of Randolph Caldecott* (London: Frederick Warne and Co. Ltd., 1976), p. 75.

53 Juliana Horatia Ewing, *Six to Sixteen*, *Complete Works*, vol. 6, p. 12. Subsequent page references are given in the text.

54 Rudyard Kipling, *Something of Myself for my Friends Known and Unknown* [1937] (London: Macmillan, 1981), p. 7.

55 Avery, *Nineteenth-Century Children*, p. 155.

56 Julia Briggs, 'Women Writers and Writing for Children: From Sarah Fielding to E. Nesbit', in Gillian Avery and Julia Briggs (eds), *Children and Their Books: a Celebration of the Work of Iona and Peter Opie* (Oxford: Clarendon Press, 1989), pp. 221–50, p. 244, p. 245.

57 Juliana Horatia Ewing, 'A Happy Family', *Melchior's Dream and other Tales*, p. 261, p. 273.

58 Juliana Horatia Ewing, 'Our Field', *A Great Emergency and other Tales*, *Complete Works*, vol. 11, p. 238.

59 Juliana Horatia Ewing, 'Snap-Dragons', *The Peace Egg and other Tales*, *Complete Works*, vol. 10, p. 148.

60 Juliana Horatia Ewing, 'A Soldier's Children', (July 1879), *Verses for Children*, *Complete Works*, vol. 9, p. 125.

61 Ronald McNeill, 'The Choice of Literature for the Young', *Parents' Review*, 8:9 (September 1897), 561–8; 624–30; Mrs. Crump, 'Living Books for the Nursery', *Parents' Review*, 14:12 (December 1903), 944–53.

62 Judith A. Plotz, 'A Victorian Comfort Book: Juliana Ewing's *The Story of a Short Life*', in John Holt McGavran Jr. (ed.), *Romanticism and Children's Literature in Nineteenth-Century England* (Athens, GA: University of Georgia Press, 1991), pp. 168–89.

63 Sheila A. Egoff, *Children's Periodicals of the Nineteenth Century: A Survey and Bibliography* (London: The Library Association, 1951), p. 16.

64 Juliana Horatia Ewing, *The Story of a Short Life*, *Jackanapes and other Tales*, *Complete Works*, vol. 15, p. 187.

65 Maxwell, *Mrs Gatty and Mrs Ewing*, p. 209.

66 Yonge, *What Books to Lend*, p. 33.

67 Judith Rowbotham, *Good Girls Make Good Wives: Guidance for Girls in Victorian Fiction* (Oxford: Basil Blackwell, 1989), pp. 189–90.

68 Ewing, *The Story of a Short Life*, *Jackanapes and other Tales*, p. 145.

69 Maxwell, *Mrs Gatty and Mrs Ewing*, p. 197.

70 Juliana Horatia Ewing, Letter to Mrs Smyth, 20 November 1881, Ethel Smyth, *Impressions that Remained*, vol. 2 (London: Longmans, Green and Co., 1919), p. 48.

71 Eden, *Juliana Horatia Ewing*, pp. 17–18.

72 Juliana Horatia Ewing, Letter to Major Ewing, 21 February 1880, Eden, *Juliana Horatia Ewing*, pp. 217–18.

73 Since the 1940s, a bowdlerised version of Ewing's tale, substituting one of

the brothers with a girl, has been included in the Brownie Guide Handbook.
74 Darton, *Children's Books*, p. 285.
75 Conversely, Eaton points out that the BBC had recently broadcast children's versions of *Jackanapes* and *Jan of the Windmill*, Anne Eaton, 'A Scientist, a Realist, and a Purveyor of Magic', in Cornelia Meigs (ed.), *A Critical History of Children's Literature*, (New York: Macmillan, 1953), p. 186.
76 John Rowe Townsend, *Written for Children* [1965] (Harmondsworth: Penguin, 1974), p. 85.
77 Humphrey Carpenter and Mari Pritchard, *Oxford Companion to Children's Literature* (Oxford: Oxford University Press, 1984), p. 171.
78 Salmon, *Juvenile Literature*, p. 132.
79 Roger Lancelyn Green, *Tellers of Tales* [1946] (Leicester: Edmund Ward Ltd., 1953), p. 92.
80 Gillian Avery, *Childhood's Patterns: A Study of the Heroes and Heroines of Children's Fiction, 1770–1950* (London: Hodder & Stoughton, 1975), p. 123.
81 R. Caldecott, Letter to Juliana Ewing, 22 January 1884, Hutchins, *Yours Pictorially*, p. 108.
82 Juliana Horatia Ewing, Letter to R. Caldecott, 29 November 1884, Hutchins, *Yours Pictorially*, p. 127.

Bibliography

Alderson, Brian, 'Tracts, Rewards and Fairies: the Victorian contribution to children's literature', in Asa Briggs (ed.), *Essays in the History of Publishing in Celebration of the 250th Anniversary of the House of Longman, 1724–1974*, London: Longman, 1974, pp. 245–82.
Auerbach, Nina and U. C. Knoepflmacher (eds), *Forbidden Journeys: Fairy Tales and Fantasies by Victorian Women Writers*, Chicago, IL and London: University of Chicago Press, 1992.
Avery, Gillian, *Childhood's Pattern: A Study of the Heroes and Heroines of Children's Fiction 1770–1950*, London: Hodder & Stoughton, 1975.
—— *Mrs Ewing*, London: Bodley Head, 1961.
—— *Nineteenth-Century Children: Heroes and Heroines in English Children's Stories, 1780–1900*, London: Hodder & Stoughton, 1965.
Bell, Edward, *George Bell Publisher, A Brief Memoir*, London: Chiswick Press, 1924.
Blom, Margaret Howard and Thomas E. Blom (eds), *Canada Home: Juliana Horatia Ewing's Fredericton Letters 1867–1869*, Vancouver, BC: University of British Columbia Press, 1983.
Brambleby, Ailsa, *The Brownie Guide Handbook*, 1968, London: The Girl Guides Association, 1979.
Bratton, J. S., *The Impact of Victorian Children's Fiction*, London: Croom Helm, 1981.
Briggs, Julia, 'Women Writers and Writing for Children: From Sarah Fielding to

E. Nesbit', in Gillian Avery and Julia Briggs (eds), *Children and Their Books: a Celebration of the Work of Iona and Peter Opie*, Oxford: Clarendon Press, 1989, pp. 221–50.

Cadogan, Mary and Patricia Craig, *You're a Brick, Angela! A New Look at Girls' Fiction from 1839–1975*, London: Victor Gallancz, 1976.

Campbell, Ian, *Kailyard*, Edinburgh: Ramsay Head Press, 1981.

Carpenter, Humphrey, *Secret Gardens: A Study of the Golden Age of Children's Literature* [1985] London: Unwin Hyman, 1987.

Carpenter, Humphrey and Mari Pritchard (eds.), *Oxford Companion to Children's Literature*, Oxford: Oxford University Press, 1984.

Collins, Louisa, *Impetuous Heart: The Story of Ethel Smyth*, London: William Kimber, 1984.

Crump, Mrs, 'Living Books for the Nursery', *Parents' Review*, 14:12 (December 1903), 944–53.

Darton, F. J. Harvey, *Children's Books in England: Five Centuries of Social Life*,1932, third edn revised by Brian Alderson, London: British Library and Oak Knoll Press, 1999.

Drotner, Kirsten, *English Children and Their Magazines, 1751–1945*, New Haven, CT and London: Yale University Press, 1988.

Eastwood, Rev. J., *History of the Parish of Ecclesfield, in the County of York*, London: Bell and Daldy, 1862.

Eaton, Anne, 'A Scientist, A Realist and a Purveyor of Magic', in Cornelia Meigs (ed.), *A Critical History of Children's Literature*, New York: Macmillan, 1953.

Eden, Horatia K. F., *Juliana Horatia Ewing and Her Books, Complete Works of Juliana Horatia Ewing*, vol. 18, London: SPCK, 1896.

Egoff, Sheila A., *Children's Periodicals of the Nineteenth Century: A Survey and Bibliography*, London: The Library Association, 1951.

Ewing, Juliana Horatia, *Melchior's Dream and Other Tales, Complete Works of Juliana Horatia Ewing*, vol.1, London: SPCK, 1894.

—— *Mrs Overtheway's Remembrances*, vol.2, London: SPCK, 1894.

—— *Old-Fashioned Fairy Tales*, vol. 3, London: SPCK, 1894.

—— *A Flat-Iron for a Farthing; or, Some Passages in the Life of an Only Son*, vol. 4, London: SPCK, 1894.

—— *The Brownies and Other Tales*, vol. 5, London: SPCK, 1895.

—— *Six to Sixteen: A Story for Girls*, vol. 6, London: SPCK, 1895.

—— *Lob Lie-by-the-fire and Other Tales*, vol. 7, London: SPCK, 1895.

—— *Jan of the Windmill: A Story of the Plains*, vol. 8, London: SPCK, 1895.

—— *Verses for Children and Songs for Music*, vol. 9, London: SPCK, 1895.

—— *The Peace Egg and Other Tales*, vol. 10, London: SPCK, 1895.

—— *A Great Emergency and Other Tales*, vol. 11, London: SPCK, 1895.

—— *Brothers of Pity and Other Tales*, vol. 12, London: SPCK, 1895.

—— *Jackanapes and Other Tales*, vol. 15, London: SPCK, 1896.

—— *Mary's Meadow and Other Tales of Fields and Flowers*, vol. 16, London: SPCK, 1896.

——*Miscellanea*, vol. 17, London: SPCK, 1896.

—— *We and the World: A Book for Boys, Part One*, vol. 13, London: SPCK, 1896.

—— *We and the World: A Book for Boys, Part Two*, vol. 14, London: SPCK, 1896.

Gatty, Mrs Alfred, *Aunt Judy's Tales*, London: Bell and Daldy, 1859.

—— *Aunt Judy's Letters*, London: Bell and Daldy, 1862.

—— *The Fairy Godmothers, and Other Tales*, London: George Bell, 1851.

—— *Parables from Nature*, London: Bell and Daldy, 1855.

Green, Roger Lancelyn, *Tellers of Tales*, Leicester: Edmund Ward Ltd., 1953.

Hoge, James O. (ed.), *The Letters of Emily Lady Tennyson*, University Park, PA: Pennsylvania State University Press, 1974.

Hutchins, Michael (ed.), *Yours Pictorially: Illustrated Letters of Randolph Caldecott*, London: Frederick Warne & Co. Ltd., 1976.

Jay, Elisabeth, '"Ye careless, thoughtless, worldly parents, tremble while you read this history!": the Use and Abuse of the Dying Child in the Evangelical Tradition', in Gillian Avery and Kimberley Reynolds (eds), *Representations of Childhood Death*, Basingstoke: Macmillan, 2000, pp. 111–32.

Kipling, Rudyard, *Something of Myself For My Friends Known and Unknown* [1937] London: Macmillan, 1981.

Knoepflmacher, U.C., *Ventures into Childland: Victorians, Fairy Tales, and Femininity*, Chicago, IL and London: University of Chicago Press, 1998.

Kuznets, Lois Rostow, *When Toys Come Alive: Narratives of Animation, Metamorphosis and Development*, New Haven, CT and London: Yale University Press, 1994.

Lang, Marjory, 'Childhood's Champions: Mid-Victorian Children's Periodicals and the Critics', *Victorian Periodicals Review*, 13:1 and 2 (Spring and Summer 1980), 17–31.

Laski, Margharita, *Mrs Ewing, Mrs Molesworth and Mrs Hodgson Burnett*, London: Arthur Barker, 1950.

McNeill, Ronald, 'The Choice of Literature for the Young', *Parents' Review*, 8:9 (September 1897), 561–8, 624–30.

Marshall, Mrs., 'Mrs Ewing', in Mrs Oliphant and Mrs Linton et al., *Women Novelists of Queen Victoria's Reign*, London: Hurst and Blackett, 1897.

Maxwell, Christabel, *Mrs Gatty and Mrs Ewing*, London: Constable, 1949.

Millington, Peter, 'Mrs Ewing and the Textual Origin of the St Kitts Mummie's Play', *Folklore*, 107 (1996), 77–89.

Molesworth, Mrs, 'Juliana Horatia Ewing', in Lance Salway (ed.), *A Peculiar Gift: Nineteenth-Century Writings on Books for Children*, Harmondsworth: Penguin, 1976, pp. 503–16.

Nesbit, E., *Long Ago When I Was Young* [1966] London: Macdonald, 1974.

Plotz, Judith A., 'A Victorian Comfort Book: Juliana Ewing's *The Story of a Short Life*', in James Holt Mc Gavran, Jr. (ed.), *Romanticism and Children's Literature in Nineteenth-Century England*, Athens, GA: University of Georgia Press, 1991, pp. 168–89.

Rowbotham, Judith, *Good Girls Make Good Wives: Guidance for Girls in Victorian*

Fiction, Oxford: Basil Blackwell, 1989.

Salmon, Edward, *Juvenile Literature as it is*, London: Henry J. Drane, 1888.

Sigler, Carol (ed.), *Alternative Alices: Visions and Revisions of Lewis Carroll's Alice Books: An Anthology*, Lexington, KY: University Press of Kentucky, 1997.

Smyth, Ethel, *Impressions that Remained*, 2 vols, London: Longmans, Green, & Co., 1919.

Townsend, John Rowe, *Written for Children* [1965] Harmondsworth: Penguin, 1974.

Yonge, C. M., *What Books to Lend and What to Give*, London: National Society's Depository, 1887.

Zipes, Jack, *Victorian Fairy Tales: The Revolt of the Fairies and Elves*, New York and London: Methuen, 1987.

7

Writing for the million: The enterprising fiction of Ellen Wood

Marie Riley

A thorough gentlewoman was she in all ways; in appearance, mind and manner. But it seemed to me a great puzzle how she could be so; or being so, that she could have married a tradesman.[1]

When the eponymous Anne Hereford first encounters her relative, Mrs Hempson, a noblewoman who has lost caste through marriage, she finds herself bewildered, both by Mrs Hempson's current standing and the status of the commercial classes she has aligned herself to. The Hempson family's social exclusion in the cathedral town of Dashleigh, like many other occurrences of class mobility in the novels of Ellen Wood, affords an opportunity to affirm that the industrial and industrious bourgeoisie, besides being in possession of their own inherent nobility and accumulated wealth, are often well connected by birth and thus demonstrably fitted to form part of the new social hierarchy. *Anne Hereford* (1868) can be read both as a female *Bildungsroman* and a murder mystery, but like many of Wood's novels serves to construct and reinforce a profile of the burgeoning middle classes for a socially aspirant readership who gained satisfaction in finding their interests and reputation advanced by one of the nineteenth century's most popular and successful writers.

Described by Malcolm Elwin in 1934 as 'the most intrinsically representative woman novelist of the mid-Victorian era',[2] and judged by her contemporary, Henrietta Keddie as 'perhaps more essentially the story-teller of her generation than most of her fellow writers',[3] Wood continues to fascinate modern readers, partly because of her ability to construct a page-turning narrative, but more significantly because her celebration of bourgeois achievement and values appeared to reflect the sensibilities and middle-brow literary tastes of the period. While sources on Wood were once limited, since the early 1990s we have seen an increase of academic interest with recent articles by Deborah Wynne, Emma Liggins, and a reprint of *East Lynne* edited by Andrew Maunder including substantial additional material that has facilitated its place on the curriculum of a number of Victorian Studies courses.[4]

The beneficiary of resurgent interest in sensation fiction and feminist reclamation of neglected women writers, Wood's reputation for conservatism renders her an unlikely recipient of Marxist analysis, but her characteristic interrogation of class boundaries can be read as articulating the ideological struggle of the mercantile middle classes to consolidate their status and cultural identity in a society in a state of flux. Following Jonathan Loesberg's influential article in 1986,[5] many commentators have read *East Lynne* (1861), Wood's most famous and successful novel, as a socio-political fable and much of Wood's other work can similarly be interpreted in this way.

Wood was born Ellen Price, in Worcester in 1814, two months after the hasty marriage of Thomas Price and Elizabeth Evans, and originated from the kind of provincial manufacturing family she habitually evoked in her fiction. The Prices had prospered from their participation in Worcester's two principal industries, gloving and malting, but suffered financial setbacks following the decline in trade when local glove manufacturing was undermined by competition from France as a result of Huskisson's 1826 Reciprocity of Duties Act; a period in Worcester's history that Wood later described in novels such as *Mrs Halliburton's Troubles* (1862) and *Mildred Arkell* (1865). After her marriage in 1836 to Henry Wood, the son of a Cheshire woollen draper, Wood and her husband settled in Boulogne where her husband, assisted by her brother, Henry Price, turned trade regulations to their advantage by importing French gloves back into the British market.[6]

It was in France in the early 1850s where Wood, by now the mother of four children, began her career as a periodical writer, submitting stories and articles to Harrison Ainsworth's *New Monthly Magazine* and later *Bentley's Miscellany*. Her first success in hardcover came with *Danesbury House* (1860) which won her the Scottish Temperance League's annual one hundred pound prize.

The sensational subject matter of her second novel, *East Lynne*, aroused interest even while it was still being serialised, and after being turned down by both Chapman and Hall and Smith and Elder, Wood was finally able to enter the mainstream fiction market by securing a publication deal with Richard Bentley. The impact of *East Lynne* was immediate, even before Samuel Lucas's influential review in *The Times* in January 1862. It was reprinted in November 1861, just two months after publication, and quickly gathered momentum, going into twenty-four editions over the next ten years. Wood's success opened up new markets for her work and she was not slow to take advantage of her opportunities. She began to diversify into other periodicals such as *The Quiver, Once a Week, Good Words* and *The Leisure Hour*, and was soon turning serial runs into three or four hardcover works a year and negotiating deals with a variety of publishers including James Nisbet and Co., Bradbury and Evans, Griffith and Farrar, and Tinsley brothers.

Popular taste, as Wood well understood, could be fickle, but she was willing to test the market with a panoply of products. In her early years as a published novel writer, Wood mixed and matched popular and up-and-coming genres and seasoned them with an additional dash of whatever topic was currently exercising the public imagination, providing the modern reader with a snapshot of mid-century fictional concerns. She served up temperance with *Danesbury House*; dealt with sensation, murder and divorce in *East Lynne*; created a hybrid church and family-orientated detective story in *The Channings* (1862); and utilised a courtroom scene featuring the dramatic testimony of a young woman in *Mrs Halliburton's Troubles*, a popular fictional device following public interest in the celebrated trial of Madeleine Smith in 1857. Apparent bigamy, made fashionable by publicity surrounding the notorious Yelverton trial surfaced in *Verner's Pride* (1863), *Oswald Cray* (1864) and *A Life's Secret* (1867) with the latter doubling as a Condition of England novel. Wood, always inclined to give weight to the power of omens and dreams, added to her repertoire a ghost story, *The Shadow of Ashlydyat* (1863), and for good measure, a boys' adventure tale, *William Allair* (1863).

Wood was widowed in 1866. The following year she acquired the ownership of *The Argosy* from Alexander Strahan and set about repairing the damage caused to the reputation of the family magazine by the serialisation of Charles Reade's scandalous and sensational historical novel *Griffith Gaunt*. A versatile and opportunist writer, she produced over forty books but is largely remembered for *East Lynne*, one of the best-selling novels of the nineteenth century, a book which over one hundred and forty years later, as Maunder confirms, 'remains a compelling read'.[7]

The initial attraction of *East Lynne* is undoubtedly its blatant sentimentality. Wood conducts a merciless assault on her readers' emotions with the story of Lady Isabel Vane, a fragile and naive young wife who deserts her worthy middle-class husband when subject to the attentions of a predatory seducer. Betrayed by her lover and then injured in a railway accident that kills her illegitimate baby, to the repeated refrain of 'never more, never more', Isabel is nudged relentlessly towards her grave. Disguised, disfigured and utterly dispirited, she returns to her marital home to take up employment as governess to her own children, and to preside helplessly over the death of her son. While even in the depths of her grief, she is forced to accede to the primacy of her usurper, a woman who has taken legal and emotional possession of the husband that Isabel has learned too late to love.

The popularity of *East Lynne* rested not just on its exploitation of sin and sentiment. It serves as a satisfying murder mystery, and at the time of publication hit a topical note in indulging the public appetite for marital disharmony brought to the fore by publicity surrounding the 1857 Matrimonial Causes Act. It touched strongly on the woman question, and as Emma Liggins argues, like much of Wood's other work, 'raised questions about women's sexual and emotional needs and how they might be accommodated into prescriptive versions of the domestic woman'.[8] Moreover, a wealth of pertinent detail about the theory and practice of mid-century household management can be found within its pages.

East Lynne did not prove to be an isolated success, nor did Wood happen upon its winning formula by chance. Her popularity was predicated not just on her storytelling skills but on her identification with the emergent bourgeoisie whose patronage of the circulating libraries could secure the career of an aspiring writer. Wood used her acuity and sound business sense to manage a successful and enduring career that withstood the hostility of critics and the literary establishment, continually bolstering support by re-positioning herself and shifting her moral and ideological messages to fine-tune them with current public opinion.

Wood's moral posturing and apparent conservatism allowed her to trespass into territory that that might have been considered inappropriate without offending the sensibilities of her readership. By 1860 when *East Lynne* commenced its serial run Wood was well-practised in such adroit handling of contentious material. From the beginning of her career as a periodical writer almost a decade earlier, she had been honing her ability both to tune into the popular Zeitgeist and to smooth over any potential indiscretions with recourse to a number of authorial devices. Her first fictional outing in 1851, 'Seven Years in the Wedded Life of a Roman Catholic,' was aimed at a specific niche in the marketplace for anti-Catholic fiction.[9] This lurid tale of priestly interference in an otherwise happy marriage culminates in bankruptcy, a bloody suicide and what is effectively child-snatching by the Jesuits. Writing somewhat in the style of the notorious *Maria Monk* (1836), a fictionalised account of life in a Montreal convent which had seen numerous reprints in Britain, Wood gives voice to fairly virulent but topical anti-Catholic sentiments. Aware of the sensitivity of her subject matter, she vindicates her stance by positioning European Catholicism in opposition to the British domestic ideal. Not only does Catholic degeneracy provide a moral threat to women via its sexually frustrated clergy, it undermines the stability of family life and encroaches illicitly upon the domestic sphere. Wood invites collusion by periodically apostrophising the reader, validating her message with recourse to her own personal experience and authority: 'Now do you believe this history? Many of you will not. Then go and live in a Catholic country as I have done.'(p. 255). These were tactics Wood was to use repeatedly in her career. By insisting on the veracity of her accounts and tempering her excesses with reassurances that deviance was being described for cautionary purposes only, Wood was able to strike the right ideological note with a broader readership with whom she forged a relationship based on assumptions about a commonality of norms and a shared value system.

During her period in France Wood frequently made use of European locations with Catholic sub-plots, although perhaps aware that this gave her serial fiction a slightly old-fashioned gothic flavour, she was beginning to intersperse more stories with a British location into her work. Alert to other topical issues in the public domain, Wood employed a masculine perspective to cover subjects further afield such as the Australian gold rush, and the Crimean War, which inspired her popular Ensign Tom Pepper series. Deborah Wynne notes how 'Wood imitates the male discourse of the *New Monthly Magazine* of the 1850s at a time when the issues of masculinity and the moral and managerial imperatives of the British Army were foregrounded by the Crimean War', but notes how quickly she was able to sense emerging changes in literary culture, returning her stories to 'a focus on female experience in the middle-class home'.[10]

Wood appeared to enjoy utilising a male narrator as evidenced by her later long-running 'Johnny Ludlow' stories, but her natural constituency was overwhelmingly feminine. One of her most notable domestic-oriented serials for *New Monthly* during this period was *Parkwater*, a cautionary tale of inappropriate social aspiration and reading for leisure, which commenced its serial run in April 1857. Its heroine, Sophia May, is a calculating social climber and an avid devotee of *E. Caterpillar's Penny Weekly Repository of Romance*, E. Caterpillar being 'a popular writer with the million'.[11] When upbraided by her mother for her proclivities for cheap romances, Sophia retorts angrily:

> 'You don't call them stupid when you read them yourself; and *you* don't like
> to be disturbed at them, though you disturb me … The other night when
> father kept asking for his supper, you were in the thick of the "Blighted
> Rose," and you wouldn't stir from it; and he had to get out the bread and
> cheese himself, and fetch the beer.'(p. 394)

Sophia, in the closing pages, faces a life of hard labour for the murder of
her illegitimate child, although reprieved from the scaffold by the last-
minute intervention of her aristocratic former suitor, two years before
George Eliot's Hetty Sorrel is rescued by Arthur Donnithorne in similar
circumstances. Rather than impressing on their daughter the value of the
work ethic, Sophia's parents had made the ultimately fatal mistake of
educating their daughter above her station, her faulty upbringing
compounded, Wood advises us, by 'being allowed the run of those wretched
weekly romances' (p. 396).

Wood, apparently oblivious to the irony of using periodical fiction to
condemn its pernicious effects, perhaps saw no contradiction in supplying
such material to a monthly magazine with a fairly middle-of-the-road
reputation, viewing it as an entirely appropriate medium from which to
admonish less discerning readers. What Wood was articulating of course,
was her contribution to the debate about the impact of mass literacy. Her
narrative serves to align her with the widespread belief that the lower
classes, rather than exercising their new skills on texts of an intellectually
or morally improving nature, preferred to indulge in more salacious and
potentially addictive reading material, a view espoused by Margaret
Oliphant who surveyed half a dozen penny periodicals for an 1855 article
for *Blackwood's Magazine* entitled 'The Byways of Literature: Reading for
the Million'.[12]

Wood is unequivocal about citing Sophia May's familiarity with the
more sensational of these magazines as a critical factor in her downfall,
and as further evidence of Sophia's flightiness, just a few days after killing
her child, she benefits from her advantageous marriage by becoming a
first class subscriber to one of the larger circulating libraries. Wood's
description of Sophia taking home six or eight volumes in a cab and
informing staff that she should require her books changed every day is
tellingly omitted from the hardcover version published ten years later, most
likely reflecting Wood's consciousness that it would be unwise for such a
popular writer to alienate subscribers. These pronouncements on the
corrosive effects of popular fiction are illustrative of the tension
experienced by those commentators who wished to position themselves
on the right side of the moral debate about reading for pleasure, but were

conscious of the commercial possibilities afforded to the writer who could exploit mass appeal. Oliphant, in her 1862 article, 'Sensation Novels,' no doubt grateful for the practice of contributor anonymity, was to condemn the 'violent stimulant of serial fiction' in the same issue of *Blackwoods* in which she was publishing her own foray into sensation writing, *Salem Chapel*.[13]

Wood's condemnation of the reading practices of young women illustrates her habitual practice of associating herself with popular opinion, but demonstrates equally her awareness, at this early stage in her career, that if she is to serve up sensational material she needs to have some regard to its status. Undiluted melodrama was poorly regarded and did not generally translate well into the more lucrative mainstream or bring sufficient celebrity to maintain a viable career. Wood needed to be tactically successful in marketing her material, not simply for Oliphant's 'multitudinous lower classes',[14] but for a wider middle-class readership in a format that was both ideologically acceptable and fictionally satisfying.

Given the disdain evident in her depiction of the May women's response to serials such as the 'The Blighted Rose', Wood was likely to have made a calculated choice about the writing of *East Lynne*, which commenced its run in January 1860, just two years after the close of *Parkwater*; weighing the appeal of its subject matter against the type of readership it might be politic to dissociate herself from. Wood maintained a close involvement in the presentation and progress of the book, priced at the reassuringly expensive thirty-one shillings and sixpence, and by now a seasoned writer, she had a number of strategies at her disposal which served to deflect criticism and cajole the reader into allowing her a degree of latitude.

Direct appeals and apostrophes had become part of Wood's authorial repertoire, and in *East Lynne* she utilises them to invite collusion and complicity at crucial points in the plot. Exhortations such as 'Oh Reader, believe me!'[15] precede warnings about the folly of abandoning husband and home, but Wood primarily intervenes to solicit a sympathetic response for her remorseful heroine; 'Poor thing! Poor Lady Isabel' (p. 335). She employs a cautious but persuasive voice to canvas on behalf of Isabel, anticipating criticism of her plea for mitigation when she describes Isabel's passion for the now inaccessible Archibald; 'I shall be blamed for it, I fear, if I attempt to defend her. But it was not exactly the same thing as though she had suffered to fall in love with someone else's husband. No one would defend *that*' (p. 656). On occasions when she is in danger of breaking down under the strain of her wayward passions, Wood interjects to address, not the reader, but Isabel herself, admonishing solemnly; 'Gently, Lady

Isabel! This is not bearing your cross' (p. 535). Such interventions point to a clear separation between her own sagacious authorial commentary and the actions of her heroine. Isabel's punishment is excessive, but this very lack of clemency allows Wood to advocate maximum compassion for her transgressor while avoiding any suspicion that her sin is being condoned. The concluding truism that 'the only way to ensure peace in the end, is to strive always to be doing right, unselfishly, under God' (p. 691) reinforces the book's ostensible Christian message. Contemporary writer Charlotte Riddell was alleged to have cynically described Wood as a 'brute' who 'throws in bits of religion to slip her fodder down the public throat'.[16] Oliphant, similarly unimpressed, commented acidly on Wood's manipulation of reader sympathies for Isabel; 'her virtuous rival we should like to bundle to the door and be rid of, anyhow'.[17] Wood's authorial devices, despite their transparency, signalled reassurance to any reader anxious about indulging in illicit pleasures, that this enthralling melodrama, unlike other potentially corrupting tales, would not offend against morality or propriety.

East Lynne was not Wood's first attempt at negotiating the difficult and sensitive subject matter of female transgression. Her apprenticeship in periodical writing had given her the opportunity to test out tales of fallen women in novellas such as *Parkwater* and shorter stories such as 'Two Phases in the Life of an Only Child' and 'Georgina Vereker' which had appeared in *New Monthly Magazine* in 1853. Wood, an early player in the emergent genre of detective fiction, was also sufficiently practised to construct the novel's substantial sub-plot concerning the murder of George Hallijohn. Many of her periodical stories feature unsolved crime, sometimes requiring expert intervention. Detective Smith, who painstakingly reviews the evidence for the murder of Sophia May's child is a forerunner of the officious detective Butterby who later features in *The Channings* and *Roland Yorke* (1869), and both characters developed from the same literary milieu as Dickens's Inspector Bucket and Wilkie Collins's Sergeant Cuff.

East Lynne grew out of a variety of influences but more specific origins can be traced. Margaret Maison's supposition that Wood drew on the work of French playwright Eugene Scribe's popular and celebrated *Ten Years in the Life of a Woman* appears credible.[18] An 1877 article in *The Argosy*, possibly written by Wood herself, hails Scribe as 'the greatest playwright of modern times', and shows an acute awareness of the financial rewards accrued by his work, focusing heavily on the enduring market value of his talent.[19] The story of Lady Isabel may have been inspired by Scribe but seemed to have been germinating for some time. In 'Millicent and Philip Crane' and its sequel 'Seven Years', published in *New Monthly Magazine* in November and December 1855, Wood had already rehearsed its twin strands. Millicent's covert meetings with her heavily disguised fugitive brother leads to jealousy, misinterpretation and the breaking of her engagement. Over a period of years, Millicent endures financial setbacks and loss of status, and eventually finds herself employed as a governess by a woman who transpires to be the wife of her former fiancé. Although the effects are not as dramatic, the emotional anguish and social dislocation suffered by the heroine clearly prefigure the situation of Isabel Vane.

While *East Lynne* was still in the early stages of serialisation, the publication of her prize-winning temperance novel *Danesbury House* finally established Wood as a named writer rather than an anonymous serial contributor. Wood was well placed to write on the subject of alcoholism following the death of one of her younger brothers in 1852 from delirium tremens, although this information and the Price family's close association with the brewing industry was scrupulously kept out of the public domain as potentially damaging to her critical and personal reputation. After the decline in glove manufacturing, Wood's family had made their living primarily as maltsters and had owned a public house, the Cross Keys in Worcester, but this kind of biographical material was never to feature in her son Charles's heavily censored memoir of her life.

Temperance fiction offered a fairly predictable route for an opportunist woman writer trying to break into the popular market, and the dramatic storyline of *Danesbury House* renders it more readable than the average novel of this type. It initially garnered some favourable reviews particularly in specialist temperance publications, and was noticed in *The Athenaeum* by Geraldine Jewsbury who was later to recommend *East Lynne* for Bentleys and serve as its proofreader. Jewsbury astutely observed that 'the authoress might write a very good novel if left to follow what whist-players call "an original lead".[20]

Wood's career trajectory had so far been fairly predictable, but the favourable reception of *East Lynne* is likely to have caused her to re-evaluate her position in the marketplace. Wood's stories and articles on Catholicism, like much topical anti-Catholic writing had been imbued with a strong low-church flavour, emphasising the importance of the Bible, railing against the sin of toiling on the Sabbath and complaining about English clergymen adorning their churches with religious images, candles and flowers. The subject matter of *Danesbury House* had rendered it similarly appropriate reading for this type of audience since temperance was a central issue in Evangelical circles. While Evangelical writers such as Emma Worboise and Hesba Stretton achieved a considerable degree of popular success, the poor status of this sub-genre of religious fiction and its associations with a lower class readership may well have influenced Wood's decision not to pursue it further. The celebrity that *East Lynne* had now conferred on Wood made her aware that she could be a player in the more prestigious arena of mainstream fiction rather than being condemned to its periphery. Although initially eager to advertise *East Lynne* on the success of *Danesbury House* she began to dissociate herself from temperance and even from the book itself, later claiming in a letter to *The Times* that *East Lynne* had been her first novel.[21] Having achieved her objective by winning the competition she largely steered clear of the issue for the remainder of her literary career, unlike her friend and contemporary, Anna Maria Carter Hall, who actively supported the temperance movement and produced tracts such as *The Drunkard's Bible* (1854) and *Digging a Grave with a Wine Glass* (1871).

Wood quickly followed *East Lynne* with *The Channings*, a book instrumental in consolidating her success. Rather than confirming a reputation as a sensation novelist, Wood changed direction and tone with a domestic story set in the fictional Helstonleigh, an alias for her native Worcester. As well as indicating her suitability for a family readership, it signalled a subtle re-positioning of her religious affiliations which had implications for the class of reader she was aiming to attract. Although Wood had eschewed any partisan religious proselytising in *East Lynne* beyond generalised Christian platitudes, her reference to 'Jesus Christ' on the deathbed of William Vane and other similar allusions still indicates something of the low-church sensibility which had pervaded much of her writing. *The Channings*, however, with its Cathedral setting and its emphasis on school life, drawing on the experiences of her five brothers who were all pupils at the Kings Cathedral School in Worcester, is more imitative of Charlotte Yonge's popular novels such as her 1856 *The Daisy Chain* in which Stoneborough School, attended by Ethel May's brothers, plays a prominent role. *The Saturday Review*, while noting that Wood's proselytising is of a less sectarian kind, draws comparisons between the two writers in its review of the book. Wood, familiar with the requisite details of Cathedral life, was likely also to have had a rival's eye on Anthony Trollope's acclaimed Barsetshire Chronicles, the fourth of which, *Framley Parsonage* (1860), had begun its highly successful serial run in the same month as *East Lynne* and had reputedly secured the future of both the *Cornhill Magazine* and of Trollope himself. At pains to emphasise this aspect of the book, Wood advised her publishers that 'the frontispiece ought to represent the Cathedral' and furnished two cathedral views for the illustrator to work from.[22] Charles Wood was later to affirm a respectable 'High and Dry' background for Wood in Worcester's cathedral precinct, distancing her as far as possible from teetotalism and any hint of Evangelical tincture and insisting that religion was never mentioned by her, being far too sacred a subject to be made a topic of conversation.

One area in which Wood has always been perceived as consistent was in promoting the social and economic ascendancy of the hard-working middle classes. *East Lynne* allows the appropriation of position and wealth by Archibald Carlyle, an industrious middle-class parvenu, from the dissipated Lord Mount Severn, and subsequently the displacement of the ornamental Lady Isabel as mistress of the country estate by efficient household manager, Barbara Hare. Effete aristocrat Sir Francis Levison, whose penchant for diamond jewellery ultimately leads to his unmasking, is thrown into Justice Hare's pond by the inhabitants of West Lynne, while Carlyle is lauded as the town's newly installed MP. Miss Cornelia pointedly draws her former sister-in-law's attention to the contrast between the upright lawyer and the drenched and despised Levison; 'The other woman who called that noble man husband left him for the other! Did she come to repentance think you?'(p. 529) thus indicating that it was Isabel's inability to distinguish genuine good breeding that proved to be her ultimate folly. Isabel's sin, in this context, can be read as the failure of the aristocracy to acknowledge the worth of the new middle classes, an error that Wood could never be prepared to countenance. Jealously guarding the status of her bourgeois hero, Wood furnished her publishers with specific instructions about the illustrations for an 1862 edition of *East Lynne*, enquiring whether 'the artist could make Mr Carlyle more of a gentleman', describing his preferred attire in detail, and for good measure insisting that he 'must be drawn as a very tall man'.[23]

In the climate that made Samuel Smiles's *Self Help* (1859) a best-seller and had ensured similar success for Dinah Mulock's *John Halifax, Gentleman* (1856), Wood's fictional outcomes supported the values and aspirations of readers rather than the prejudices of critics. *The Saturday Review*, amused by Wood's depiction of Archibald Carlyle, found it 'a little hard to suppress a smile at the thought that in *East Lynne,* this king of men is a country attorney',[24] and later that year claimed the heady achievements of the Halliburtons to be unrealistic and unattainable, 'a sort of pious fraud' perpetrated on the type of poor boy likely to be inspired by Smiles's biographical subjects.[25] Samuel Lucas, despite the enthusiasm evident in his seminal *Times* review of *East Lynne* was clear that, although he found the novel 'highly *entertaining*' it was, as he concludes simply 'a first-rate story' albeit one which had brought Wood 'into the foremost rank of her class'.[26] Lucas here is primarily concerned with literary categories rather than socio-economic ones, but the two were not entirely unrelated and the issue of social class was for Wood's critical reputation and readership at least as significant as that of gender. *The Christian Remembrancer*, drawing attention to her 'persistent use of certain vulgarisms' and pronouncing with mock solemnity 'We do not know what to say of the courage which shall plunge boldly into the manners of a society of which the writer has not the remotest experience'[27] reflected the tone of many reviewers, and it soon became evident that Wood was to be the subject of disdain by critics who routinely sneered at her grammar and ridiculed her depictions of the aristocracy.

Wood fought back against this kind of insidious sniping with an attack on critical integrity in *Roland Yorke* in which the review columns of *The Snarler* are used as a vehicle for personal spite and self-aggrandisement. More typically, she reacted to such disparagement by embracing with pride the bourgeois identity that critics were to find so amusing and turning it to commercial advantage by positioning herself as the authentic voice of the mercantile middle-class, a strategy designed to win success in the circulating library rather than the review columns. While not averse to incorporating elements of aristocratic life into her novels, she was primarily concerned with aligning herself with the norms and values of a lower middle-class readership, using fiction as a medium to validate bourgeois ambition, and consistently promoting the values of hard work, self-help and thrift as the key to upward mobility. Social aspiration for the lower classes such as Sophia May's family is disapproved of as 'false gentility' but for well-connected, middle-ranking tradespeople, it facilitates the establishment of a natural order based on justice and merit.

Wood's narratives consistently argued for a shifting of class signifiers. Wood's men of commerce are notable for their education and refinement. Mr Ashley, the glove manufacturer in *Mrs Halliburton's Troubles*, supposedly modelled on Wood's own father, is a classical scholar, immediately recognisable as 'a thorough gentleman'.[28] Austin Clay, who acts as clerk to a firm of builders and contractors in *A Life's Secret*, is similarly cultured, well-educated and personable. In *Anne Hereford* the young heroine is pleasantly surprised by Mrs Hempson's husband, a linen draper and silk mercer, described as 'tall, bright, handsome'. She acknowledges him to be 'a far more gentlemanly man' (p. 179) than those she had encountered in more prestigious company.

Wood trumpeted the supremacy of the entrepreneurial classes but she exhibited a keen interest in their vicissitudes. Recurring themes of bank failures, embezzlement, bankruptcy and the collapse of speculative business ventures in novels such as *Verner's Pride*, *The Shadow of Ashlydyat*, *George Canterbury's Will* (1870), and *The Master of Greylands* (1873) serve to articulate the period's characteristic preoccupation with financial instability and the struggle to consolidate a class identity in an apparently prosperous, but potentially shifting and uncertain social and economic climate. Financial hardship looms large in Wood's novels and serials, echoing her own precarious economic circumstances. Accused by her critics of having an inadequate grasp of good society, Wood is precise about lower middle-class poverty. Her homilies of self-advancement were written with the conviction of a woman who understood the practical difference that an additional pound a week could make to the management of a household, and moreover, could suggest numerous innovative ways in which that pound might be pursued. In *Edina* (1876), the Raynors rent four shabby rooms for eight shillings a week in South London, and are only able to avoid destitution through the industry of their children. The young Charles Raynor brings home a wage of between fifteen and eighteen shillings as a copying clerk to a firm of solicitors while his younger sister, Alice, earns thirty guineas a year as a governess, a situation that closely mirrors that of Wood's own circumstances during the writing of *East Lynne*. The Woods had returned to South London after Henry's business ventures had failed and were scraping a living in a cheap lodging house. Henry was never to work again and Wood, battling ill-health and a painful curvature of the spine, was writing for the family's financial survival aided by the support of nineteen-year-old Charles who was employed as a clerk for a firm of stockbrokers. The desperate straits of the Channings, Halliburtons and other struggling families give Wood the opportunity to outline many alternate strategies of economic survival. Jane Halliburton narrowly avoids eviction and having her furniture seized by a bailiff who takes up residence in her living-room, a situation Wood refers to in detailed and familiar terms. Jane supplements her income by letting out rooms with a view of the Malvern Hills for one pound a week, although this necessitates borrowing strips of bedside carpet for the bare floor. She also earns six shillings a week working discreetly from home, stitching elaborate French point on gloves from the local manufactory where her young son, William, labours for four shillings. 'We pity the trials and endurance of the poor,' counsels Wood, 'but, believe me, they are as nothing compared with the bitter lot of reduced gentlepeople' (p. 300).

Wood used her background in trade to lend veracity to her treatment of manufacturing in books like *Mrs Halliburton's Troubles* in which she extolled the glove industry as an exemplar of practical capitalism, and to lay claim to an authoritative voice on the subject of industrial unrest in her notorious strike novel, *A Life's Secret*, in which feckless and work-shy 'Slippery' Sam Shuck exploits a climate of unrest to line his pockets as a trade union agitator. Wood's espousal of anti-union sentiments were certainly authentic and no doubt struck a chord in some quarters, but such attitudes did not win universal approval and Wood, unusually seems to have miscalculated the response to her anonymous contribution to this debate. Serialisation of the novel sparked protests and threats of broken windows at the offices of *The Leisure Hour*, a Religious Tract Society publication issuing from Paternoster Row. In an exercise in damage limitation, the proprietors inserted an editorial note at the end of Chapter 8 assuring readers that 'Sam Shuck and his followers represent only the ignorant and unprincipled section of those who engage in strikes' and asserting that working men are entitled to combine in pursuit of better wages and working conditions 'provided there be no interference with the liberty of masters and fellow-workmen'.[29]

Aware that publication might re-ignite controversy, and perhaps unwilling to associate her name with sentiments that might prove damaging, Wood did not immediately follow up the serialisation with a hardcover version. Although the book was distributed in the United States in 1862, it was another five years before it was published in Britain at a time when her fictional output was beginning to flag. Mindful of the story's previous reception, she utilised her preface to justify her stance and remind readers that she wrote from personal experience; 'it is thought that the pictures of the social misery induced by the strike (or lock out) as described in the story which it fell to my lot to see something of, may possibly be felt as a warning, and act for good now' (v–vii). This was not enough to satisfy critics such as John Cordy Jeaffreson who claimed that Wood 'gives offensive utterance to the worst prejudices of those sections of the prosperous middle classes that are most strongly opposed by their selfish interests to trades' unions'.[30]

Wood's experiences of the vagaries of industrial capitalism informed her subject matter, but more significantly made her cognisant of the fact that what she was selling was a commodity like any other. The Price and Wood families had provided a model of entrepreneurial practice, adapting to changes in legislative and economic practices, pursuing alternate careers and businesses, and diversifying according to the requirements of the market. Wood's two sisters had supported themselves by keeping a school in Worcester which they later combined with a lodging house, and Wood profited from their labours by utilising fictionalised accounts of their experiences in her 'House of Halliwell' series for *Bentley's Miscellany*. Female economic activity was a necessary component in the struggle for prosperity and one that Wood repeatedly endorsed in her fiction. She demonstrated the requisite flexibility of the entrepreneurial middle classes with a capacity for modifying her merchandise in order to ensure its compliance with the demands of the literary marketplace.

Wood's industry at this juncture of her career was expedient in business terms, as Henrietta Keddie observed 'she knew how to make hay when the sun shone', but it did little to enhance her critical standing.[31] Reviewing *Mrs Halliburton's Troubles* in *The Athenaeum* Eleanor Eden noted 'It is not likely that writing at this extravagant rate, she can keep up her reputation to the standard expected from the author of "East Lynne".[32] *The Saturday Review*, complaining of Wood's haste and carelessness in writing *Verner's Pride*, advised, that Wood 'would do wisely to remember that a work is generally good in proportion to the amount of thought spent on it', while its review of *The Shadow of Ashlydyat* complains that Wood, emboldened by the success of *East Lynne*, 'has gone on ever since at the rate of a novel every three months, each successive production weaker and more carelessly written than its predecessor'.[33] Geraldine Jewsbury, finding *Oswald Cray*, 'dull and long drawn out' speculated whether Wood was 'suffering under the fatigue of writing so many long stories, with scarcely an interval of rest between them'.[34]

Wood could not maintain such a punishing schedule and by the mid–1860s she had already produced her best work. The longevity of her career was made possible not by a prolific output but by careful husbanding of resources prepared for by a lifetime of thrift and good management. Her only new published novel in 1865 was *Mildred Arkell*, an extension of a story she had originally written for *New Monthly Magazine* in 1854. Its sequel the following year, *St Martin's Eve* (1866), in which mentally unstable Charlotte Norris deliberately causes the death of her five-year-old stepson probably represents Wood's attempt to cash in on the infamous Road Murder following the publication of Constance Kent's confession to the killing of her half-brother in *The Times* in August 1865. The book was plundered from the same serial run as *Mildred Arkell*, but lacking sufficient material to pad out a three-volume novel, Wood grafted on some of her

European Catholic stories from the same era. The various sub-plots sit uneasily together, but Wood realised that she had the potential to augment her output by dipping into the ready fund of work she had produced for Harrison Ainsworth in the 1850s, work for which she had sensibly retained the copyright. Publisher William Tinsley, writing in 1900 suggested that Wood's stories 'were so well linked together that the expert reader could hardly imagine that such was the case' and suggested that Wood had subverted Ainsworth's preference for shorter serial fiction by purposefully forging connecting links between her stories: 'Indeed, there can be no doubt Mrs. Wood had an idea when she first wrote them of welding them together at some future time if she had the chance'.[35]

Sharp-eyed critics were not so generous in their assessment. *The Red Court Farm* (1868) brought together two serial runs that had appeared in *Bentley's Miscellany* in 1857, leading Jewsbury to admonish that the novel contains 'two plots rolled into one'. Jewsbury's allegation that the two stories have little in common and 'are only bound together by a few loose tendrils growing out of one plot and spreading into the other' could fairly be applied to a number of Wood's later works, but the practice made sound commercial if not artistic sense.[36] Wood's critical reputation was now at its lowest point and the scale of her output was reducing yearly. Her purchase of *The Argosy* in 1867 was timely, acting as a spur for some new work such as *Anne Hereford*, a first-person narrative set in a Belgian *pensionnat*, reminiscent of Charlotte Brontë's *Villette*. Keeping profits within the family, she paired her leading title with her son Charles's debut novel, *Buried Alone* (1868) and employed Charles as co-editor and regular contributor on travel writing. For a writer who had already passed her peak of popularity, editorial control allowed Wood a means of promoting and profiting directly from her own work, and enabled her to harvest her earlier fiction by reprinting work that had appeared in the 1850s in *New Monthly Magazine* and *Bentley's Miscellany*. By following up with a subsequent hardcover version Wood was frequently able to maximise profits by ensuring three exposures for a single piece of work. *Parkwater* was given another resuscitation after a gap of eighteen years, commencing its serial run in *The Argosy* in January 1875, finding publication with Richard Bentley alongside a number of other stories entitled *Told in the Twilight* (1875), and then repackaged again the following year under its own original title. Short stories, articles, two-part serials or shorter serial runs were often reissued in this way with the occasional addendum 'an old story reprinted'.

In the last decade of her life Wood produced little new work although her creation of the Johnny Ludlow series was successful in enabling her to continue to write episodically without having to labour over a long drawn-out plot. The practice of recycling her work continued several years after her death under the editorship of Charles, who re-published thirty or forty-year old works such as *The Story of Charles Strange* (1888), *The House of Halliwell* (1894) and *Ashley* (1897), both in serial form and hardcover.

The key to Wood's phenomenal success lay in her adaptability and opportunism which manifests itself in her ability to identify her target market and tailor her material accordingly. Despite her uneasy relationship with a sceptical literary establishment she succeeded in capturing an unsophisticated and morally conservative readership, meeting a public demand for readable and melodramatic fiction by delivering it in a format that did not compromise their status or sense of propriety. *The Saturday Review,* notwithstanding its impatience with the careless workmanship evident in *Verner's Pride,* had been forced to concede; 'Of a circulating library story, the book before us is a perfect type'. Despite the novel's numerous limitations the reviewer recognises the book's place in the literary hierarchy, admitting; 'it is nonetheless removed from the tedious trash which constitutes so large a part of our ephemeral literature' (p. 280).

Wood's life mirrored her work, validating her premise that the work ethic offered social ascendancy and redemption from adversity. She reaped the benefits of good financial management, her pragmatism and sound business sense ensuring her enduring success. An analysis of the totality of her writing career is revealing of her relationship to the commodification of texts during this period and of how she negotiated cultural and ideological practices that may have conflicted with her commercial instincts, attuning herself to the popular market to access space and gain empowerment within the publishing arena.

Notes

1 Ellen Wood, *Anne Hereford*, 3 vols (London: Tinsley Bros., 1868), vol. 1, pp. 178–9.
2 Malcolm Elwin, *Victorian Wallflowers* (London: Jonathan Cape, 1934), p. 232.
3 Henrietta Keddie, *Three Generations: The Story of a Middle-Class Scottish Family* (London: John Murray, 1911), p. 319.
4 Andrew Maunder (ed.), *East Lynne* (Peterborough, Ontario: Broadview, 2000); Emma Liggins, 'Good Housekeeping? Domestic Economy and Suffering Wives in Mrs Henry Wood's Early Fiction', in Emma Liggins and Daniel Duffy (eds) *Feminist Readings of Victorian Popular Texts: Divergent Femininities* (Aldershot: Ashgate, 2001), pp. 53–68; Deborah Wynne, '"See

What a Big Wide Bed It Is!" Mrs Henry Wood and the Philistine Imagination',
in Liggins and Duffy (eds), *Feminist Readings*, pp. 89–107; and Deborah
Wynne, 'Ellen Wood's *East Lynne* in the *New Monthly Magazine*', *The Sensation
Novel and the Victorian Family Magazine* (Basingstoke: Palgrave, 2001), pp.
60–82.

5 Jonathan Loesberg, 'The Ideology of Narrative Form in Sensation Fiction',
Representations, 13 (Winter 1986), 115–38.

6 My biographical information on Wood has been obtained from parish
records, General Register Office certificates, wills, census material and similar
primary sources. I am indebted to a number of people who aided my research
including Susan Moncrieff, Susan Hughes, David Everett and Bruno
Haffreingue.

7 Maunder (ed.), *East Lynne*, p. 36.

8 Liggins, 'Good Housekeeping', p. 65.

9 Ellen Wood, 'Seven Years in the Wedded Life of a Roman Catholic', *New
Monthly Magazine*, 91 (1851), 255.

10 Wynne, 'A Big Wide Bed', p. 100.

11 Ellen Wood, 'The Lawyers' Servants', *New Monthly Magazine* 109 (1857), 393.
Subsequent page references are given in the text.

12 Margaret Oliphant, 'The Byways of Literature: Reading for the Million',
Blackwood's Magazine, 84 (1858), 201–16.

13 Margaret Oliphant, 'Sensation Novels', *Blackwood's Magazine*, 91 (1862), 568.

14 Oliphant, 'The Byways of Literature', p. 204.

15 Maunder, *East Lynne*, p. 334.

16 Elwin, *Victorian Wallflowers*, p. 241, cites this remark from Charlotte Riddell.
It originates from Harry Furniss's book, *Some Victorian Women, Good, Bad
and Indifferent* (London: John Lane, 1923), p. 6. Furniss, who worked as an
illustrator for *The Argosy*, omits Wood's name from his account.

17 Oliphant, 'Sensation Novels', p. 567.

18 Margaret Maison, 'Adulteresses in Agony', *The Listener* (19 January 1961),
134.

19 'Eugene Scribe', *The Argosy*, 23 (June 1877), 429–32. Unsigned articles in *The
Argosy* were frequently written by either Wood herself or her son, Charles.
Wood seems a more likely candidate in this case since Charles was too young
to appreciate Scribe in his heyday.

20 Geraldine Jewsbury, 'Danesbury House: Prize Tale', *The Athenaeum* (24 March
1860), 407.

21 Wood was writing in rebuttal to an attack in *The Times* by Caroline Norton
who had claimed that Wood's publishers used the byline 'by the author of
East Lynne' because 'it was the only one of her works that had made a
permanent impression on the reading public' *The Times* (25 October 1871,
p. 6). Wood responded, 'East Lynne was my first novel; and therefore I (not
my publishers) retain it as my distinguishing title.' *The Times* (28 October
1871), p. 6.

22 Ellen Wood, Letter to Messrs Dalziel (19 September 1862), Harry Ransom Humanities Research Center, The University of Texas at Austin.
23 Ellen Wood, Letter to Messrs Dalziel (19 September 1862).
24 'East Lynne', *The Saturday Review* (15 February 1862), 187.
25 'Mrs. Halliburton's Troubles', *The Saturday Review* (13 December 1862), 714.
26 Samuel Lucas, 'East Lynne', *The Times* (25 January 1862), 6.
27 'Our Female Sensation Novelists', *The Christian Remembrancer*, 46 (July 1863), 216.
28 Ellen Wood, *Mrs Halliburton's Troubles*, vol. 1 (London: Richard Bentley and Son, 1862), p. 216.
29 'A Life's Secret', *The Leisure Hour* (20 February 1862), 117.
30 John Cordy Jeaffreson, 'A Life's Secret', *The Athenaeum* (2 November 1867), 570.
31 Keddie, *Three Generations*, p. 322
32 Eleanor Eden, 'Mrs Halliburton's Troubles', *The Athenaeum* (6 December 1862), 731.
33 'Verner's Pride', *The Saturday Review* (28 January 1863), 279–80; 'The Shadow of Ashlydyat', *The Saturday Review* (16 January 1864), 82.
34 Geraldine Jewsbury, 'Oswald Cray', *The Athenaeum* (24 December 1864), 859.
35 William Tinsley, *Random Recollections of an Old Publisher* (London: Simpkin Marshall and Co., 1900), p. 131.
36 Geraldine Jewsbury, 'The Redcourt Farm', *The Athenaeum* (25 July 1868), 107.

Bibliography

The Argosy, 23, 'Eugene Scribe' (1877), 429–32.
The Christian Remembrancer, 46, 'Our Female Sensation Novelists' (July 1863), 209–36.
Eden, Eleanor, 'Mrs. Halliburton's Troubles', *The Athenaeum* (6 December 1862), 731.
Elwin, Malcolm, *Victorian Wallflowers*, London: Jonathan Cape, 1934.
Furniss, Harry, *Some Victorian Women, Good, Bad and Indifferent*, London: John Lane, 1923.
Hall, Anna Maria, *The Drunkard's Bible*, London, 1854.
—— *Digging a Grave with a Wine Glass*, London, 1871.
Jeaffreson, John Cordy, 'A Life's Secret', *The Athenaeum* (2 November 1867), 570.
Jewsbury, Geraldine, 'Danesbury House: Prize Tale', *The Athenaeum* (24 March 1860), 407.
—— Oswald Cray', *The Athenaeum* (24 Dec. 1864), 859.
—— The Redcourt [sic] Farm: a Novel', *The Athenaeum* (25 July 1868), 107.
Keddie, Henrietta, *Three Generations: The Story of a Middle-Class Scottish Family*,

London: John Murray, 1911.

The Leisure Hour, 'A Life's Secret' (20 February 1862), 117.

Liggins, Emma, 'Good Housekeeping? Domestic Economy and Suffering Wives in Mrs Henry Wood's Early Fiction', in Emma Liggins and Daniel Duffy (eds), *Feminist Readings of Victorian Popular Texts: Divergent Femininities*, Aldershot: Ashgate, 2001, pp. 53–68.

Loesberg, Jonathan, 'The Ideology of Narrative Form in Sensation Fiction', *Representations*, 13 (Winter 1986), 115–38.

Lucas, Samuel, 'East Lynne', *The Times* (25 January 1862), 6.

Maison, Margaret, 'Adulteresses in Agony', *The Listener* (19 January 1961), 133–4.

Maunder, Andrew (ed.), *East Lynne*, Peterborough, Ontario: Broadview, 2000.

Monk, Maria, *Awful Disclosures of Maria Monk and Thrilling Mysteries of a Convent Revealed*, Philadelphia: T. B. Peterson, 1836.

Mulock, Dinah Maria, *John Halifax, Gentleman*, 3 vols, London: Hurst and Blackett, 1856.

Norton, Caroline, *The Times*, 25 Oct. 1871, 6.

Oliphant, Margaret, 'The Byways of Literature: Reading for the Million', *Blackwood's Magazine* 84 (1858), 201–16.

—— Sensation Novels', *Blackwood's Magazine*, 91 (1862), 564–84.

Romer, Robert, 'George Canterbury's Will', *The Athenaeum* (12 March 1870), 351.

The Saturday Review, 'East Lynne', (15 February 1862), 186–7.

—— The Channings' (10 May 1862), 540–1.

—— Mrs. Halliburton's Troubles' (13 December 1862), 717–4.

—— Verner's Pride' (28 January 1863), 279–80.

—— The Shadow of Ashlydyat' (16 January 1864), 82–3.

Smiles, Samuel, *Self Help*, London: John Murray, 1859.

Tinsley, William, *Random Recollections of an Old Publisher*, London: Simpkin, Marshall and Co., 1900.

Wood, Charles W., *Buried Alone*, London: Tinsley Brothers, 1868.

—— Mrs Henry Wood: In Memoriam', *The Argosy*, 43 (1887), 251–70, 334–53, 422–42.

Wood, Ellen, 'Seven Years in the Wedded Life of a Roman Catholic', *New Monthly Magazine*, 91 (1851), 245–55.

—— A Word to England on the Spread of Catholicism', *New Monthly Magazine*, 97 (1853), 182–92.

—— The Sequel to "A Word to England"', *New Monthly Magazine*, 97 (1853), 335–42.

—— Two Phases in the Life of an Only Child', *New Monthly Magazine*, 98 (1853), 144–57.

—— Georgina Vereker', *New Monthly Magazine*, 98 (1853), 349–61.

—— A Record of the Gold-Fever', *New Monthly Magazine*, 100 (1854), 58–72.

—— Millicent and Philip Crane', *New Monthly Magazine*, 105 (1855), 334–47.

—— Seven Years', *New Monthly Magazine*, 105 (1855) 401–13.

—— The Lawyer's Servants', *New Monthly Magazine*, 109 (1857), 393–408. (The

commencement of *Parkwater* which runs April–December 1857)
— *Danesbury House*, Glasgow: Scottish Temperance League, 1860.
— *East Lynne*, 3 vols, London: Richard Bentley and Son, 1861.
— *The Channings*, 3 vols, London: Richard Bentley and Son, 1862.
— *Mrs Halliburton's Troubles*, 3 vols, London: Richard Bentley and Son, 1862.
— *The Shadow of Ashlydyat*, 3 vols, London: Richard Bentley and Son, 1863.
— *Verner's Pride*, 3 vols, London: Bradbury and Evans, 1863.
— *William Allair*, London: Griffith and Farrah, 1863.
— *Oswald Cray*, 3 vols, Edinburgh, Adam and Charles Black, 1864.
— *Mildred Arkell*, 3 vols, London: Tinsley Brothers, 1865.
— *St Martin's Eve*, 3 vols, London: Tinsley Brothers, 1866.
— *A Life's Secret*, 2 vols, London: Charles W. Wood, 1867.
— *Anne Hereford*, 3 vols, London: Tinsley Brothers, 1868.
— *The Red Court Farm*, 3 vols, London: Tinsley Brothers, 1868.
— *Roland Yorke*, 3 vols, London: Richard Bentley and Son, 1869.
— *George Canterbury's Will*, 3 vols, London: Tinsley Brothers, 1870.
— *The Master of Greylands*, 3 vols, London: Richard Bentley and Son, 1873.
— *Told in the Twilight*, 3 vols, London: Richard Bentley and Son, 1875.
— *Edina*, 3 vols, London: Richard Bentley and Son, 1876.
— *Parkwater*, London: Richard Bentley and Son, 1876.
— *The Story of Charles Strange*, 3 vols, London: Richard Bentley and Son, 1888.
— *The House of Halliwell*, 3 vols, London: Richard Bentley and Son, 1894.
— *Ashley*, London: Richard Bentley and Son, 1897.
— Letter to *The Times* 28 October 1871, 6.
— Letter to Messrs Dalziel, 19 September 1862. The Harry Ransom Humanities Research Center, The University of Texas at Austin.
Wynne, Deborah, *The Sensation Novel and the Victorian Family Magazine*, Basingstoke: Palgrave, 2001.
—''' See What A Big Wide Bed it is!" Mrs Henry Wood and the Philistine Imagination', in Emma Liggins and Daniel Duffy (eds), *Feminist Readings of Victorian Popular Texts: Divergent Femininities*, Aldershot: Ashgate, 2001, pp. 89–107.
Yonge, Charlotte, *The Daisy Chain*, London: John W. Parker and Son, 1856.

8

Behind the scenes, before the gaze: Mary Braddon's theatrical world

Valerie Pedlar

Mary Braddon's reputation in the 1860s was – as it still is – as a writer of sensation fiction. She was unapologetic about this, but her letters to her mentor, Edward Bulwer Lytton, testify to the pressure under which she worked, which she felt prevented her from writing as artistically as she might have done. Since she was writing in order to support herself and her mother (and later a large family of children), she needed to produce work that was popular and that brought in the money. Until the 1870s, by which time she was financially more secure, she churned out fiction for the cheaper periodicals, at the same time as working on sensation novels that were the subject of critical attack for their immorality and lack of realism. However, even as early as 1864, she tried her hand at a more 'literary' novel, *The Doctor's Wife* (featuring, ironically enough, a writer of popular sensation fiction), which was modelled on Gustave Flaubert's *Madame Bovary*. And in the course of the eighty-two novels that were written during a career of over fifty years, she turned to other genres, writing novels of character, simple love stories, stories of imperial adventure, detective stories and historical romance. Tempting as it is to categorise her fiction, in truth most of her novels show a mix of genres. *The Fatal Three*, for instance, is an interesting novel from 1888, in which psychological analysis is married with sensational elements and the plot is based on the contemporary and contentious issue of marriage to a deceased wife's sister, a variation on the theme of bigamy that was so popular in sensation fiction.

Through the surviving one-sided correspondence, Robert Wolff, in what has been for many years the standard biography, has reconstructed part of the story of her early attempts to get published under the guidance of a Yorkshire businessman, John Gilby, 'the Beverley Maecenas'.[1] He urged her to concentrate on poetry, but while she was working on 'Garibaldi' and other poems, she started writing fiction, and *Three Times Dead*, her first novel, was published in Yorkshire in 1860. Gilby was not, however, her only mentor, since at about this time she had also met John Maxwell, the proprietor of *The Welcome Guest* as well as of the more prestigious *Temple Bar*. Wolff conjectures that there was not only a business, but also a romantic rivalry between these two men, and that the role of adviser was coupled with that of suitor. If Gilby failed to attract Braddon, Maxwell, with a wife in an asylum near Dublin and five children to care for, was hardly the most eligible suitor. Nevertheless, she put herself into business and quasi-marital partnership with him, and eventually, after the death of his wife in 1874, they became legally husband and wife.

In 1860 her first short story was published in *The Welcome Guest* and in 1861 Maxwell republished *Three Times Dead*, slightly revised, as *The Trail of the Serpent*. *The Welcome Guest* was a short-lived magazine and folded in 1861, whereupon the staff were moved over to a new publication, *Robin Goodfellow*, a weekly sixpenny magazine, which was designed to continue the 'genteel fiction' of its predecessor,[2] and at the same time, another weekly magazine, *The Halfpenny Journal*, was launched as an enterprise to attract the lower class reader. To this Braddon contributed seven or eight novels in instalments between July 1861 and June 1865, in what Wolff calls 'literary hackwork' (p. 119). Wolff is harsh in his assessment of this extremely popular (in one sense of the term) fiction writing; *The Black Band*, for instance, he describes as 'an example of MEB's penny-dreadfuls ... those diffuse, pedestrian, primitive efforts to entertain the nearly illiterate' (p. 121). It was not long, though, before Braddon achieved spectacular success with *Lady Audley's Secret* in 1862. Originally published in instalments in *Robin Goodfellow*, the work was abandoned in 1861 when the magazine failed after thirteen issues, and Braddon started work on *Aurora Floyd*. But, encouraged by popular demand, she returned to *Lady Audley's Secret* and serialisation recommenced in Ward and Lock's *Sixpenny Magazine*, a monthly 'for all classes and all seasons'.[3] Even before the last (twelfth) instalment was out, the novel had been published in the standard three-volume format favoured by the circulating libraries by Tinsley Bros in October 1862, and it ran to eight editions before the end of the year. Tinsley also published her three novels from 1863, *Aurora Floyd*, *Eleanor's Victory* and *John Marchmont's Legacy*. Thereafter she was published by either Maxwell or Ward, Lock & Tyler until 1871, when Maxwell became her sole publisher, except for a single novel in 1874, *Lost for Love*, which was handled by Chatto & Windus. From 1887 her publishers were Spencer Blackett, who published one novel; Simpkin Marshall, who published fifteen novels; Hutchinson, who published eight, and Hurst and Blackett, who published four.

In 1866 Maxwell sold *Temple Bar*, and founded a new magazine, *Belgravia*, aimed at a lower middle-class reader, and intended primarily as a vehicle for the serial publication of Braddon's fiction. She was also its editor, and in it she published her tribute to Bulwer Lytton after his death in 1873. She had already had eight novels serialised in *Belgravia*, when she was approached by the owner of another periodical, the Lancashire *Bolton Journal and Guardian*, which had been started in 1871. William Francis Tillotson was anxious to lift his sales by including fiction written by well-known authors. He offered a flat rate for serial publication, but left the copyright for book publication in the hands of the author. Enticed by the thought of being introduced to new readers, who would then want to read her previous books, Braddon was the first established writer to join Tillotson and she kept up the connection until 1887. For four years she produced one novel a year for *Belgravia* and at least one for Tillotson. Then in 1876 *Belgravia* was sold to Chatto & Windus and Braddon severed her connections with it. It was not long, however, before she started another periodical, the Christmas annual, *The Mistletoe Bough*. Until 1887 she wrote for it, collected material and edited it; thereafter her son, Will, took over the collecting and editing, though she continued to write for it until it closed in 1892.

Mary Braddon was born in 1837, the year of Queen Victoria's accession. She died on 4 February 1915 and, as Jennifer Carnell points out, the evening papers carried the news of her death as the headline, despite the war.[4] In 1862, Henry Mansel had castigated Braddon and others for churning out a diseased literature, written for a corrupt age.[5] The morning after her death *The Times* commemorated her achievements very differently:

> No one would place Miss Braddon among the outstanding and enduring figures of English fiction. But she knew exactly what a healthy-minded public, just beginning to need relaxation from an increasingly exacting social life, was likely to require. 'Lady Audley's Secret' was a fair representative of her immense library of fiction. Her skill in the manipulation of plots, her unfailing resource in the invention of character and incident, never failed her; her vigour, fluency and literary skill were as conspicuous in her seventieth novel as in her first.[6]

Writing was Mary Braddon's second choice of career; her first was the stage, when she needed to find money to support herself and her mother. Robert Lee Wolff speculates that Braddon was on the stage, under a *nom de thâ tre* as Mary Seyton, for just three years. However, more recent research by Jennifer Carnell has shown that her theatrical career probably lasted for eight years between 1852 and 1860. Wolff locates the start of her acting career in 1857 at the Assembly Rooms in Beverley, Yorkshire, with the part of Mrs Sternhold in Tom Taylor's three-act drama, *Still Waters Run Deep*. As Carnell points out, it would have been very unlikely, even in the days before institutional drama schools, and even in the provinces, for a middle-class woman to have stepped on to the professional stage for the first time in a major role. This was in fact one of the most important roles that Braddon was to play, and it was typical in that she was cast as much older than her actual age.

Braddon's first billing is at the Theatre Royal, Southampton in 1853, where she is described as 'Miss Mary Seyton, from the Theatre Royal, Bath'. Although her name does not appear in the playbills for the Bath theatre, she may have appeared there only for a short time late in the season, sufficient simply to give her billing at Southampton that extra touch. Together with Adelaide and Clara Biddle, two sisters from a theatrical family, she is classed as a 'walking lady', an actress who played minor roles. Adelaide Biddle was already well experienced, soon progressed to leading lady, and married Charles Calvert, who was already playing as leading man. Adelaide Calvert's memoirs provide not only evidence of Braddon's early acting career, but a contemporary picture of a young woman who was clearly not typical of the actresses of the time. Since they lived in nearby lodgings, the two sisters and Calvert were invited to tea on Sundays by Braddon and her mother, who was her constant chaperone. Adelaide comments that she and Mary 'were omnivorous readers', embracing 'everything from Carlyle to Ruskin to Harrison Ainsworth and Fenimore Cooper'.[7] Between 1853 and 1859 Braddon played in London, Beverley, Hull, Brighton and Coventry (the latter two towns with Henry Nye Chart's company, which she joined in the summer of 1857), but apart from the odd juicy role, she did not really progress beyond 'walking ladies'. She met up with Adelaide Calvert again in Brighton in 1859 and played Celia to Mrs Calvert's Rosalind, but by this time there were signs that her attention to her work was slipping: 'half her speeches were impromptu (though, somehow, she always managed to alight on the last three or four words correctly)'.[8] Calvert concluded that her heart wasn't in it: 'She was writing a novel, and her theatrical work was a secondary consideration'.[9] Finally, she held a benefit night, shared with two other actresses, on 29 February 1860, and when the company went to Cheltenham, she left for Beverley to continue her writing career.

Given Braddon's years on the stage, it is not surprising that she herself wrote for the stage. What is surprising is that her plays were not more

successful. Her first play was *Loves of Arcadia* (1860), and the Mary Braddon
website lists fourteen more written between then and 1904, most of them
dating from the last twenty years of the century.[10] Far more popular were
the adaptations of her novels, although, as she complained, these
adaptations brought her little income.[11] In *Women and Victorian Theatre*,
Kerry Powell notes that contemporary discussion mostly concerned the
adaptations by men of other men's work, but in fact over one hundred
productions on the Victorian stage can be identified as transcriptions by
men of stories by women.[12] Since the original author had no control over
the stage script it was quite likely that adaptations lacked subtlety and the
power of the original was lost or distorted. Powell comments, for instance,
that all three adaptations of *Lady Audley's Secret* from this period make
Lady Audley unambiguously mad. Furthermore, Ruth Burridge
Lindemann shows that, ironically, those plays that adapt novels with
theatrical scenes or characters, actually erase or diminish those elements.
She sees this as a sign of middle-class anxiety about the theatre's lack of
respectability. Braddon, on the other hand, equally concerned about moral
rectitude, 'writes middle-class morality, industry, and economic necessity
into her theatrical character references'.[13]

In what follows I shall be elaborating on the issue of the moral stance in
Braddon's fiction, as I distinguish three ways in which Braddon's theatrical
experience enters into her fictional writing. In the first place, she
incorporates characters who are professional actors or otherwise involved
in theatre life, and uses the theatrical context as part of her fictional world,
as in *Eleanor's Victory*, *John Marchmont's Legacy*, *Rupert Godwin*, *Dead-
Sea Fruit*, *Hostages to Fortune*, *A Strange World*, and three of the short
stories in the collection entitled *Under the Red Flag*.[14] Secondly, she weaves
in reference to plays and well-known characters, especially Shakespearian,
as in *The Doctor's Wife*.[15] Finally, she draws on theatrical effects, particularly
those of melodrama, in her use of tableaux, in her representation of
emotional states through the description of physical appearance rather
than psychological analysis, and through the use of descriptions of setting
and place to intensify the emotional impact and foreshadow the passions
to be portrayed, rather like the use of musical underlay in stage melodrama.
Through the representation of the theatrical world in contrast with other
social contexts Braddon comments on moral values, favouring the
traditional Christian virtues of compassion, generosity and purity of spirit.
Furthermore, it is in drawing comparisons and making reference to
Shakespearian and other well-known characters from the 'classics' of
English literature as well as characters and scenes from the world of theatre,

that she is able to highlight the degree to which role-playing is part of everyday life, and to draw attention to the theatricality of ordinary domestic existence. Finally, the way in which Braddon draws on theatrical effects contributes to the popularity (in the sense of appeal to a mass market) of her novels, since the intensity of the visual experience makes for easy assimilation. Martin Meisel has shown the extent to which Victorian cultural forms were inclined towards visual representation: 'In the nineteenth century all three forms [novels, pictures and plays] are narrative *and* pictorial; pictures are given to storytelling and novels unfold through and with pictures'.[16] A readership accustomed to the semiotics of melodrama could recognise without effort the signifiers of guilt, innocence, and a range of emotional states without the necessity for lengthy narratorial explanations. As Meisel goes on to say, 'The shared structures in the representational arts helped constitute ... a popular style' (p. 4). The last part of this chapter, then, will show how Braddon gives her work the appeal and ease of assimilation that comes from representation that relies primarily on the intensity of visual imagery.

The most obvious way in which Braddon draws on her theatrical experiences is in the representation of theatre, backstage and front of house, of performances and their audiences, of actors, actresses and the other people who work in the theatre. It is a world of pretence and make-believe, but it is also a world of real hard work, and often real poverty. There is a sharp distinction between the life of the provincial player and that of the actor in a London company, but there is also a distinction between the small, out-of-the-way London theatres and the fashionable playhouses of the West End. Most frequently Braddon features the drab and dirty world of provincial and obscure London theatres, where the costumes are shabby and far from clean, the scenery creaking and where there is a company that 'asks no more from existence than that its swift-recurring Saturday shall witness the payment of every man's salary'.[17] Even a production at a major London theatre can be portrayed as dismayingly unalluring. When Edward Arundel visits Drury Lane Theatre in 1838, at the beginning of *John Marchmont's Legacy*, he finds a 'dull production', which even the performance of a great actor is unable to enliven.[18] But this is only the backdrop for the supernumerary who turns out to be Edward's old schoolmaster, who has fallen on hard times and who now presents a 'degrading spectacle':

> The feeble frame, scarcely able to sustain that paltry one-sided banner ...
> two rude daubs of coarse vermilion upon the hollow cheeks, the black
> smudges that were meant for eyebrows, the wretched scrap of horsehair

> glued upon the pinched chin in dismal mockery of a beard; and through all
> this the pathetic pleading of large hazel eyes, bright with the unnatural lustre
> of disease, and saying … 'Do not look at me; do not despise me; do not even
> pity me. It won't last long'. (pp. 12 –13)

John Marchmont fails to conform to the standards of theatre, since not
only does his make-up fail to convince, revealing only its own artificiality,
but the expression of his eyes ('Do not look at me') subverts the theatre's
purpose of display.

The major ambition of many an actor is to make the move to London,
but, once there, he is likely to face the antagonism and arrogance of the
established London players. But Braddon uses just this situation to
highlight the hidden moral qualities of the acting fraternity. In 'At Daggers
Drawn', the recruitment of a provincial 'low comedian', Joseph Munford,
is a cause of concern to the resident comedian at the Royal Terence Theatre
in London, who sees him as a deadly rival.[19] When, however, the new arrival
falls ill and therefore into severe financial difficulty, the great Tayte doesn't
hesitate to offer support and when Munford no longer qualifies for the
salary that the theatre manager has so far been paying with more than
usual generosity, it is Tayte who out of his own pocket continues the
payments. It is only at the point of death, and the final moments of the
story, that Munford discovers that it was his rival and not the manager
who was paying him:

> 'James Tayte,' he cried, 'I did not think there was so good a man upon this
> earth!'
>   He groped feebly for the hand of his benefactor, found it, pressed it to his
> lips, and, kissing it, died. (p. 252)

Again in *Eleanor's Victory* the theatre is promoted as the source of moral
rectitude.[20] Braddon refers to the theatrical world through the character
of Richard Thornton, violinist, scene-painter and translator. The novel
starts in Paris where he is copying the scenery, 'picking up' (presumably
copying) the music and translating the script of a play called *Raoul
l'Empoisonneur*, so that it can be performed at the 'transpontine' theatre
where he works in London. The practice of translating, or more commonly,
adapting plays from the French was widespread in England in the mid-
nineteenth century. Richard, like Sigismund Smith, the sensation novelist
in *The Doctor's Wife*, cheerfully accepts an artistic life that is based on
practicality, rather than inspiration. It is Richard, though, who is Eleanor's
first rescuer, when, her father having met with some gambling companions,
she is left to find her way home on her first evening in Paris. If the father–

daughter relationship, as so often in Braddon, shows the parent's self-centredness, financial irresponsibility and lack of concern for his child that it is difficult not to attribute to Braddon's own experience, Richard represents the selfless caring that is frequently associated with the poorer members of the theatrical professions in her fiction. He and the aunt with whom he lives have little room in their house, and small financial resources, yet they share both with the young girl after her father's sudden death. They also offer their morality of Christian forgiveness, which she, intent on avenging her father's death, is unable to share.

The question of morality is a central concern in the representation of the actresses who figure so significantly in Braddon's fiction. As Tracy C. Davis points out in her study, *Actresses as Working Women*, the stage was one of the few employment opportunities open to women.[21] The profession as a whole was characterised by a heterogeneity of experience, competence, salary and social class. Although the general perception among the middle class was that acting was an unsuitable occupation for respectable women, and this attitude is certainly reflected in Braddon's fiction, it was nevertheless middle-class women who, in the absence of formal training, were best prepared: 'As long as the profession lacked systematic training schools with low or free tuition, middle-class recruits tutored in singing, dancing, languages, and recitation at home or in girls' school had the best chance of getting employment in dramatic lines' (p. 12). Davis writes, furthermore, about the personal qualities required of an actress: 'assertiveness and self-negation, flamboyance and modesty, intellectuality and emotiveness, and active and reactive qualities' (p. 15), a combination, in fact, of masculine and feminine qualities. This requirement for an actress to combine contradictory qualities was matched by other paradoxes in their lives. Expected to represent stereotypical female objects of male desire, they were in fact living lives of masculine independence; putting themselves on show night after night, they had at the same time to make clear that they were not for sale. Davis traces the parallels between the situation of the actress and that other professional with whom she was so often identified – the prostitute. To counteract this dangerous identification, actresses strove to assert the propriety of their private lives.

Actresses in Braddon's fiction are usually reputable figures, working to support a parent or children, but they are not usually good or committed actresses. In *Dead-Sea Fruit* Lucy St Albans (neé Alford) is encouraged by her father (who has become impoverished through drink) to go on the stage, when she expresses her enthusiasm for the art. She labours away in the provinces, then gets a miserable London engagement, in which she plays Pauline, the leading-lady in *Lady of Lyons* by Braddon's mentor, Edward Bulwer Lytton. This is the role that Braddon recognises as the pinnacle for any provincial actress: 'Where is the juvenile actress – unknown, perhaps, to metropolitan fame, but famous in her particular sphere – whose Pauline is not her strong point?'.[22] But Lucy's performance is poor and the production terrible. Like Mr Wopsle in *Great Expectations*, Lucy discovers that migration to the London theatre does not necessarily bring success or credit. As in 'At Daggers Drawn', we have a vivid picture of the antagonism and arrogance of the metropolitan towards the provincial player. In the end, when her father is arrested for debt and then dies, her self-appointed guardian, Laurence Desmond, arranges for her to take a job as a governess in Ireland. In 'Across the Footlights' Rosalie Morton, another daughter having to support a parent (in this case her mother), appears as the fairy queen in the pantomime at Helmstone-by-the-sea.[23] Later, when her husband dies leaving her with two children to support, she again returns to the stage, but is only too ready to give it up when her daughter makes an advantageous marriage that removes the necessity to work.

Violet Westford, the heroine of *Rupert Godwin*, is forced to go on the stage when she, her mother and brother are left destitute.[24] Her first sortie into the world of employment, reversing the path taken by Lucy Alford, is, typically enough, as a governess, but when a malicious falsehood claiming that her mother is immoral is told to her employer, thus leading to her dismissal, she obtains work as a *figurante*, the Queen of Beauty, in the last scene of a burlesque;[25] with nothing to say she has simply to wear a wonderful costume and 'sit in statuesque repose upon a gilded throne and look beautiful' (p. 120). In this novel, the moral probity of the heroine is indubitable, but the theatre is a mixed environment, and another actress, better established, but jealous of Violet's role in the burlesque is instrumental in her abduction to the very different environment of the Moat. Instead of a theatrical transformation scene, there is a textual transformation as the novel shifts into the gothic mode, and Violet is thrust into the role of a gothic heroine.

Justina Elgood in *A Strange World* presents a more complicated example, but the point about moral rectitude remains.[26] The novel opens with the description of a rural scene, in which the two figures are explicitly alienated:

> Two figures are seated in a corner of the meadow, beneath the umbrage of an ancient thorn, not Arcadian or pastoral figures by any means; – not Phillis the milkmaid, with sunbrowned brow and carnation cheeks, not Corydon fluting sweetly on his tuneful pipe as he reclines at her feet; – but two figures

which carry the unmistakable stamp of city life in every feature and every garment. (p. 9)

But although the man, who turns out to be Matthew Elgood, is endemically and irredeemably urban, the girl, despite her apparent estrangement from the country scene, is in some way reclaimed by nature. Here she is simply compared with 'a fast-growing weed', but as the description continues we find that she is sitting with 'her lap full of bluebells and hawthorn' (p.10) and as she gazes at the cathedral towers in the distance she notices a bird's nest behind a gargoyle and wishes she was a bird in that nest. As if to emphasise her estrangement from the world that Elgood represents, she is represented as antipathetic to the stage and in fact not a very good actress; for her it means drudgery:

> I wish I could earn a good salary, father, for your sake; but I should never be fond of acting. I've seen too much of the theatre. If I'd been a young lady, now, shut up in a drawing-room all my life, and brought to the theatre for the first time to see 'Romeo and Juliet', I could fancy myself wanting to play Juliet; but I've seen too much of the ladder Juliet stands on in the balcony scene, and the dirty-looking man that holds it steady for her, and the way she quarrels with Mrs. Wappers the nurse, between the acts. I've read the play often, father, since you've told me to study Juliet, and I've tried to fancy her a real living woman in Verona, under a sky as blue as these flowers – but I can't – I can only think of Miss Villeroy, in her whitey-brown satin, and Mrs. Wappers, in her old green and yellow brocade, – and the battered old garden scene – and the palace flats we use so often – and the scene-shifters in their dirty shirt-sleeves. All the poetry has been taken out of it for me, father. (p. 12)

Justina's vivid backstage perspective shows a reality that contrasts with the 'reality' she is looking for in drama. She can neither enter into the poetry of Shakespeare's text, nor are her professional skills sufficient to rise above the constraints of miserably inadequate means of creating an illusion. Nevertheless, Justina does become a successful actress, not in Shakespeare, but playing the heroine in a fashionable comedy, and as she becomes established as a star in the theatrical scene, there is great emphasis on the naturalness of her acting: 'She was … natural yet artistic – free from all trick, unaffected, modest, yet with the impulsive boldness of a true artist' (p. 227). In fact the opening opposition of the rural with the urban, of the natural with the theatrical, is further complicated at the novel proceeds.

At the beginning Justina's life in a world of tawdry theatricality is contrasted with Madge Bellingham's life as she moves from the hardships of impoverished gentility to the comfort of marriage to a wealthy Cornish landowner. Unusually for Braddon, the audacious crime that underpins the plot is committed by a male rather than a female protagonist. Churchill Penwyn, an intelligent and ambitious lawyer, murders his younger cousin, James, in order to inherit the Penwyn estate in Cornwall, and thus have the financial security to marry Madge. The murder having been committed, and the marriage solemnised, Madge and Churchill set up as respectable and dutiful landlords in Cornwall. Stereotypically, Churchill takes upon his shoulders the responsibility for their material comfort and the financial improvement of the estate, while Madge, an adoring wife, finds herself the custodian of Christian values in their marriage. Compared with the criminal secrets of Penwyn Manor the secrets of the theatrical family of Matthew Elgood are free of shame. It is these secrets that Maurice Clissold, a gentleman-detective in the mould of Robert Audley or the less gentlemanly Richard Thornton of *Eleanor's Victory*, sets out to uncover. He has been friend and mentor to the murdered James, and after the latter's death becomes friend, lover and eventually husband of Justina. The uncovering of the secrets of Elgood's past reveals that Justina is only an adopted daughter of the actor; when all the facts are revealed she is discovered to be the true heir to the Penwyn estate. She leaves the stage, and, refusing to appropriate Penwyn Manor, lives in contentment with her husband in a newly-built house nearby.

From the opening pages, Braddon has granted the theatre a kind of moral respectability by associating it with the church. In the scene I have already quoted from it is the cathedral that is the focus of Justina's attention, and the theatre itself is built close to the cathedral: 'The theatre stood in the angle of a small square, almost overshadowed by the towers of the cathedral, as if the stage had gone to the church for sanctuary and protection from the intolerance of bigots' (p. 23). The theatre, though, is a fragile home for Christian values; Braddon is acutely aware of the disreputable side of the life of provincial touring, and represents theatrical people as quick to seize any source of enjoyment. But, however hard-drinking and fond of food and however chaotic their lifestyle, they, like the circus people in *Hard Times*, are good-hearted and support each other in their difficulties. Nevertheless, by showing Justina's unease in this environment at the beginning of the novel, and at the end by making her forsake the stage, where she has found considerable success, and restoring her to the rural environment to which she more 'naturally' belongs, Braddon indicates a lack of confidence in the theatre as a suitable context for the conventionally virtuous.

A similar uncertainty becomes apparent in Geraldine Jewsbury's *The Half Sisters* (1848).[27] Like Braddon, Jewsbury uses the theatrical context to provide a contrast: one sister is an actress, the other wife to a busy industrialist. The main focus of the novel is the rise of Bianca, from her arrival in England, with her impoverished and half-insane mother, to her establishment as a leading actress in London. But Jewsbury both assesses acting and its cultural significance differently from Braddon, and adopts a less popular approach. Whereas Braddon shows great awareness of the artistry, dedication and need for training of the professional actress, she does not, as Jewsbury does, reflect on the spiritual aspects of the art of acting. Jewsbury, through the dialogue between Bianca and her mentor, the 'great actor', who is never named, reflects with great earnestness on the mission of acting, on its responsibilities as an art form. Furthermore the intertwining of acting and life is explored in meditative as well as in more dramatic ways, as the novel traces the actress's romantic relationships with the worthless Conrad (who deserts her) and the steadier and devoted Lord Melton (who marries her).

One crisis of the plot comes when Melton, already passionately in love himself, has promised to find out whether Conrad has any serious intent towards Bianca. Before he can do so, Bianca overhears Conrad talking to some friends at an after-theatre party: 'The Bianca is a very good girl … but she is the last woman in the world I would marry' (p. 208). When Melton comes to find her, she looks terrible and he wants to take her home, but she protests in the language of the theatre: 'No, no, I tell you, I am quite able to go through my business' (p. 209). And indeed she acts her way superlatively through the rest of the evening: 'Bianca, who did not in general excel in this species of light skirmish, seemed that evening inspired, and was brilliant enough to have established a dozen reputations' (p. 210). Ironically, at this moment of effortful acting, a young admirer whispers to Conrad: 'You would hardly suppose, to look at her, that she was an actress' (p. 210). The intertwining of acting and living is finally broken, and a happy ending contrived, when she awakes to her love for Melton and without hesitation gives up the stage when she marries him. Again, it seems that the virtuous heroine must in the end forsake the theatre.

Braddon does represent an accomplished and successful actress in *Hostages to Fortune*.[28] Like Jewsbury's Bianca, she is devoted to her art, but unlike Bianca, her moral standards are questionable. As in *A Strange World*, there are contrasting worlds, but whereas in the latter, the contrast is between the fundamentally commendable moral standards of the theatrical world and the moral blemishes in the apparent rural idyll, in *Hostages to*

Fortune the moral ranking goes in reverse order. In this novel the brittle reality of the commercial world of the theatre is contrasted with two idylls: that of the Welsh countryside, home of Editha Morcombe, and that of the Devonian past of the writer, Herman Westray and the actress-manageress, Myra Brandreth. The link between the three worlds is made through Herman, who marries Editha and whisks her away to Fulham, where, like David Copperfield and Dora, they set up extravagant and unsuccessful housekeeping.[29] Unable at this stage to fully embrace the Christian virtues represented by Editha, Herman turns towards Myra, in search of professional stimulation and conversational excitement. Metropolitan life generally is shown to be giddy and godless, but Myra is to some extent aloof. There is nothing shoddy about her life – at least in its material aspects; her theatrical company is carefully chosen and well turned out, and in her private life she is discreet in clothing and lifestyle. Her tasteful and well-ordered home contrasts with the shambles at Fulham, and her understanding of theatrical effect is vital in bringing Herman's comedies to life on the stage. The emphasis in the way a theatrical text is discussed and treated is on visual effect. As Kate Mattacks points out, Myra 'translates the text into a bodily text which ensures its success with an audience trained in the reading of legible somatic signs'.[30] To this extent the novel suggests an analogy between Herman/Myra's play texts and Braddon's own work, for it is her skill in making her writing visually appealing, in creating 'legible somatic signs' for the reader, that helped to create her popularity as a novelist. The parallel extends also to the plot, since both explore the proposition that, as the cynical man-about-town, Hamilton Lyndhurst, puts it: 'A man can love honestly but once in his life' (p. 180). Lyndhurst, furthermore, attacks the need for didacticism in art: 'The greatest works of literary art have been innocent of moral teaching' (p. 180). But Braddon's fiction is not innocent of moral teaching. Myra's desire to re-possess Herman, her first lover, leads her to devise with Hamilton a scheme to compromise Editha. The scheme ultimately fails, Editha and Herman live happily ever after, and Myra's downfall and moral disgrace is confirmed, ironically enough, in her last theatrical success. Having brought back to England a French play that she manages to produce without alterations to satisfy English censorship, she achieves an astonishing success in it. But, drained by the nightly performances, she falls ill and at the end of the novel we see her being wheeled in a bath chair, paralysed and insane. Herman, meanwhile, re-discovers his love for Editha, resolves to submit his writing in the future 'to her refining taste' (p. 334), and retires to live with her in the Welsh countryside, forsaking the metropolis and the stage.

Mattacks argues that *Hostages to Fortune*, like so much other sensation fiction plays on the conflation of theatre and home.[31] I should like now to turn to a novel where the theatre is not specifically present, though it is implied in various ways as the home becomes an acting space. *The Doctor's Wife*, Braddon's homage to *Madame Bovary*, is set partly in the fictional town of Conventford, which represents the Coventry that Braddon visited as an actress.[32] In this nondescript town, the young Isabel Sleaford acts as nursery-governess in Charles Raymond's undemanding household. Even though this position has rescued her from her chaotic and somewhat mysterious family, she is bored and dissatisfied with her life, imaginatively exploring possibilities of fulfilment. Acting is one of these: 'Sometimes, when the orphans were asleep, Miss Sleaford let down her long black hair before the little looking-glass, and acted to herself in a whisper … Sometimes she thought of leaving friendly Mr Raymond, and going up to London with a five-pound note in her pocket, and coming out at one of the theatres as a tragic actress' (p. 74). There is a distinction between these two fantasies; wholly unrealistic, the idea of actually going on the stage is never remotely possible, but being an actress in her own life is. As the novel goes on Isabel assuages her boredom by imagining herself as, or comparing herself with different heroines drawn from drama, poetry and prose fiction, including both Florence and Edith Dombey. Sometimes it is not clear to what extent the fantasy is in Isabel's imagination and to what extent it derives from the way that Isabel is represented through theatrical analogy. For instance, as she wanders in the garden after her charges are asleep: '[she] stole softly down and went out into the garden to walk up and down in the fair moonlight; the beautiful moonlight in which Juliet had looked more lovely than the light of day to Romeo's enraptured eyes; in which Hamlet had trembled before his father's ghostly face' (p. 73). In context this passage reads as poetic allusion on the part of the narrator, but later in the paragraph the romantic allusion is captured in free indirect speech: 'She was getting quite old … she was nearly eighteen! Juliet was buried in the tomb of the Capulets before this age, and haughty Beatrix had lived her life, and Florence Dombey was married and settled, and the story all over' (p. 73).

But Isabel also imagines herself in more generic roles. Even as she agrees to marry George Gilbert, the humble and dedicated provincial doctor, she imagines herself in the *role* of bride and wife, with him in a supporting role: 'He was the bridegroom, the husband; a secondary character in the play of which she was the heroine' (p. 99). Later, a bored wife, her visions of a sentimental friendship with Roland Lansdell are abruptly brought to an end when he sends her a letter in which he announces his intention of leaving England for some time to come. The narrator typically, and crisply, balances sympathy with judgement and criticism: 'She was very wretched, very foolish' (p. 221). Sitting at her mirror, as she had been when 'acting to herself' (p. 74), Isabel experiences real suffering; she is no longer 'acting', but exaggerated expression of her feelings leads to their representation in theatrical terms, and the thought of her life being finished is given literal expression in the idea of suicide:

> And now it was all over, and she would never, never, never, never see him again! Her life was finished. Ah, how truly he had spoken on the battlements of the ruined tower! and how bitterly the meaning of his works came home to her to-day! Her life was finished. The curtain had fallen, and the lights were out; and she had nothing more to do but to grope blindly about upon a darkened stage until she sank in the great vampire-trap – the grave. A pale ghost, with sombre shadowy hair, looked back at her from the glass. Oh, if she could die, if she could die! She thought of the mill-stream. (p. 222)

Her thoughts of death, generated by the theatrical imagery, pass to the thought of Ophelia and a picture that recalls Millais's famous painting, and thence to thoughts of what lies beyond death, whereupon the narrator takes up the theatrical allusions with a further reference to *Hamlet*, explicitly comparing Isabel's fear of the hereafter with that of Shakespeare's tragic hero. These theatrical allusions, then, draw attention to Isabel's over-fondness for playing roles of her own choosing rather than living the roles allotted to her by provincial society, thus reminding us of the theatricality of ordinary domestic life, of the extent to which living *is* role-playing. At the same time the continual narratorial comparisons between her circumstances and those of Shakespeare's heroes and heroines elevates the predicaments of Braddon's characters, conferring a solemnity that dignifies the ordinary, even as the narrator reminds us of their littleness: 'I know that she was alike wicked and silly; I know that it must be difficult to win sympathy for a grief so foolish, an anguish so self-engendered; but her sorrow was none the less real to her because it seems foolish in the eyes of wisdom' (p. 223).

The Doctor's Wife is not written in Braddon's most popular style; there are long passages which analyse in detail the consciousness of both Isabel and her lover, Roland Lansdell, and there are similarly long passages of narratorial reflection and moralising. But the novel introduces an element of metafictionality through the character of Sigismund Smith, the sensation writer, who had an 'enthusiastic devotion to his profession' (p. 49) and who holds forth with great volubility about the particular techniques and strategies of sensationalism, thus emphasising the difference from the more reflective, introverted 'telling' that is the predominant mode for the novel itself. More usually, however, Braddon writes with an emphasis on visual description, using what might be called 'dramatic' techniques. Winifred Hughes has noted sensationalism's characteristic employment of setting to convey or intensify emotional effect.[33] Braddon manages this with great artistry in, for instance, *Lady Audley's Secret* as she moves from the languid, Mariana-like scene presented at the opening of the novel, via a brief description of the setting sun seen by George Talboys on board ship as he returns from Australia, to the passionate description of the effect of the setting sun on Audley Court, thus linking the two different environments and hence the characters inhabiting them, and transforming the placidity of the old house with a fiery foreboding. It is as though, in a novel that owes much to Tennyson, 'Mariana' has acquired the emotional intensity of *Maud*. Very different, though no less intense, is the emotional effect created in the description of Editha's ferry-crossing in *Hostages to Fortune*, where the pitching and tossing of the vessel, the confusion and the bleakness of the dawn-scene at Ostend, mirror her emotional turmoil and distress, and, further, suggest that there is still more distressing emotion to come. This novel is written in the present tense which, appropriately enough for a novel that is so focused on theatre, intensifies the dramatic effect.

The sense of the novel as a dramatic script is increased by Braddon's use of direct rather than indirect or free indirect speech, by her representation of characters' thoughts through (unheard) direct speech, by the description of actions and facial expression and by the avoidance of long passages of narratorial commentary. At moments of emotional drama theatrical poses are described, as for instance in *A Strange World*, when to please his wife, Churchill agrees to give up the Penwyn estate, even though Justina has said he can keep half of it. She exclaims, 'Churchill, my own true husband', and then we are presented with a simply-posed tableau signifying wifely devotion: 'She was on her knees by his side, her head lying against his breast, her eyes looking up at him with love unspeakable' (p. 366).

Braddon's characteristic reliance on visual means of representation is partnered by an interest in the reading of facial expression and in acts of looking. In *Eleanor's Victory*, for example, where several of the characters are quite deliberately playing roles that confuse their identity, Eleanor is forced to conceal her real identity in order to accept the post of companion to young Laura Mason. There she meets the man she holds responsible for the death of her father. Now known by his real name of Launcelot Darrell, he has masqueraded under the name Robert Lance while living in Paris, where he has been a gambling acquaintance of Eleanor's father. As Eleanor pursues her plan of revenge against him, she alternates the roles of incompetent detective and Greek tragic heroine; in both the face and the gaze play an important part. Her method of detection is to study the face of her enemy in the hope that he will give himself away. As a tragic heroine it is her own face that possesses the potential to give her away. When Richard joins her as a fellow amateur detective, he asks how she has investigated Darrell's 'antecedents':

> 'I have watched him very closely,' she said, 'and I've listened to every word he has ever said –'
> 'To be sure. In the expectation, no doubt, that he would betray himself by frowns and scowls, and other facial contortion, after the manner of a stage villain'. (p. 215)

It is Richard who introduces a more 'scientific' method of detection, in which he traces material clues to follow Launcelot Darrell's movements and to deduce what they might mean. Nevertheless, the visual is still important. Darrell is struggling to make a career as a painter, and Richard, as an artist himself (though, as Darrell is quick to point out, in the inferior genre of scene-painting), realises that the man's work will betray his preoccupations. In fact the examination of his portfolio very quickly supplies a résumé of his various places of residence, and since the Paris pictures are signed with the pseudonym, suspicions are strengthened about his illicit residence in that city. Faced with what to her is incontrovertible proof of Darrell's guilt, Eleanor slips again into her world of revenge:

> The scene-painter … knew that Eleanor stood behind him, erect and statuesque, with her hand grasping the back of his chair, a pale Nemesis bent on revenge and destruction … looking round at that pale young face, Richard saw how terrible was the struggle in the girl's breast, and how likely she was at any moment to betray herself.
> 'Eleanor,' he whispered, 'if you want to carry this business to the end, you must keep your secret. Launcelot Darrell is coming this way. Remember that an artist is quick to observe. There is the plot of a tragedy in your face at this moment.' (p. 223)

Richard, a man of the theatre, in the earlier comment points out the difference between the way people behave in life and the way they act in melodrama, but here he is forced to recognise that people may 'betray' themselves by facial expression in life, as readily as on the stage.

Even in her most 'popular' fiction, fiction that was written for the cheap weekly magazines, Braddon's interest in eyes, in the act of looking and in the interplay of gazes is not without subtlety. When, in *Rupert Godwin*, Violet finds herself posed as the Queen of Beauty, passive as a statue, she has nothing to say or do and the only activity possible for her is to look at the audience. The episode comprises a polyphony of gazes. As she waits onstage, Violet faces the 'prospect of finding herself the focus of all the eyes in the crowded house' (p. 120), yet the moment of curtain-up is represented from her point of view. As the 'confused mass of faces and glittering lamps' that first presents itself to her eyes resolves into individual faces, she is able to look around and sees her lover, George Stanmore. He is totally ignorant of her fate at this point in the novel and his eyes are 'fixed upon vacancy' (p. 121), but she fixes her gaze on him and is startled by her recognition of a similarity between his eyes and those of an unfriendly fellow actress, Esther Vanburgh (who turns out to be his half-sister). George in his turn, it is revealed, has been attracted by a similarity in the eyes of the Queen of Beauty to those of his sweetheart. But if the eyes are a medium of recognition, they can also be deceived. In this instance Violet's identity is masked by her costume and by her distance from the spectator, who is without opera glasses. This scene gives Violet superiority of knowledge up to a point, but she fails to understand how profoundly she is disguised. The next time the *tableau* is described she is represented as the vulnerable object of the magnified male gaze. Adopting a neutral stance, the narrator describes how Violet attracts the attention of the ill-intentioned men scrutinising her through opera glasses from their box. Thus aided, her 'wicked' uncle is able to penetrate her theatrical disguise. It is her theatrical status as a woman on display, advertising her charms to the men in the audience, however unconsciously and innocently, that renders Violet the object of sexual desire.

As Louis James has pointed out, popular fiction of the nineteenth century has much in common with popular drama; they share 'the same approach to style, plot, moral outlook, and character portrayal – that of melodrama'.[34] This popular approach is one that appeals primarily to the visual sense; avoiding the philosophical ruminations of George Eliot or the detailed psychological analysis of Trollope, visual imagery is employed to make more vivid both the moral messages and the psychological analysis of characters and relationships. Refusing to align himself with the contemporary view of sensation fiction as immoral and diseased, Henry James remarked in a review of *Aurora Floyd* in the *Nation* (1865) that Braddon may have taken advantage of the 'romance' of 'vice', but 'she has done it with … a strict regard to morality'.[35] Her representations of the world of the theatre are fully alive to its reputation for loose morals and the common assumption that actresses were no better than prostitutes. However, like Dickens, Braddon shows that although the life of the players may not conform to the standards of respectability that were promoted by the middle class, nevertheless the actors themselves, hard-working professionals, who are impelled, like any middle-class professional or entrepreneur, by the need to succeed and make money, can rise to superior heights, overcoming professional competition to support their colleagues. By drawing on her theatrical experiences for the content of her novels, Braddon not only provides a flamboyant setting and characters, lending to the domestic the charm of the exotic, but she also conveys a moral message that is firmly grounded in traditional Christian values, however ambivalent she may be about theatre as an environment for the virtuous heroine.

Notes

1 Robert Lee Wolff, *Sensational Victorian* (New York and London: Garland, 1979).
2 Wolff, *Sensational Victorian*, p. 119.
3 Wolff, *Sensational Victorian*, p. 5.
4 Jennifer Carnell, *The Literary Lives of Mary Elizabeth Braddon: A Study of her Life and Work* (Hastings: The Sensation Press, 2000).
5 [Henry Mansel], 'Sensation novels', *Blackwood's Edinburgh Magazine*, 91 (1863), 482–514.
6 *The Times* (5 February 1915), 9.
7 Richard Foulkes, *The Calverts: Actors of Some Importance* (London: The Society for Theatre Research, 1992), p. 8.
8 Carnell, *Literary Lives*, p. 71.
9 Carnell, *Literary Lives*, p. 74.
10 www.chriswillis.freeserve.co.uk.
11 She herself could retain copyright of stage performances if there was one performance of her script; copyright of the novel was only infringed if the dramatic adapter had his or her version published.
12 Kerry Powell, *Women and Victorian Theatre* (Cambridge: Cambridge University Press, 1997).
13 Ruth Burridge Lindemann, 'Dramatic Disappearances: Mary Elizabeth Braddon and the Staging of Theatrical Character', *Victorian Literature and Culture* (1997), 279–91, 288.
14 The novel that is generally taken to be most autobiographical in its use of a theatrical background, *A Lost Eden*, dates from 1904. I have, however, confined

the discussion in this chapter to novels written within the Victorian period.

15 She is not alone, of course, in doing this. Othello, for instance, stands as a bench-mark for male jealousy, and it is not uncommon to find that novelists who are dealing with this issue refer explicitly to Shakespeare's character: for instance Trollope (*He Knew He Was Right*) and Reade (*Griffith Gaunt*).

16 Martin Meisel, *Realizations: Narrative, Pictorial, and Theatrical Arts in Nineteenth-Century England* (Princeton, NJ: Princeton University Press, 1983), p. 3. Subsequent page references are given in the text.

17 Mary Elizabeth Braddon, *Dead-Sea Fruit* [1868] (London: Simpkin, Marshall, Hamilton, Kent & Co. Ltd., 1891), p. 105.

18 Mary Elizabeth Braddon, *John Marchmont's Legacy* [1863] (Oxford: Oxford University Press, 1999). Subsequent page references are given in the text.

19 Mary Elizabeth Braddon, 'At Daggers Drawn', in *Under the Red Flag and other tales* [1883] (London: J. and R. Marshall, n.d.).

20 Mary Elizabeth Braddon, *Eleanor's Victory* [1863] (Stroud: Alan Sutton Publishing, 1996). Subsequent page references are given in the text.

21 Tracy C. Davis, *Actresses as Working Women* (London: Routledge, 1991). Subsequent page references are given in the text.

22 Mary Elizabeth Braddon, 'Lord Lytton', *Belgravia* (1873), 73–88, 87.

23 Mary Elizabeth Braddon, 'Across the Footlights', in *Under the Red Flag and other tales* [1883] (London: J. and R. Marshall, n.d.).

24 Mary Elizabeth Braddon, *Rupert Godwin* [1867] (London: Simpkin, Marshall, Hamilton, Kent & Co. Ltd., n.d.). Subsequent page references are given in the text.

25 The mid-Victorian burlesque frequently (as here) combined parody with gorgeous spectacle.

26 Mary Elizabeth Braddon, *A Strange World* [1875] (London: Simpkin, Marshall, Hamilton, Kent & Co. Ltd., n.d.). Subsequent page references are given in the text.

27 Geraldine Jewsbury, *The Half Sisters* [1848] (Oxford: Oxford University Press, 1994). Subsequent page references are given in the text.

28 Mary Elizabeth Braddon, *Hostages to Fortune* [1875] (London: J. and R. Maxwell, 1878). Subsequent page references are given in the text.

29 The comparison is explicitly noted by Editha herself, p. 171.

30 Kate Mattacks, 'After Lady Audley: M. E. Braddon, the Actress and the Act of Writing in *Hostages to Fortune*', in Emma Liggins and Daniel Duffy (eds), *Feminist Readings of Victorian Popular Texts: Divergent Femininities* (Aldershot: Ashgate, 2001), p. 80.

31 The extent to which sensation fiction recognised the home as a place of performance is discussed by Lyn Pykett, *The Sensation Novel: from The Woman in White to The Moonstone* (Plymouth: Northcote House, 1994) and Jenny Bourne Taylor, *In the Secret Theatre of Home: Wilkie Collins, Sensation Narrative, and Nineteenth-Century Psychology* (London: Routledge, 1988).

32 Mary Elizabeth Braddon, *The Doctor's Wife* [1863] (Oxford: Oxford

University Press, 1999). Subsequent page references are given in the text.
33 Winifred Hughes, *The Maniac in the Cellar: Sensation Novels of the 1860s* (Princeton, NJ: Princeton University Press, 1980).
34 Louis James, *Fiction for the Working Man* (London: Oxford University Press, 1963), p. 147.
35 Henry James, 'Miss Braddon', *Notes and Reviews* [1921] (New York: Books for Libraries, 1968), p. 11.

Bibliography

Braddon, Mary Elizabeth, *Loves of Arcadia*, unpublished, 1860.
—— *Three Times Dead*, London: W. & M. Clark and Beverley, Empson, 1860.
—— *The Black Band* [1861] London: George Vickers, 1877.
—— *The Trail of the Serpent* [1861] New York: The Modern Library, 2003.
—— *Lady Audley's Secret* [1862] Oxford: Oxford University Press, 1987.
—— *Aurora Floyd* [1863] Oxford: Oxford University Press, 1996.
—— *Eleanor's Victory* [1863] Stroud: Alan Sutton Publishing, 1996.
—— *John Marchmont's Legacy* [1863] Oxford: Oxford University Press, 1999.
—— *The Doctor's Wife* [1864] Oxford: Oxford University Press, 1999.
—— *Rupert Godwin* [1867] London: Simpkin, Marshall, Hamilton, Kent & Co. Ltd., n.d.
—— *Dead-Sea Fruit* [1868] London: Simpkin, Marshall, Hamilton, Kent & Co. Ltd., 1891.
—— ' Lord Lytton', *Belgravia* (1873), 73–88.
—— *Lost for Love*, London: Chatto and Windus, 1874.
—— *A Strange World* [1875] London: Simpkin, Marshall, Hamilton, Kent & Co. Ltd., n.d.
—— *Hostages to Fortune* [1875] London: J. and R. Maxwell, 1878.
—— *Under the Red Flag and Other Tales* [1883] London: J. and R. Marshall, n.d.
—— *The Fatal Three* [1888] Stroud: Sutton Publishing Limited, 1997.
—— *Rough Justice* [1898] London: Simpkin, Marshall, Hamilton, Kent & Co. Ltd., 1899.
—— *A Lost Eden*, London: Hutchinson, 1904.
Carnell, Jennifer, *The Literary Lives of Mary Elizabeth Braddon: A Study of her Life and Work*, Hastings: The Sensation Press, 2000.
Davis, Tracy, C., *Actresses as Working Women*, London: Routledge, 1991.
Foulkes, Richard, *The Calverts: Actors of Some Importance*, London: The Society for Theatre Research, 1992.
Hughes, Winifred, *The Maniac in the Cellar: Sensation Novels of the 1860s*, Princeton, NJ: Princeton University Press, 1980.
James, Henry, 'Miss Braddon', *Notes and Reviews* [1921] New York: Books for Libraries, 1968.
James, Louis, *Fiction for the Working Man*, London: Oxford University Press, 1963.

Jewsbury, Geraldine, *The Half Sisters* [1848] Oxford: Oxford University Press, 1994.

Liggins, Emma and Daniel Duffy (eds), *Feminist Readings of Victorian Popular Texts: Divergent Femininities*, Aldershot: Ashgate, 2001.

Lindemann, Ruth Burridge, 'Dramatic disappearances: Mary Elizabeth Braddon and the Staging of Theatrical Character', *Victorian Literature and Culture* (1997), 279–91.

[Mansel, Henry], 'Sensation novels', *Blackwood's Edinburgh Magazine*, 91 (1863), 482–514.

Mattacks, Kate, 'After Lady Audley: M. E. Braddon, the Actress and the Act of Writing in *Hostages to Fortune*', in Emma Liggins and Daniel Duffy (eds), *Feminist Readings of Victorian Popular Texts: Divergent Femininities*, Aldershot: Ashgate, 2001.

Meisel, Martin, *Realizations: Narrative, Pictorial, and Theatrical Arts in Nineteenth-Century England*, Princeton, NJ: Princeton University Press, 1983.

Powell, Kerry, *Women and Victorian Theatre*, Cambridge: Cambridge University Press, 1997.

Pykett, Lyn, *The Sensation Novel from The Woman in White to The Moonstone*, Plymouth: Northcote House, 1994.

Taylor, Jenny Bourne, *In the Secret Theatre of Home: Wilkie Collins, Sensation Narrative, and Nineteenth-Century Psychology*, London: Routledge, 1988.

Wolff, Robert Lee, *Sensational Victorian*, New York and London: Garland, 1979.

The Times, 'Miss Braddon', 5 February 1915.

www.chriswillis.freeserve.co.uk.

9

'LOVE': Rhoda Broughton, writing and re-writing romance

Shirley Jones

> It is said that our Rhoda herself was once thought improper. 'I began my career,' said she with a joyful snort, 'as Zola, I finish it as Miss Yonge; it's not I that have changed, it's my fellow country-men.'[1]

Rhoda Broughton here identifies the polarities of her contemporary reputation. She made a dramatic entry onto the literary scene with two immensely popular and critically divisive 'sensation' novels and after a long career found herself reviewed as a purveyor of safe pleasurable stories.[2] A similar contrariness is to be found in biographical accounts of Broughton. She is usually described as leading a sedate and uneventful life and at the same time she has a public persona which is represented as highly social, witty and daring in her conversation. To some she is a formidable figure, in 1874 an observer wrote: 'She walked about in such a "strong-minded" manner, stared at people and talked loud, and showed by every look and action that she knew perfectly well that she was the most important person there.'[3] In contrast to the 'strong-minded' and self-satisfied figure described above, Broughton appears to others to exemplify the Victorian amateur lady writer. After Broughton's death in 1920, Marie Belloc Lowndes, a close friend, states that 'she was curiously humble about her books. It was almost as if she was content to regard her literary gift as a kind of elegant accomplishment'. This comment is taken from the foreword Belloc Lowndes wrote to Broughton's posthumously published *A Fool in Her Folly*.[4] In this work, Charlotte, the would-be-writer heroine spends ten minutes facing the challenge of a blank page before she takes up her pen:

> There could at least be no doubt about what the title was to be, and I inscribed it hastily in capitals:
>   'LOVE'

It did not take long to write the great monosyllable, nor to make a dash
after it! (pp. 25–6)

Charlotte's writing of desire comes to a very bitter end and curiously
Broughton's lifetime of writing is completed with a tale which considers
'professional authorship as not at all suitable for ladies'.[5] But Broughton's
own career 'spans the distance between the "Girl of the Period" and the
"New Woman".[6] And throughout her writing life she wrote romantic
fiction; as Ernest Baker states, her subject matter was consistently 'nothing
but love'.[7]

Broughton describes how she started her writing career on 'a certain
wet Sunday afternoon when she was about twenty-two; she was distinctly
bored by a stupid book which she was trying to read, when "the spirit
moved her to write". She 'wrote swiftly and in secret, until at the end of
six weeks she found a vast heap of manuscript accumulated, to which she
gave the title of "Not Wisely, but Too Well". In January 1865 she showed
the manuscript to her uncle (by marriage), Sheridan Le Fanu, who
published the novel as a serial in the *Dublin University Magazine* (August
1865–July 1866) and suggested book publication to George Bentley.[8]
Bentley turned the novel down on the grounds of taste but accepted
Cometh Up as a Flower (which appeared in the *Dublin University Magazine*,
July 1866–January 1867) as a replacement and Broughton worked upon
revisions of the first novel which was eventually published by the Tinsley
Brothers.[9] Both novels were published in volume form in the same year,
1867, thus the peculiarities of Broughton's style were clearly and doubly
established with the public.[10]

Broughton was first published at the age of twenty-four and her career
was to last until her death in 1920. She produced twenty-six novels and
a collection of supernatural short stories. The best bibliography available
at present is to be found in Marilyn Wood's *Rhoda Broughton (1840–
1920), Profile of a Novelist*.[11] Despite the initial problems Bentley became
the chief publisher of Broughton's work. Many of Broughton's novels
appeared first in serial form in *Temple Bar* before volume publication.[12]
All of her novels from *Red as a Rose is She* in 1870 until *Dear Faustina* in
1897 (with the exception of the collaborative *A Widower Indeed*, 1891)
were published by Bentley.[13] In 1898 after the death of George Bentley,
Macmillan took over the copyright of Broughton's novels and published
her new work from 1899 until 1910. From 1912 Broughton published
three novels with Stanley, Paul and Co., and the posthumously printed
A Fool in Her Folly was published by Odhams. Broughton's earlier novels
appear in very many editions, consequently it is still possible to buy

these works second-hand but the later one-volume novels are treasures now rarely found.

Although seemingly not writing with the same financial imperative as many women writers (she never had a family of children to support), Broughton did not see herself undersold and kept a healthy interest in the earnings of other novelists.[14] Percy Lubbock states that Broughton's income from writing was significant in maintaining her social life and her seasonal visits to London.[15] Wood speculates that Broughton gave financial help to her relatives.[16] Although Broughton lost her scandalous early status and her popularity diminished with time, she never lost an audience. However, when she adopted the one-volume form from 1892 onwards she was paid pro rata, so her income considerably lessened.[17] Despite living in straitened circumstances in later years (Lubbock describes Broughton as 'poor'), Wood notes that Broughton left 'effects' valued at over £6,000 which seems a fair sum for a single woman in 1920, but of course notions of wealth are relative.[18]

In *Rhoda Broughton* Wood admits that finding biographical information about her subject is difficult: 'Even those who were quite close to her at various times in her life admitted total ignorance of much of her personal history'. Before her death Broughton destroyed all her correspondence.[19] Born on 29 November 1840, Broughton was the third child of Rev. and Mrs Delves Broughton, she had two older sisters and a younger brother. She was born at Segrwyd Hall, near Denbigh in Wales. She lived for most of her youth at Broughton Hall, Staffordshire. Broughton's mother died in 1860 and her father died in 1863. Broughton then moved to Surbiton where her sisters lived together. In 1864, her sister Eleanor married William Newcombe and Broughton was invited to live with her sister and brother-in-law at Upper Eyarth in Denbighshire. The Newcombes lived here for fourteen years and had two sons. When William Newcombe died, Broughton and her sister moved to Oxford. They lived in Oxford from 1878–1889 and in Richmond from 1890–1899. When Eleanor died Broughton moved to Headington Hill, near Oxford to live with a cousin. She stayed here until her death.

One assumes from reading Broughton's novels that she travelled in Europe.[20] She gives detailed descriptions of many locations in France, Italy, Switzerland and Germany.[21] She had many friends including Ethel and Matthew Arnold, Mary Cholmondley, Thomas Hardy, Henry James and Andrew Lang.[22] Broughton was very fond of dogs, and dogs feature as distinctive characters in many novels.[23] Unsurprisingly she was concerned for animal welfare and wrote an appeal to raise money for a rest home for horses.[24] Broughton was not associated with any kind of politically progressive or radical movement, she did not call herself a feminist. R. C. Terry, making a timely comparison in 1983, describes her as a 'Tory lady and iron maiden' who 'maintains a pleasing asperity and within her limitations contributed to the growing consciousness among women of their need for greater freedom, even though, as she grew older, larger changes than she could encompass had occurred.'[25]

Broughton never married and no one has named a lover, although Michael Sadleir asserts that an early unhappy love affair must have contributed to her depiction of lovers:

> There can be no shadow of doubt that the ill-fated love-affair of Char and Bill Drinkwater [in *A Fool in her Folly*] is the love-affair of Nell and Dick McGregor in *Cometh Up*, of Kate and Dare Stamer in *Not Wisely*, and of Rhoda herself, in her excited book-stimulated teens, and some discreditable unknown. If this be granted, the slant of all her work is accounted for, and the feverish element in the first two novels seen to be natural and inevitable. The abandon of her heroines' love-making, which so scandalized the 'sixties, was too fresh in her memory to be tuned to period taste, and the heart-break of her deserted girls was, for all its exaggeration, written from experience and not imagined.[26]

It is difficult to challenge or confirm Sadleir's theory. It is perfectly possible that Broughton's lifelong obsession with romance stemmed from unresolved personal experience, alternately a well-read young woman with a talent for observation and a fertile imagination could produce the 'feverish element' that Sadleir describes.

Broughton's critical reputation is still based on her earlier novels. Sadleir argues that 'the tyranny of the serial and three-decker convention' that Broughton submitted to in order to earn 'the larger payment which a full length fiction could command' resulted in the production of inferior fiction. It was only when Broughton resolved to give up writing three-volume novels that 'she found *herself*'.[27] And yet: 'probably hardly anyone nowadays has even heard of *Mrs. Bligh, Scylla and Charybdis, Dear Faustine* (sic), *A Waif's Progress, The Game and the Candle, Mamma, The Devil and the Deep Sea*, while every fiction-conscious reader knows, at least by name, *Cometh up as a Flower, Not Wisely but Too Well, Goodbye Sweetheart, Nancy* and *Belinda*' (p. 85). In Sadleir's view it is ironic that Broughton is best known for her lesser works. Undoubtedly Broughton's later slim volumes are spare, elegant and understated and deserve a wider readership.

In the late twentieth century Broughton's early work has been studied within the overlapping contexts of popular Victorian fiction, sensation fiction and the culture of women's reading. Her work has therefore largely been analysed as part of a phenomenon (sensation fiction/popular writing) at a particular historical moment (the 1860s and 1870s).[28] In an essay of this length I can only work with a limited number of texts but I want to extend the chronology of the texts discussed. I shall look first at the sensational start to Broughton's career, reviewing *Not Wisely, but Too Well* (1867), *Cometh Up as a Flower* (1867), *Red as a Rose is She* (1870) and *Good-bye Sweetheart!* (1872), then move to two *fin de siècle* texts, *Dear Faustina* (1897) and *The Game and the Candle* (1899) and then return to a deliberately belated 'Victorian' novel, *A Fool in Her Folly* (1920).[29] I want to explore the way that Broughton worked experimentally with the romance genre, how she constructed and reconstructed the concept of love, how she wrote the romance plot again and again but resisted formulaity, and finally how she re-read, re-wrote, and reviled her own early work in the posthumously published *A Fool in Her Folly*.

Many contemporary critics of Broughton quote Margaret Oliphant's *Blackwood's Edinburgh Magazine* article 'Novels' (1867) which finds popular women writers of the day largely responsible for the moral decline of the English novel.[30] Oliphant's outrage is amusing to a modern reader, but there is a tone of genuine distress which disturbs and also a sharp critical intelligence which astutely identifies many of the distinctive features of the contemporary Victorian heroine. Oliphant takes offence at women writers who make public women's desires and whose heroines revel in physicality; 'She waits now for flesh and muscles, for strong arms that seize her, and warm breath that thrills her through, and a host of other physical attractions, which she indicates to the world with a charming frankness' (p. 259). Broughton's identity as a 'sensation' writer rests entirely on her depiction of the excessively sensual and sexual. Adultery, or the possibility of it, is the most common 'crime' featured in her novels. Mysteries are always mysteries of the heart, and the supernatural when invoked is a mark of a disturbed state of mind.[31]

In her later survey *The Victorian Age of English Literature* (1892) in a chapter on 'The Younger Novelists', Margaret Oliphant summarises Rhoda Broughton's career thus, her 'novels, with that rashness which sometimes characterises women of genius, impatient of the supposed trammels of the conventional, were apt at first to play overmuch with those questions of "Passion" (as if there was but one passion in the world!) ... and were full of love-scenes too warm'.[32] Oliphant's emphasis here is still on the early novels and on the undoubted fact that Broughton's work is obsessed with 'questions of "Passion"'. She was wrong to assert that Broughton wrote about only one passion; there were other forms of love that Broughton wrote about, most significantly the love between family members. Though Broughton always worked with a romance plot, love did not always mean romance.

In 1867 Oliphant identified one of the hallmarks of the sensation heroine as her motherless status. This is true of the vast majority of Broughton's novels, in fact most of her heroines are not merely motherless but orphans (Broughton's own biography may be relevant here). As Oliphant states, this motherless position allows heroines a certain kind of liberty and vulnerability:

> Ill-brought-up motherless girls, left to grow anyhow, out of all feminine guardianship, have become the ideal of the novelist. There is this advantage in them, that benevolent female readers have the resource of saying 'Remember she had no mother,' when the heroine falls into any unusual lapse from feminine traditions.[33]

In Broughton's four early novels, only Nell in *Cometh Up as a Flower* has a parent living, and though the two share an idealised relationship, her father contributes substantially to the tragedy of Nell's romantic life. Kate in *Not Wisely, but Too Well*, Esther in *Red as a Rose is She*, and Lenore in *Good-bye Sweetheart!* are all orphans. Initially for Kate, her dead mother is a significant moral force until she becomes involved with Dare and cannot bear to look upon her image: 'She had exchanged her dead mother for living Dare, it seemed, and she clasped her bargain to her heart, and repented not of it' (p. 92). Desire for Dare represents growing up and growing away and Kate embraces this. For all these young heroines romantic love represents the ultimate experience that life can offer. For Kate, desiring Dare symbolises her abandonment of conventional morality and the throwing away of her socially acceptable self; at the same time her sensual self will find fulfilment. Dare is simply a projection of Kate's daring, her willingness to go beyond the proscribed path. He recognises her as 'one of those who would think the world well lost for love' (p. 30). Though Kate is saved from eloping with Dare, the path she eventually follows, working with the poor, functions as a retreat from the social world she was born into and represents too a suicidal urge. She rejects physical well-being and gives up her body to the demands of the spiritual. James Stanley, the poor clergyman who seeks to guide Kate's spiritual path offers an ironic reflection of Kate's love for Dare. As Kate loves James only as a brother, they both share the experience of a hopeless romantic love. His death, worn out by his ministry, foreshadows hers years later.

In all of these early novels the imaginative possibilities of the romantic tale are constructed in relation to the absolute finality of death. We know from the opening chapter of *Not Wisely, but Too Well* that Kate is dead. Her journey from innocence through temptation to probable salvation is (as the title indicates) a fable of misplaced but genuine love. After Dare's death Kate knows that to find any rest she has to wear her body out and she begs her sister: 'O Maggie, Maggie! let me go away and try to pray and work and *tire* myself into belief and peace again' (p. 355). Despite their very different moral values, death for Kate, Dare and James is the price of thwarted desire.

Cometh Up as a Flower charts Nell Le Strange's progress from graveyard to grave. It opens with Nell meditating quite cheerfully on where she will be buried when she dies and ends with her final words of prayer. It is in the graveyard on a beautiful May evening that Nell meets her one and only romantic love, Dick McGregor, a tall, blond and handsome soldier. He is as good as Dare Stamer is bad. Although Nell asserts that their first meeting is not like the meeting of a hero and heroine in a novel (p. 4), in retrospect it would seem to be love at first sight. On their fourth meeting Nell confesses to her readers that she is in love: 'for love him I did, though I have not said much about it, as it is no use dwelling on unpleasant truths' (p. 44). The controversial qualities of this novel lie not in the desire expressed for the wicked love object as in *Not Wisely, but Too Well* but in the first-person articulation of physical attraction. Nell knows she should not be saying what she is saying, her previous reticence is proof of this, yet she insists also on the undeniablity of her feelings. As in *Not Wisely* a substantial presence is described, admired and regretted when absent:

> Oh, my Dick, my bonny, bonny sweetheart! how goodly you were then! are you goodlier now, I wonder, in that distant *Somewhere* where you are; or when we meet next, shall we be two bodiless spirits, sexless, passionless essences, passing each other without recognition in the fields of ether? God forbid that it should be so! (p. 70)

Love-making is a pleasure that Nell enjoys: 'he kisses me softly, and I forget to be scandalized' (p. 72). Unlike Kate whose conscience at least recognises a maternal viewpoint, Nell revels in her motherless state: 'it was to me a matter of unfeigned and heartfelt gratulation that my mother had died in my infancy' (p. 27). She appreciates both the 'freedom' that this gives her and the close relationship that this gives her with her father: 'some one else would have been nearer his heart than I' (p. 28). But the love that Nell feels for her father hinders her romance with Dick. After Nell's scheming materialist sister Dolly puts an end to the correspondence between Nell and Dick (by hiding letters from Dick to Nell and forging a letter from Nell to Dick); Nell agrees to marry a suitor who has her father's approval. Having seemingly been rejected by Dick, Nell sacrifices herself in marriage to Sir Hugh Lancaster to please her father and rescue the family's reputation. Though Adrian Le Strange is cheered by the marriage he dies soon after and Nell is left with Sir Hugh, a kind but much older man. Nell finds his physical attentions repulsive. One night Nell is left alone having recently heard that Dick McGregor's regiment has been called to India and she fears she will never see him again. She has an 'overpowering mad longing … to go to him to ask him why he had been so cruel to me, to ask him to take me with him to that far sultry land' (p. 247). In an exemplary moment of transcendence, Nell's desire is fulfilled:

> The fire burnt cheerily; the wax candles shed a soft lustre round them; the old china on the mantel-shelf and table and cabinet looked comfortable and snug and homelike; but I felt stifled, choking. I went to the window, opened it, and stepped out into the verandah … It was not cold and I felt to breathe freer, leaning my face among the wet ivy, which climbed and twisted round the further pillar of the verandah.
>
> 'It was here he kissed me; it was here he took me in his arms', said I to myself, nestling my head among the dripping green. 'I thought I was going to spend my life with him, and now I am alone, alone for evermore! Great God, now (sic) unbearable!'
>
> Suddenly there comes a lull between two rainbursts; the moon comes sweeping out from behind a great cloud shoulder; the Portugal laurel beside me shakes and rustles; and from behind it a man steps out suddenly – steps out into the moonlit gravel walk, where the pebbles are glittering like so many diamonds. (p. 247)

The ideal home that Nell's marriage has brought her is a prison. She is suffocating and seeks escape outside its doors. The storm, of course, expresses Nell's desperation, by the light of the moon she watches her emotion externalised and gains relief. In nature she can speak her mind, in recalling her intimacy, she recreates it and conjures up the image of her lover. He steps out into the natural spotlight and the scene is set for romantic resolution. He is real, he is a true lover, pebbles have been turned into diamonds. All of Broughton's early heroines have this ability to call up their lovers through the strength of their longing, to move from the ordinary to the extraordinary; this is the essence of the appeal of romance, love transforms life. The omnipresence of death merely heightens the vitality of such moments.

Once Nell and Dick have reached the emotional climax of their romantic experience there is nothing left but to die. Although Nell in her 'insanity' begs Dick to take her with him, he refuses: 'Do you think I'm such a brute as to be the ruin of the only woman I ever loved?' (pp. 251–2). As marriage is impossible, they part. Dick dies of 'fever and ague at Lahore'(p. 280), Nell dies of consumption; able, she says 'to watch the steps of my own dissolution' (p. 281), fearing that she will not get to heaven: 'All the love and aspirations I had to bestow had been squandered on that intense earthly passion which seemed to be eating up body and soul. It was too late to mend now, but I was sorry it had been so' (p. 283). In opposition to the earthly passion, Nell tries to imagine the unimaginable and picture 'that land of unpictured, *unpicturable* passionless bliss' (p. 284).

Esther Craven, the heroine of *Red as a Rose is She* is like Kate and Nell an innocent; an orphan, the love of her life is her brother Jack. With few companions and an almost pathological desire to please she unwisely accepts Robert Brandon's marriage proposal. She doesn't exactly say 'yes' but she doesn't precisely say 'no' either (p. 22). She allows him to live in hope that she might come to love him. When Bob tells his family the arrangement becomes more formally defined and Esther finds herself in an uncomfortable situation. Bob is a good man but quite unlike the ideal lover that Esther had imagined: 'Miss Craven's ideal is dark; at seventeen, most ideals are dark: he has long, fierce, sleepy, unfathomable eyes. Robert is straw-coloured; his eyes are blue; very wide awake: they say exactly what his tongue does'. The difference between the ideal and the real here is rather like the difference between Dare and Dick; Bob, like Dick is a soldier. The ideal 'inspires fear equally with love; you can imagine his being harsh, fierce, cruel, to the woman he loves'. But of Bob, Broughton writes: 'Esther can indulge no faintest hope that he will bully her' (pp. 56–7). Although Broughton makes fun of Esther's ideal, she then offers him up to the reader. Esther goes to stay with some distant relatives and there he is: Esther unsurprisingly falls instantly in love. St John Gerard is (ironically given his name), a hero in the Rochester mould, and there is a Blanche Ingram kind of love rival in the figure of Constance Blessington.[34] St John is twice as old as Esther and has suffered in love, he is wary of a new romance, nevertheless he falls for Esther. The pleasure and pain of their relationship is explored over the next two-and-a-half volumes. They exchange much flirtatious and indeed serious banter, and Esther teases St John for his upholding of sexual double standards, but melodrama is the dominant mode of this coupling. Esther agrees to marry St John without telling him about Bob, but when St John finds out he is understandably unhappy and expresses himself with typical understatement: "'You are a murderer!" he answers, with fierce vehemence, looking at her once again as she had asked him – looking at her with wrathful, reluctant passion, but not kindly. "You have murdered my whole future –?" "If I am a murderer, I am a suicide too" (pp. 208–9), Esther replies. Again, Broughton makes the connection between loving and living, thwarted love and death. Gerard leaves home and before any amends can be made Esther is called away to see her sick brother. Jack dies and Esther is in fact now suicidal. As she kisses her dead brother goodbye she hopes she will catch the diptheria that has killed him. She neglects her health and own welfare. She is now penniless and homeless, and although Bob's family take her in she does not like being dependent on them, especially as Bob has released her from the engagement. Of course, it transpires that the only employment she can find is as a companion to Constance Blessington's elderly aunt and uncle. Constance is now engaged to St John, so it is only a matter of time before Esther and St John meet.

Again there are misunderstandings and problems to be waded through before true love can be acknowledged but the change in Esther's circumstances contributes to the renewed sympathy that St John feels for her. In Esther's work 'there is nothing to endure, nothing to enjoy; it is essentially negative, flat, stale, sterile' (p. 309). It is winter and she goes on 'long damp evening rambles' (p. 353), thinking nothing of her health and always of her brother. When St John arrives at Blessington Court (not having been told by Constance of Esther's presence) he is horrifed by the total lack of pity he finds for her plight. St John's sympathy is tested when he suspects (wrongly) that Esther is flirting with a gentleman visitor but then Constance finds St John and Esther together and mistakenly suspects the same. After harsh words from Constance, St John breaks off their engagement. Esther's virtue is confirmed but her sense of pride will not allow her to renew her engagement to St John. Esther says they must part, St John says 'death is the only "goodbye" I will accept as valid between us' (p. 431). Inevitably Esther is taken seriously ill and as she lies on what she has been told will be her deathbed, Esther asks to see St John '*now – at once – before I die!*' (p. 441, original emphasis). Safe in the knowledge of her death she reaches 'out her slight, weary arms to him – "kiss me, St. John!"' (p. 443). Then:

> Without a word he gathers her to his breast; fully understanding, in his riven heart, that this embrace, which she herself can ask for, must indeed be a final one; his lips cling to hers in the wild silence of a solemn last farewell.
> 'I'm glad you are not angry with me now,' she whispers, almost inaudibly;

and then her arms slacken their clasp about his bronzed neck, and her head droops heavy and inert on his shoulder.

And so they find them half an hour later: he, like one crazed, with a face as ashen white as her own, clasping a lifeless woman to his breast. (p. 443)

Broughton ends her penultimate chapter with these lines and then begins the final chapter by bringing Esther back from the dead. Esther is the first Broughton heroine privileged with a happy ending and this is the first of many endings to tease the reader with a sudden twist. In this instance Wood quite rightly sees Broughton as taking a cliché and turning it comically. But the frequency of such endings in Broughton seems to be both part celebration of authorial power (why shouldn't a plot turn unexpectedly?) and also a genuine belief in the myriad possiblities of life and love. The happy ending does not in fact bring closure. The last words of the novel are spent on Bob, who, like his forerunner, Dick, dies abroad, but not before he has heard of Esther's impending marriage and sent the best wedding gift he could afford. Bob is the true hero of the novel, growing in romantic stature as the novel progresses, although in no way suicidal ('with no life-hating madness' (p. 450)), symbolically he dies of unrequited love. Like James in *Not Wisely*, he is one of many male lovers in Broughton's work who offer self-denying devotion to heroines who desire others. The reader is always made aware of paths not chosen.

Good-bye Sweetheart! could be described as a darker re-working of *Red as a Rose is She*. The heroine and hero of *Good-bye Sweetheart!*, Lenore Herrick and Paul Le Mesurier are more extreme versions of the naturally flirtatious Esther Craven and the foolishly jealous St John. In fact the distinctive depiction of Lenore and Paul defines them perhaps more properly as anti-heroine and hero and points the reader to one of the novels that finds echoes in this text. Whereas *Red as a Rose* alludes to *Jane Eyre*, *Good-bye Sweetheart!* seems to be informed by the combatitive and experimental elements of *Villette* (1856).[35] It is Jemima, Lenore's older confirmed spinster sister who most resembles Lucy Snowe: she is described in the novel as being one of life's 'spectators' (p. 253) and by Eliza Lynn Linton as 'tart and priggish'.[36] But Lenore is, as Lucy Snowe was intended to be, a challenge to the reader. Though young and beautiful, she is 'not ladylike' (p. 152) and she 'hate[s] children' (p. 173). She is spoilt, wilful and reckless. Her insistence on always having her own way is explained by her upbringing:

'Once, long ago, when I was little, I was very, *very* ill – I'm not over strong now, though you would not think it to look at me – and the doctor said I was to have whatever I asked for, for fear of bringing on a fit of coughing if I screamed; and the consequence was that if I ever wanted anything I always threatened to break a blood-vessel, and straightway got it.' (p. 41)

The rosy redness of Esther's frequently flushed cheeks which signals her vulnerable sensuality and inabilty to cover her desire, becomes here in Lenore a violent image, a threat to self and others. The love story that develops from the meeting of Lenore and Paul is chararacterised by such excesses of expression. Jemima describes Paul's name as 'an ugly, abrupt little name' (p. 140) which reminds one of Monsieur Paul Emanuel, but Paul Le Mesurier does not offer Lenore the kind of sustenance that Brontë s hero ultimately offers her heroine. The relationship of Lenore and Paul is a battle of heart and will from start to finish.

The novel is set at first in France, then there is a return to England where everything goes wrong, and then finally the characters end their emotional journey in Switzerland. The novel charts a movement from the ridiculous to the sublime: the meeting of Lenore and Paul is farcical, but the ending amidst the Alpine scenery is genuinely pathetic. Lenore and Jemima are 'two innocents travelling about the Continent with a young man in our train' (p. 5), the young man, Frederick, is the first of Lenore's lovers in the novel, he is swiftly despatched when Lenore becomes attracted to Paul. Paul, a mere acquaintance of Frederick's is immediately perceived as a challenge by Lenore. When invited by Frederick to visit the two young women, Paul turns the offer down, Frederick takes great pleasure in repeating his words: 'one has enough of women in England' (p. 8). Lenore is captivated by the idea of this 'interesting misogynist' (p. 8). She vows to see him before nightfall and borrows a maid's outfit to achieve her aim. In the guise of a Breton peasant she visits the hotel where Frederick and Paul are staying and as she is acting as a waitress to Paul, he comments to Frederick on her looks: 'Do they grow them like this here? Because, if so, we had better import a few.' When he asks Lenore: '*Comment vous appellez-vous, ma chère?*' and tries to take her hand, she replies affronted 'in very good English' (p. 15). Lenore is embarrassed and ashamed by being found out, and disappointed too as Paul has 'a rather ugly tanned face' (p. 16). Paul is amused, he defines Lenore as a 'Girl of the Period' but asserts: 'From all such "Good Lord Deliver us!"' (p.16).

As the narrative progresses Paul and Lenore fall in love. Paul loves Lenore despite himself; she is 'the exact opposite of everything he has hitherto thought good and fair in woman' (p. 112). To Jemima, Lenore says: 'One loves because one loves – because one cannot help it, and because one would not, if one could' (p. 142). The novel explicitly deals with the power struggle that is their relationship and, again, like *Red as a Rose*, the double standards of patriarchy. In the early days of their courtship Paul states that 'every woman needs some one to keep her in order' (p. 43), Lenore, unsurprisingly disagrees: 'There is not that man living that could keep me in order; I would break his heart, and his spirit, and everything breakable about him, first' (p. 43). The problem for Lenore though (and this is the disturbing and difficult aspect of the book) is that she loves the man who believes in such views and lives in a society which condones them. Neither the ideological context nor the individual constitutions of Paul and Lenore allow for an equal contest. The lovers know this too:

> 'Paul, never pretend to be jealous of me again! It is patent to everybody that I love you a hundred times better than you do me; you know it yourself, and I – I am not blind to it.'
>
> 'Bosh!' says Paul, turning away uneasily, not feeling exactly guilty; for he does love her heartily, yet with an uncomfortable lurking sensation that there is a grain of truth in what she asserts.
>
> 'It is the way of the world, I suppose,' says the girl, sighing. 'One gives, and the other takes; it would be superfluous for *both* to give, would not it? Perhaps some day – some far-off day – the balance will be changed, and we shall love each other equally; till then'. (p. 191)

The 'far-off day' never comes but through loving Paul, Lenore does experience the ultimate joy that Broughton can bestow her heroine. Engaged to Paul and reunited with him in England, Broughton writes: 'Lenore is *absolutely* happy!' Typically she continues: 'It is something to have been able once to say that; but why do not people know *when* to die?' (p. 180). Life persists, and minutes later Lenore finds out about Paul's cousin who has been a ministering angel to his father:

> Nothing has happened: the fire still radiates warmth from its deep red heart. The footmen are carrying round sweet-breads, and fricandeaus, and timbales, and all manner of nice things. Sylvia and Jemima are still smiling, but yet – but yet – Lenore has made one step, a very little step indeed, but still a step, down from her pinnacle of heavenlike bliss. (p. 181)

Although in the end Paul marries the conventional cousin, it is not desire for her that provokes the split between himself and Lenore. Rather it is the conflict that arises out of Paul's jealousy and desire to dictate the pattern of Lenore's behaviour. Practically, it would be quite easy for Lenore to follow Paul's wishes, not to flirt with a third suitor, Charlie Scrope, to only dance with Paul, but she acts with a 'perverse determination' which he does not humour. (p. 247) She maintains her position of self-assertion which is paradoxically also a masochistic move. When Paul concludes 'it would have been a thousand times better if we had never met', we are told that: 'a pain like knife goes through her HEART, but she makes no sign' (p. 258). After Paul has left her, she tells Scrope 'I have been amusing myself cutting my own throat' (p. 262).

Lenore does make attempts to get Paul back. Jemima sums up the situation: 'the question is, how can you live best: with your dignity and without Paul, or with Paul and without your dignity?' Lenore confesses that she 'would eat all the dirt that ever was in all the world to get him back again' (p. 275), but eating dirt, in the form of writing Paul a letter of apology, does not work. In the end, after a foolish plan to marry Scrope, Lenore succumbs to the disease of a broken heart.

In Switzerland where Lenore is resident with her sisters for the benefit of her health, she is treated to one last meeting with Paul. The encounter recalls Nell's final scene with Dick but with a twist. Lenore is alone, outside, thinking of Paul and the moon is rising when 'here he comes, out of the rock-shadow into the light!' (p. 368). After the shock of finding each other they talk and exchange their versions of what had happened between them and Broughton reminds us of the former scene: 'Now that it is all clear between them, now that all clouds of misconception have been swept away, now that they are all alone here in the moonlight, surely he will take her in his arms' (p. 374). But though there is a kind of rapprochement, there is no embrace. Paul tells of his forthcoming marriage and Lenore 'receives a mortal blow' (p. 376). It is not Paul but Jemima and Charlie Scrope, another of Broughton's unrequited lovers, that watch over Lenore in her last days.[37] Scrope, yielding to Lenore's last wish to see Paul, journeys to find him but returns with the news that 'it was his wedding-day when I got there' (p. 449). Appropriately, therefore, when absolutely all hope is gone, Lenore dies.

As discussed earlier, *Good-bye Sweetheart!* is an experimental text and part of this experiment is found in the shaping of the novel into parts, 'Morning', 'Noon' and 'Night' and the use of two modes of narration, third person and first person. Most of the quotations given here have come from the third-person sections, 'What the Author Says' which is where the scenes of Lenore and Paul alone are found. The first-person narrative 'What Jemima Says' posits a highly subjective view of Lenore's romantic life by the sardonic self-derogatory elder sister who asserts that it is 'a mercy' that 'one's *palate* outlives one's *heart*; one can still relish red mullet when one has lost all appetite for moonshine' (p. 227). Though Jemima's voice is often cynical, as Lenore's health deteriorates Jemima lovingly and sympathetically charts her sister's decline. Through Jemima too, Broughton also provides an alternative vision of a woman's life where romance is not an available option. In this, therefore, Broughton is much harder (or is it wiser?) than Charlotte Brontë who provides even Lucy Snowe with a suitor. In Jemima and Lenore, Broughton exemplifies the 'sense' and 'sensibility' of the two much more famous sisters of Jane Austen's novel.[38] At the end of *Good-bye Sweetheart!* Broughton leaves sister and lover bereft with no trace of a possible romance between them.[39] When Charlie returns to Lenore with his news of Paul, Jemima describes the lover 'putting me aside' but Jemima describes her sister's silence and quotes the last words: 'Gone thro' the strait and dreadful pass of death' (pp. 449–50).

Contemporary feminist theories of romance provide a useful frame through which to view Broughton's work. Although Janice Radway's pioneering work, *Reading the Romance* focused on formulaic romantic fiction many of her insights on the readership of romance seem appropriate to Broughton as writer and reader. Radway writes of twentieth-century readers identifying romance reading as a means of release from their social roles as wives and mothers.[40] For Broughton's young heroines, romantic activity and fantasy provides escape from the boredom of young women's lives. In the repetition of the reading of formulaic work Radway asserts that readers are attesting to dissatisfaction with what life offers as romance (patriarchal heterosexuality) as much as to obsession with the idea of romance.[41] In Broughton's obsession with romance which leads to experimentation rather than formulaity we can see too a questioning of the genre she chose to work within as well as a serious consideration of what love might be. Pamela Gilbert argues that Broughton's novels 'are only nominally about love' and that 'the designation of love story focused critics' watchfulness on the representation of passion and left Broughton free to make social commentary relatively unassailed.'[42] But Broughton's exploration of the conventions of romance in life and fiction is part of her social commentary and not in opposition to this. Thus Broughton's work moves with her times, in looking now at *Dear Faustina* I shall consider how Broughton charts the romantic life of a New Woman.

There are a variety of New Women in *Dear Faustina* (1897), although Broughton herself does not use the phrase. Most significant are Althea Vane, the young heroine; Mrs Vane, her mother; the eponymous Faustina Bateson (originally an associate of Mrs Vane); and Miss Cressida Delafield, a would-be disciple of Faustina. The novel makes fun of all these women to varying degrees but at the same time feminist and socialist views are voiced and through the characters of Althea and the hero, John Drake, given respect. We first meet Althea at a turning point in her life, her father has recently died and her mother sees this moment as the opportunity to escape from her conventional role and abandon her children. She makes a speech to Althea and her four siblings articulating the political rights of the situation and promptly disappears from the novel. The figure of the mother then, so often an absent presence in Broughton's work, here absents herself from the text. This is an original move which once again renders a heroine vulnerable and parentless. It is Althea's older sister, Clare who functions as the traditional woman who attempts to look after Althea's physical and moral well-being. Clare is engaged to be married, and Althea watches with distaste as her sister goes off on honeymoon: 'what an awful fate, to be vanishing into a fen alone with William Boteler for a whole fortnight' (p. 69). As the Vane residence is to be sold, Clare offers Althea a home with herself and her future husband. Althea is able to turn down this offer as Faustina invites her to share her flat. There is a rivalry for influence on Althea throughout the novel and neither the 'old' nor the 'new' woman can offer her entirely what she needs.

At the opening of the novel Althea is in love with the ideals of social progress and the romance of its pursuit. She is also devoted to Faustina. When Clare suggests that Althea herself will soon marry, their conflict of views on Faustina is voiced. Althea says: 'I shall never marry. You know that I have a horror of it.' Clare retorts: 'I know … that of late you have chosen to say so, and I also know to what influence to attribute it; but when once you have got away from that influence −' Althea is adamant: 'I have no wish … to get away from it, since it is far the noblest I have ever known' (pp. 37–8). On the evening after Clare's wedding Althea admits to Faustina that 'till you came I had quite as much inclination towards love and marriage as the average girl is usually credited with.' Faustina, in her 'partiality' has defined Althea as 'above the average' and 'lifted a corner of the veil' on marriage (pp. 75–6). Faustina and Althea enjoy a romantic friendship. In the opening chapter Broughton writes that Faustina 'has sat down by her young friend, and is speaking in that tone of passionate caressingness which used to belong to Love, but which female friendship has lately stolen from his quiver' (p. 2). Faustina is the dominant, more 'masculine' partner, with her 'short hair parted on one side' (p. 7). She is however finally revealed to be unworthy, a woman who will use Althea to further her ambition in inappropriate ways. Althea is not the first young woman to have fallen for Faustina and Faustina is happy to substitute Miss Delafield for Althea as soon as Althea is proved to be inadequate to her needs. That Faustina preys on young, innocent, idealistic women is made clear in the novel. Althea's life has been dramatically altered by her father's death and her mother's quest for freedom and she needs more sensitive guidance through her new life.

The sensitive guide is found in the form of John Drake, an old friend and comrade of Faustina's who (usefully) knows her personal history. From their very first meeting Drake offers Althea help (initially with Faustina's inebriated maid, who Althea innocently believes to be ill). Drake's socialist credentials are impeccable. Faustina explains how he gave up £20,000 a year on the strength of his beliefs: 'his father owns a chemical factory in the East End, and when John found the poisonous conditions under which the hands spent their lives, he refused to touch a penny of money wrung from the wretchedness of hundreds of his fellow-creatures' (p. 120). Most of Drake's time is spent working at the 'Settlement' in Canning Town, which offers practical, educational and moral guidance to the working classes. What is equally important in this novel is his old-fashioned sense of morality and old-style chivalry. As Althea gradually becomes disillusioned with Faustina, and equally dispirited by the prospect of a life like Clare's, she comes to appreciate the value of a man like Drake.

Drake understands how alienated Althea feels, that she is cut adrift from her family and yet is the kind of woman who would enjoy the intimacies of family life. Althea's difference from Faustina is signalled when Althea talks of 'love and warmth and family life, which, after all, are three good things.' 'Love and warmth' are available elsewhere says Faustina, and family life 'is generally more of a hamperer than a help' (p. 42). Drake steps into the gap in Althea's existence left by her father. When Althea, feeling despondent after 'failing' Faustina in a task she has set, goes for a walk to Old Chelsea Church, she ponders her past: 'The past to the girl always means her father – means graceful tastes, leisurely cultivation, tender high-breeding, nice honour. With a rush of bitter discouragement she feels how far, in the short space from his death, she has travelled from them all – all but the last, *nice honour*.' (p. 208) Althea is pondering whether this moral sense is something to be proud of if it hinders her political use to Faustina and she wonders precisely how she can work for social progress. At this point, Drake, who knows about Althea's disappointment, enters the church and offers support and salvation:

> There is no mistaking the out-and-out partizanship bespoken by both voice and eye, and a small stir of comforted warmth makes itself felt about her heart. Her own family misunderstand and chide her; her chosen guide has weighed her in the balance and found her wanting. But this comparative stranger – oh no! no longer that – himself proved capable of the highest

self-sacrifice, recognizes through the wretchedness of her performance the high reality of her endeavour – recognizes it as the truly noble are ever quick to recognize the dimmest spark of nobility in others. (pp. 212–13)

Both Althea and Drake perceive what is best in each other. Drake who is consistently defined in terms of nobility introduces Althea to the Settlement, where she, like he, is a great success. Drake makes scrupulous arrangements for her first visit there by arranging for a newly-married 'female friend and fellow-worker' to act as a chaperone. One evening Althea herself arranges 'to give tea and entertainment to the club of factory girls', all is going well until there is a rush upon the buffet table which Althea is standing behind: 'the pressure around her is growing suffocating, and in another second she feels that it must pin her crushed and helpless against the wall' (p. 262). Drake, of course, is on hand to save Althea: 'was she ever before so glad to see him? though even at this moment it flashes upon her as a revelation that she has never been anything but glad – and, putting her behind him, he stands shieldwise before her' (p. 264). Drake's defence of Althea is almost mock heroic in presentation but it affirms rather than denies his role as shining knight. Drake is affected more by the incident than Althea and he fears she will not visit again but Althea has enjoyed herself 'if it were not for Faustina and all I owe her, I should like to come among you for good!' (p. 269)

Drake has one more maiden to save before Althea achieves her desire. Miss Cressida Delafield, encouraged by Faustina, and inadvertantly inspired by Althea, is willling to give up her family for and spend her fortune on the pursuit of 'rescue work'. Lady Lanington, Cressida's mother begs Althea to help her deliver her daughter from this fate. When Althea finds Faustina is unwilling to dissuade Cressida from her intention they argue and Althea leaves. Althea's exemplary morality is explored, she parts from Faustina because of her fear for Cressida and she is horrified by Faustina's perception of her relationship with Drake. Faustina says that Althea is 'the cat's-paw of John Drake' and she predicts that their relationship will not end in marriage (p. 305). Broughton's image of Althea's despair encapsulates the vulnerable idealism of both traditional and progressive women: 'She had carried her white maiden pennon so high; and now it lies draggled and defiled in the filth of the public street' (p. 310). This image illustrates how even the most virtuous of women are subject to the violence of misinterpretation. When Drake makes a timely appearance and offers to help, Althea begs him not to listen to any insinuations that Faustina might make about her. Althea has to seek shelter with her sister and wait for news from Drake.

Drake is successful in his appeal to Faustina to protect Cressida; in essence he 'blackmails' her with the threat of the withdrawal of the pecuniary support he has been providing her for years. We learn that in the past Faustina had broken the marriage laws in some (unspecified) way but that he had remained loyal to her because her 'convictions *were* convictions' (p. 356). Now he is as disillusioned as Althea.

Although Drake sends Althea a telegram and a letter explaining that Cressida Delafield is safe, with gentlemanly decorum he does not outline Faustina's past failings. The time Althea spends with her family only confirms how 'absolutely out of touch' she feels with them. At last Drake visits and he finds Althea resting in the verandah: 'a more exquisite picture of opulent idleness it would be difficult to see, or one more unlike that working woman whom she had been so proud to call herself' (p. 379). Drake explains that he has not visited earlier because he thought he 'must be associated with the most painful and repulsive experience' of her life. He assumes she is happy now but Althea says 'I am miserable.' He is shocked: 'I had such an impression of perfect well-being – of the right woman in the right place.' Althea is roused: 'The right woman in the right place – lying in a wicker chair doing nothing; that is all you think I am fit for' (pp. 388–9). After further discussion when Althea's need for serious work is clearly signalled, Drake confesses that he has come to see if Althea wants to join the Settlement. She asks what she can do and Drake explains that she could join the new Women's Settlement and start 'a co-operative workroom' based on needlework and dress-making. Althea is delighted, Drake has recognised her 'one gift'. In keeping with the thematic structure of this novel, Althea's future employment reconciles traditional feminine values with a pioneering social spirit. Althea gets her work and her man, she will live in the Women's Settlement and he in the Men's. This is the ultimate romantic ending for Broughton's very particular protagonists. Love for Althea Vane and John Drake is a noble comradeship and a model of modern romance, both 'are silent for a while, a delightful dawning sense of the unity of interest that is the future to connect their lives giving their spirits that sort of hush that comes with the real dawn' (pp. 398–9). Althea's ideals and their fulfilment are beyond even the imagining of Broughton's early heroines.

The Game and the Candle (1899), by contrast to *Dear Faustina*, charts a journey not into an idealised future but to disillusion. This is a novel which explores the central mystery of romantic love and asks "Is it *real*?" (p. 226). As a novelist of romantic fiction for over thirty years Broughton ought to be supremely well-qualified to answer the question but typically she leaves the reader with much to ponder. Jane Etheredge, the heroine of *The Game and the Candle*, escapes from a loveless marriage when her much older invalid husband finally dies. It is clear that this man is an emotional tyrant. He attempts to maintain his power even after death but Jane's moral integrity and romantic optimism, initially at least, defend her from his abuse. On his deathbed, Henry Etheredge reveals that he is aware of Jane's love for another man. Jane and her lover, whose romance had developed over a six-month period had not pursued an adulterous relationship and had parted at Jane's insistence. Henry had overheard this parting five years ago. As a condition of her inheritance, Henry demands that Jane promises that she will not resume her relationship with this man. Jane refuses.

Despite being cast out of her marital home (a large country house and estate) after her husband's death, Jane cheerfully embraces the modest single life she must lead. She moves to a small house in Richmond and intends to mourn respectfully for a year (although she often has trouble keeping up a suitably subdued appearance). Jane is, she says 'a new woman in a brand-new world', but not a 'New Woman' (p. 77). She sustains herself throughout her time of mourning with her memories and her fantasies of the future. She spends most of her time quite happily alone although she has a concerned friend in Willy Clarendon, her husband's former secretary, and new acquaintants in his sisters, Flora and Mabella. Clarendon is devoted to Jane, but like James, Bob and Charlie from former novels, he is destined to remain an unrequited lover.

Through Jane, Broughton explores the romantic's ability to live on nothing but reminiscence and daydreams. And offering an absurd reflection of Jane's state, is Lady Barnes, the only other person who knows of the existence of Jane's lover. Lady Barnes had been at the house party when Jane and Jack Miles met, and like Jack, she has not seen Jane for five years. When Jane and Lady Barnes accidently meet, Lady Barnes sets herself up as the lovers' mediator. Having never 'had any vivid personal interest in my own life' she says 'I seem to live *intensely* in my friends' (p. 131). Lady Barnes had seen Jack in the United States and she talks of how he looked: bronzed, with bleached hair, 'the picture of blond virility'. She tells Jane that Jack had said several times that he was at 'a loose end'. Both Lady Barnes and Jane read this as a sign of fidelity. Lady Barnes constructs a fiction of ideal love about Jane and Jack, this is of course what Jane wants to hear. She sees Jane as a woman who has sacrificed all for love and Jack as 'a Crusader that has lost his way in the centuries, with a lady's glove in his helm, and "Faithful unto death" written across his shield' (p. 106). She writes to Jack to let him know where Jane is now living.

Jack turns up unexpectedly at Jane's house and for moments they experience 'divine oblivion' as 'they stand clutching one another, as if to wring from the past and concentrate in one all the foregone embraces of six harvestless years' (p. 155). But this reunion is too soon, only eight months after Etheredge's death, and Jane insists on waiting another four months before they meet again. Lady Barnes arranges a houseparty in Scotland where they can be together. In the intervening time Jack is in London, making acquaintance with and spending money on Mabella Clarendon. When September arrives, Jane 'has nothing to do but go up [to Scotland] and possess the Promised Land' (p. 205). The end of her journey is by a steamer which will be met by a small boat from her destination. When the small boat arrives she runs down 'the swaying, slippery wetness into the outstretched arms that snatch her into their safe keeping before her foot can touch the rocking boat, and Eden's gates are open at last' (p. 219). The presentation of passion in 'wetness', through 'wetness' is entirely typical of Broughton and here signals the dangers of sensuality and the vulnerabilty of the heroine.[43] The 'safe keeping' of Jack's arms when Jane is between the 'swaying' and 'rocking' boats is ironic. There is nothing solid beneath her feet; later 'the idea strikes her, though in her present state of exaltation it has no power to alarm her, of how very little she really knows him' (p. 222).

The days that follow are an unsettling mix of joy and discomfort. Jane says that she and Jack must 'talk rationally', she wants to know about his life over the past six years. Jack prefers to live in the present and answer her questions by kisses. She discovers his intellectual limitations and his crude and flirtatious manners. He has been left money by a woman he supposedly hardly knew. Nevertheless Jane and Jack plan to marry and Jane resolves to adapt, if 'theirs is to be that ideal union which she had pictured, it must be by the suppression of one half of her own nature' (p. 262). But this self-denying 'ideal' is not to be. Jane sees Jack comforting a tearful Mabella Clarendon first with words, and then with a kiss. Finally Jane 'sees her deity as he is' (p. 281).

After the initial shock Jane acts quickly, she leaves Scotland and returns home to brood on the devastation of her life, 'she has nothing left in this or any other world' (p. 280). On the floor 'where she has cast herself, she writhes in an agony of self-contempt. Has her love then, when stripped of its fine clothes, been nothing but sensuality? (p. 282). Broughton does not answer this, she leaves her reader to mull over Jane's mistakes. By what critieria are we to judge love? Jack arrives speedily, 'handsomer than ever' and argues that the incident with Mabella was 'nothing'. He says: 'I have never loved, never shall love, any woman in the world but you.' His 'own absolute belief in the sob-broken assertion' is insisted upon and his further claim to love Jane more than she loved him is absolutely validated when Jane says: 'I never loved you' (pp. 285–6). She elaborates: 'I never loved you. I loved someone that was masquerading in your shape.' Jack leaves and the reader, like Jane, is left to contemplate her epiphany. In terms of the romance genre, this ending is paradoxical, at once an anti-romantic ending in the disillusioned parting of the lovers, but at the same time a confirmation of the desirabilty of true love. Jane's realisation of the inadequacies of both self and other do not shatter the ideals of romance.

Broughton's last book, *A Fool in Her Folly*, published posthumously in 1920 is a fascinating final working through of Broughton's obsession with romantic love. Although Sadleir argues that the book was not necessarily written last nor intended for publication its subject matter positions it appropriately as a concluding work.[44] The novel has a first-person narrator, a woman of eighty who looks back on her youth. The narrator emphasises the very different moral and cultural environment of the mid-Victorian period; when she looks back she sees a vanished world. At the age of twenty, the heroine, Charlotte (Char) Hankey, lives a seemingly peaceful existence within an ideal (indeed, idealised) family. She has a reserved but wise father and an angelic mother. Char has a younger sister Sophy, and an older sister Harriet, engaged to a cleric. The family live a quiet rural life. The disruption to this idyll comes from Char's reading and writing.

Char explores the further reaches and higher shelves of her father's library. Her parents trust her to choose books with propriety. However Char enjoys reading which she knows would not be considered appropriate. One Sunday morning Char's appearance attracts attention, her eyes are red and sore and she is excused from church attendance. Her family do not know that she has spent the last two nights reading a book then considered most unsuitable for young ladies, *Guy Livingstone*.[45] The reading inspires Char and she takes full and ironic advantage of her absence from church to embark on a great undertaking. She will write a novel.

Her novel is called *Love* although both the younger and older versions of Char admit that at this point in her life all her experience of romantic love is secondhand. Char embarks on her narrative, a highly derivative tale informed by a heady mix of contemporary fiction, French novels and Romantic poetry. Her chief role model is Charlotte Brontë. Char reveals to us what she has learned of love through quotation. She chooses a 'motto' for each chapter. (This of course, could be seen as parodic of the excessive use of quotation in Broughton's early works.) Char works on her novel very early and very late, in secret because she knows that if her older sister or parents found out about her writing they would be 'shocked'. However Char still fantasises about the day that her genius will be revealed to her appreciative family. Despite such fantasies Char is serious about her writing. Throughout the novel she is a stern critic of her own work, willing to cut, re-draft and re-write. She has intentions to destroy the whole of her first draft when it is discovered (but not read) by her younger sister Sophy, and then read by her governess who then takes the manuscript to their mother. Both parents read the text and their reaction is dramatic and surprising both to the early twentieth-century and twenty-first-century reader. The parents are horrified by their daughter's work, and insist on the destruction of the manuscript and Char's promise not to write again. They also decide that Char must be sent away until she sees sense and becomes a reformed character; crucially the mind revealed in the manuscript could pollute Sophy, so separation is a necessary emergency measure. As readers we can only imagine, or indeed fail to imagine what kind of work Char has constructed.[46] She refuses to repent and asserts her right to creativity. But even the younger Char can see that her parents act only with the best intentions, as the separation will be as painful for them as it will be for Char. But the modern reader is likely to sympathise with Char's right to self-determination even accepting the inferior quality of her work. And the older Char emphasises that this drama of revelation is historically specific belonging explicitly to an earlier era and so rather a curiosity than a current concern.

And so Char is sent away and of course, it is now that she learns about love and the realities of relationships between men and women, and the role that fantasy plays within the construction of romantic narratives. She is sent to stay with an aunt, Florinda, who she knows very little about except that she was married for twenty years to a tyrant. Char is surprised and delighted by Florinda who is anxious for the comfort of her niece and unwittingly gives her the freedom to express her creativity. There are mysteries to the aunt's life which nurture the development of Char's fiction. Her aunt has an obvious admirer in the local squire, St John Delaval, her late husband's cousin but there seems to be some barrier to a more public relationship. There is a poor old lady in the village (Miss Strong of Sunbeam Cottage) who, touched with a little romance herself (a portrait of an earl in her meagre dwelling), seems to know something about the aunt's romance. And there is a handsome young man, William Drinkwater, who offers help to Char on her arrival at Frampton but who is despised by the squire and is a source of anxiety for the aunt. Char has plenty to occupy her and she finds the entanglements of Frampton of great assistance in imbuing her re-writing of *Love* with realism.

Char starts re-writing her novel and falls in love with Drinkwater. As she starts to uncover the romantic mysteries around her she decides that the squire's distrust of Drinkwater is mere prejudice. She pledges herself to Drinkwater but his response is equivocal and he is finally proved dishonourable. His 'interest' in Char is a device to bring him closer to the aunt for whom he nurtures an unreciprocated desire. Char is saved before she commits a more dangerous folly (sexual intimacy), in her distress she writes to her mother agreeing to any conditions she names as long as she can return. Char returns a chastened and submissive daughter, 'crushed and humiliated' by her 'unspeakable folly' (p. 350). Her parents are sensitive to the change in her. She gives up writing and she rejects the notion of romantic love in print or in human form:

> There was a pitiable new humility about me – a bottomless distrust of that self which had precipitated me into such a chasm. I never entered the library without a shudder, or glanced at its top shelves, whence *Manon* and *Héloise* grinned at me like mocking demons; and if accident put into my hands a tale of love, I threw it down with nausea. Thus I walked through life. 'A good, conscientious girl, dull, but rather pretty,' was the verdict of my acquaintances …
>
> I believe that I might have had admirers; but at the merest hint of anything approaching tenderness in look or voice I bucked and shied away so violently that my not very vehment aspirants quickly desisted, and carried their sighs and censers elsewhere. (p. 351)

Like Jane Etheredge in *The Game and the Candle*, Char's sense of self is undermined by her experience of misplaced desire. She cannot trust herself to re-experience romance in life or in her reading. Char's sisters marry and her parents die. She is the spinster daughter who cares for them to the end, grateful that God 'suffered me to hold each dying hand in mine till death loosened its clasp' (p. 352). The final words of the novel summarise fifty years of life in as unromantic a manner as possible. There is no happy ever after for Char, she is a dutiful wife seemingly finding her vocation in self-abnegation. Presumably there are no children to hold Char's hand at her decent death as a widow of a man with no name and no physical attractions. Char achieves angelic status before death:

> A year later I married – chiefly, I think, because I had got into the habit of 'looking after' people; and my future husband was glaringly in need of care. But I might have employed the phrase of George Whitefield, who, when

proposing marriage to his future wife, added that he thanked God that there was not the slightest mixture of carnal love in his feeling for her.

And now my husband, good man, has departed too. I am eighty years old, and there is nothing left for me but to die. I hope I shall do it decently. (p. 352)

Michael Sadleir describes this novel as 'unmistakable autobiography' but if *A Fool in Her Folly* is autobiographical in terms of the early bitter experience of love then it is still posits an alternative fictional ending.[47] Although we might read Char's passionless marriage as analogous to Broughton's spinsterhood, the fact of Broughton's career remains. Char destroys her own writing (finally throwing the fragments of her manuscript from the train) and her sensuality is contained. She retreats from the world to devote herself to her parents. The real love of Char's life is her mother. By contrast, Broughton did write her novels in spite of possible family objection and despite, or maybe because of, unhappiness in love. While we can only speculate on Broughton's romantic life, her writing life reveals an author embracing the romance form, (re-)creating passion and exploring romantic possibilities. What Broughton denies Char as a writer, she allows herself, she writes and re-writes her love story, pursuing personal desire for public pleasure.

Notes

1 Percy Lubbock, *Mary Cholmondeley: A Sketch from Memory* (London: Jonathan Cape, 1928), p. 25.
2 Marie Belloc Lowndes, foreword to Rhoda Broughton, *A Fool in Her Folly* (London: Odhams Press Limited, 1920), p. 5.
3 Quoted in Michael Sadleir, *Things Past* (London: Constable, 1944), p. 91.
4 Lowndes, foreword to Broughton, *A Fool in Her Folly*, p. 6.
5 Lowndes, foreword to Broughton, *A Fool in Her Folly*, p. 6.
6 Walter Sichel, 'Rhoda Broughton', *The Reader* (August 1917), 138–41, quoted in Marilyn Wood, *Rhoda Broughton (1840–1920): Profile of a Novelist* (Stamford: Paul Watkins, 1993), p. 116.
7 Ernest A. Baker, *The History of the English Novel: Yesterday* (London: H. F. and G. Witherby, 1939), p. 211.
8 Helen C. Black, *Notable Women Authors of the Day, Biographical Sketches* (Glasgow: David Bryce and Son, 1893), pp. 41–2.
9 For a discussion of the revisions made to *Not Wisely, but Too Well* before publication in volume form see Sally Mitchell, *The Fallen Angel: Chastity, Class and Women's Reading, 1835–1880* (Bowling Green, OH: Bowling Green University Press, 1981), p. 83; and Helen Debenham, 'Rhoda Broughton's *Not Wisely But Too Well* and the Art of Sensation', in Ruth Robbins and Julian

Wolfreys (eds), *Victorian Identities: Social and Cultural Formations in Nineteenth-Century Literature* (London: Macmillan Press, 1996), p. 14.

10 Rhoda Broughton, *Cometh Up as a Flower* [1867], 2 vols (Stroud: Alan Sutton, 1993); Rhoda Broughton, *Not Wisely, but Too Well* [1867], 3 vols (Stroud: Alan Sutton, 1993).

11 Wood, *Rhoda Broughton*, pp. 175–91.

12 Eleven of Broughton's novels were published in serial form in *Temple Bar*, for dates of serial publication see Wood, *Rhoda Broughton*, pp. 175–91.

13 Rhoda Broughton, in collaboration with E. Bisland, *A Widower Indeed* (J. R. Osgood, McIlvaine and Co., 1891).

14 Wood quotes Broughton's letter to Bentley in 1879 which compares her own earnings with those of Miss Laffan and Helen Mathers, see Wood, *Rhoda Broughton*, p. 56.

15 Lubbock, *Mary Cholmondeley*, p. 42.

16 Wood, *Rhoda Broughton*, p. 57.

17 Sadleir argues that Broughton largely maintained 'her earning power' but the payments he quotes as paid for Broughton's novels indicate a considerable drop in actual income, Sadleir, *Things Past*, p. 113. Wood substantially repeats this information, see Wood, *Rhoda Broughton*, p. 95.

18 Lubbock, *Mary Cholmondeley*, p. 42; Wood, *Rhoda Broughton*, p. 121.

19 Wood, *Rhoda Broughton*, p. 6.

20 Wood does not discuss any instances of foreign travel but Black mentions a trip to Algeria, *Notable Women Artists*, p. 43.

21 Novels with foreign locations include: *Good-bye Sweetheart!* (London: Richard Bentley and Son, 1872); *Belinda* (London: Richard Bentley and Son, 1883), *The Devil and the Deep Sea* (London: Macmillan and Co., 1910).

22 Wood, *Rhoda Broughton*, p. 5.

23 Dogs feature prominently in *Joan*, 3 vols (London: Richard Bentley and Son, 1876), *Belinda*, 3 vols (London: Richard Bentley and Son, 1883), and *The Game and the Candle* (London: Macmillan and Co., 1899). In *The Devil and the Deep Sea* (London: Macmillan and Co., 1910), the story of the male protagonist tells of a car crash caused by avoiding running over a dog is crucial to the understanding of character in the novel.

24 'A Home of Rest', *Temple Bar*, 370 (September 1891), 68–72.

25 R. C. Terry, *Victorian Popular Fiction, 1860–80* (London: Macmillan Press, 1983), p. 131.

26 Sadleir, *Things Past*, p. 87.

27 Sadleir, *Things Past*, pp. 85–6. Subsequent page references are given in the text.

28 See Mitchell, *The Fallen Angel*; Terry, *Victorian Popular Fiction*; Kate Flint, *The Woman Reader, 1837–1914* (Oxford: Clarendon Press, 1993); Lyn Pykett, *The Sensation Novel from 'The Woman in White' to 'The Moonstone'* (Plymouth: Northcote House, 1994); Debenham, 'Rhoda Broughton's *Not Wisely But Too Well* and the Art of Sensation'; Pamela K. Gilbert, *Disease,*

Desire and the Body in Victorian Women's Popular Novels (Cambridge: Cambridge University Press, 1997).

29 Rhoda Broughton, *Red as a Rose is She*, 3 vols, 1870 (London: Macmillan and Co., 1899); *Dear Faustina*, (London: Richard Bentley and Son, 1897).

30 Mrs Oliphant, 'Novels', *Blackwood's Edinburgh Magazine*, 102 (1867), 257–80. Subsequent page references are given in the text. See also Flint, *The Woman Reader*, p. 275; Pykett, *The Sensation Novel*, p. 7, p. 141; Gilbert, *Disease, Desire and the Body*, p. 122, p. 134.

31 See, for example, *Red as a Rose is She* (1870) where Esther's literal and metaphorical isolation at Blessington Court inspires gothic imaginings.

32 Mrs Oliphant and F. R. Oliphant, *The Victorian Age of English Literature*, 2 vols (London: Percival and Co., 1892), vol. 2, pp. 206–7.

33 Oliphant, 'Novels', p. 265.

34 Charlotte Brontë s *Jane Eyre*, 3 vols (London: Smith, Elder, and Co., 1847) features characters called St John Rivers and Blanche Ingram (though Constance Blessington is as fair as Blanche is dark). Esther's employment at Blessington Court, her lonely walks and the gothic atmosphere of her room, particularly at night, all recall Brontë s novel. For a detailed consideration of how Broughton's *Not Wisely but Too Well* re-writes *Jane Eyre* see Debenham, 'Rhoda Broughton's '*Not Wisely But Too Well* and the Art of Sensation', pp. 12–15.

35 Charlotte Brontë, *Villette*, 3 vols (London: Smith, Elder and Co., 1853). Direct reference is made to *Villette* on p. 116 of *Good-bye Sweetheart*.

36 Eliza Lynn Linton, 'Miss Broughton's Novels', *Temple Bar* 80 (June 1887), 196–209, p. 206.

37 Charlie Scrope is an interestingly feminised suitor to Lenore. Initially on meeting her, he admits to Jemima that Lenore "frightens" him (p. 137). He is petite and and pretty, and is described as a doll (p. 308). When Paul has left her, Lenore proposes to Scrope and he blushes like a schoolgirl (p. 299).

38 Elinor and Marianne Dashwood are the central characters of Jane Austen's *Sense and Sensibility*, 3 vols (London: T. Egerton, 1811). Direct reference is made to *Sense and Sensibility* on p. 154 of *Good-bye Sweetheart*.

39 A possibility of romance between Jemima and Scrope was suggested when Scrope first enters the novel, see p. 94 and p. 157.

40 Janice A. Radway, *Reading the Romance: Women, Patriarchy, and Popular Literature* [1984] (London: Verso, 1987), p. 11.

41 Radway, *Reading the Romance*, p. 14.

42 Gilbert, *Disease, Desire and the Body in Victorian Women's Popular Novels*, pp. 113–14.

43 See for example, the ending of *Belinda*, 3 vols (London: Richard Bentley and Son, 1883) where the eponymous heroine resolves to leave her husband for her lover, the scene is set in a rainy Lake District and the lover is called Rivers.

44 Sadleir, *Things Past*, p. 88.

45 George Alfred Lawrence, *Guy Livingstone* [1857] (Leipzig: Bernard Tauchnitz, 1860).

46 This is also true of the novel that the heroine, Emma Jocelyn, writes in Broughton's *A Beginner* (London: Richard Bentley and Son, 1894).
47 Sadleir, *Things Past*, p. 86.

Bibliography

Austen, Jane, *Sense and Sensibility*, 3 vols, London: T. Egerton, 1811.

Baker, Ernest A., *The History of the English Novel: Yesterday*, London: H. F. and G. Witherby, 1939.

Black, Helen C., *Notable Women Authors of the Day: Biographical Sketches*, Glasgow: David Bryce and Son, 1893.

Brontë, Charlotte, *Jane Eyre*, 3 vols, London: Smith, Elder and Co., 1847.

——*Villette*, 3 vols, London: Smith, Elder and Co., 1853.

Broughton, Rhoda, *Not Wisely, but Too Well* [1867] 3 vols, Stroud: Alan Sutton, 1993.

—— *Cometh Up as a Flower* [1867] 2 vols, Stroud: Alan Sutton, 1993.

—— *Red as a Rose is She* [1870] 3 vols, London: Macmillan and Co., 1899.

—— *Good-bye Sweetheart!* [1872] 3 vols, London: Richard Bentley and Son, 1882.

—— *Nancy*, 3 vols, London: Richard Bentley and Son, 1873.

—— *Joan*, 3 vols, London: Richard Bentley and Son, 1876.

—— *Twilight Stories*, London: Richard Bentley and Son, 1879.

—— *Second Thoughts*, 2 vols, London: Richard Bentley and Son, 1880.

—— *Belinda*, 3 vols, London: Richard Bentley and Son, 1883.

—— *Doctor Cupid*, 3 vols, London: Richard Bentley and Son, 1886.

—— *Alas*, 3 vols, London: Richard Bentley and Son, 1890.

—— *A Widower Indeed*, in collaboration with Elizabeth Bisland, J. R. Osgood, McIlvaine and Co., 1891.

—— 'A Home of Rest', *Temple Bar*, 370 (September 1891), 68–72.

—— *Mrs. Bligh*, London: Richard Bentley and Son, 1892.

—— *A Beginner*, London: Richard Bentley and Son, 1894.

—— *Scylla or Charybdis?*, London: Richard Bentley and Son, 1895.

—— *Dear Faustina*, London: Richard Bentley and Son, 1897.

—— *The Game and the Candle* [1899] Leipzig: Bernhard Tauchnitz, 1899.

—— *Foes In Law*, London: Macmilllan and Co., 1900.

—— *Lavinia*, London: Macmillan and Co., 1902.

—— *A Waif's Progress*, London: Macmillan and Co., 1905.

—— *Mamma*, London: Macmillan and Co., 1908.

—— *The Devil and the Deep Sea*, London: Macmillan and and Co., 1910.

—— *Between Two Stools*, London: Stanley, Paul and Co., 1912.

—— *Concerning a Vow*, London: Stanley, Paul and Co., 1914.

—— *A Thorn in the Flesh*, London: Stanley, Paul and Co., 1917.

—— *A Fool in Her Folly*, London: Odhams Press Limited, 1920.

Debenham, Helen, 'Rhoda Broughton's *Not Wisely But Too Well* and the Art of Sensation', in Ruth Robbins and Julian Wolfreys (eds), *Victorian Identities: Social* and *Cultural Formations in Nineteenth-Century Literature*, London: Macmillan Press, 1996.

Flint, Kate, *The Woman Reader,1837–1914*, Oxford: Clarendon Press, 1993.

Gilbert, Pamela K., *Disease, Desire and the Body in Victorian Women's Popular Novels*, Cambridge: Cambridge University Press, 1997.

Linton, Eliza Lynn, 'Miss Broughton's Novels', *Temple Bar*, 80 (June 1887), 196–209.

Lubbock, Percy, *Mary Cholmondeley: A Sketch from Memory*, London: Jonathan Cape, 1928.

Mitchell, Sally, *The Fallen Angel: Chastity, Class and Women's Reading, 1835–1880*, Bowling Green, OH., Bowling Green University Press, 1981.

Oliphant, Mrs. Margaret, 'Novels', *Blackwood's Edinburgh Magazine*, 102 (September 1867), 257–80.

Oliphant, Mrs. Margaret, and F. R. Oliphant, *The Victorian Age of English Literature*, 2 vols, London: Percival and Co., 1892.

Pearce, Lynne and Jackie Stacey (eds), *Romance Revisited*, New York and London: New York University Press, 1995.

Pykett, Lyn, *The Sensation Novel from 'The Woman in White' to 'The Moonstone'*, Plymouth: Northcote House, 1994.

Radford, Jean (ed.), *The Progress of Romance: the Politics of Popular Fiction*, London and New York: Routledge and Kegan Paul, 1986.

Radway, Janice A., *Reading the Romance: Women, Patriarchy, and Popular Literature* [1984] London: Verso, 1987.

Sadleir, Michael, *Things Past*, London: Constable, 1944.

Sichel, Walter, 'Rhoda Broughton', *The Reader* (August 1917), 138–41.

Terry, R. C., *Victorian Popular Fiction, 1860–80,* London: Macmillan Press, 1983.

Wood, Marilyn, *Rhoda Broughton (1840–1920): Profile of a Novelist*, Stamford: Paul Watkins, 1993.

Index

'The Flint and Hart Matronship' 58
Hallowed Spots of London 48, 50
'The Hatton Garden Spoon' 56–7
The Lady Herbert's Gentlewomen 47–8, 50, 51, 58
The Life of Josiah Wedgewood 46, 47, 48, 49, 51
Lilian's Golden Hours 50
'Lis's Culture' 55
'Lucy Dean; The Noble Needlewoman' 51, 54
Mainstone's Housekeeper 47, 48, 49, 51
'My Work as a Decorator' 57
The Nine Hours Movement 50
'Scenes in the Life of an Authoress' 47
'The Shop at Barrow' 55
'A Soul Amongst the Vagrants' 54
Struggles for Fame 46, 47, 50
'The Thorn and Then the Rose' 59
'A Winter and its Spring' 50, 58
'A Woman's Pen' 59
Meyer, Susan 9
Meyer Spacks, Patricia 8, 9
Miles, A. H., 24, 25
Mill, John Stuart 26, 67–8, 72
Millais, John Everett 200
Mistletoe Bough, The 188
Mitchell, Charlotte 94
Mitchell, Sally 56
Moers, Ellen 8, 98
Molesworth, Louisa 14, 111–34, 135, 147–8, 156, 157
Carrots: Just a Little Boy 116–17, 120, 124–5
The Carved Lions 121, 123, 125
A Christmas Child 117
Christmas Tree Land 127, 128
Cicely: A Story of Three Years 114
The Cuckoo Clock 121, 122, 124, 128
Four Winds Farm 125

Grandmother Dear 126
Hathercourt Rectory 114
Hoodie 117
Lover and Husband 114, 116
Miss Bouverie 114
My New Home 125–6
'My Pink Pet' 111
Not Without Thorns 114
Rosy 124
She was Young, and he was Old 114
The Tapestry Room 112–13, 121
Tell Me a Story 113, 117, 119
The Wood Pigeons and Mary 127
Molesworth, Richard 113, 115
Molesworth, Violet 113
Monthly Packet, The 91, 106, 112, 118, 137
Morgan, Charles 121
Morning Chronicle 91
Morris, William 90, 119
Mozley, Anne 92
Mozley, Charles 93
Mozley, Harriett 95
Mozley, John 93

Nesbit, Edith 95, 96, 97, 127, 128, 129, 150, 151
Newgate novel 47
Newman, John Henry 26, 93
New Monthly Magazine 166, 169, 172, 173, 179, 180
Nonconformity 69
Norton, Mrs 3

Oddfellow's Magazine, The 47
Odhams 209
Oliphant, Mrs Margaret 5, 8, 92, 94, 121–2, 170, 172, 212–13
Autobiography 9, 10
'The Byways of Literature: Reading for the Million' 170
Miss Marjoribanks 92
'Novels' 212
Salem Chapel 171